WORKING OUTSIDE

A Career and Self-Employment Handbook

WORKING

OUTSIDE

A Career and Self-Employment Handbook

BY PEGGY HARDIGREE

HARMONY BOOKS
New York

Published simultaneously in Canada by General Publishing
Company, Ltd. Printed in the United States of America.

Designed by Elyse Shick

Library of Congress Cataloging in Publication Data

Hardigree, Peggy Ann, 1945-
    Working outside.

    1. Vocational guidance.   2. Occupations.
I. Title.
HF5382.H37   1980   331.7'02   79-23170
ISBN: 0-517-537753
        0-517-540088 pbk.

10   9   8   7   6   5   4   3   2   1
First edition

To Lonzie Mays, who had faith

Acknowledgments

My thanks to all the outdoor workers who gave so freely of their time and made this book possible, with an extra nod of gratitude toward the staff at Assateague Island National Seashore, where I received more help than any writer has a right to expect. Thanks also to Congressman Tony Hall of Ohio, who, at the time it was sorely needed, gave his help in cutting away miles of bureaucratic red tape.

CONTENTS

Forestry Aides and Technicians · Smokejumpers · Fire-control Aides, Fire Lookouts, and Fire Dispatchers · Fire-control Officers · Forest-fire Staff Officers

Part Two

INTRODUCTION

It is possible to leave behind the noise, smog, and congestion of the city and find a richly rewarding, meaningful way of life in the great outdoors. Despite the claims of the early critics of the environmental movement, the struggle to improve our environment—to gain the fullest use of our natural resources without destroying them—has created a wealth of career opportunities. You can take advantage of them.

There is enormous satisfaction to be found in good, wholesome, useful outdoor work. Whether your interest lies in helping to preserve an endangered species and its habitat, preventing soil erosion, improving the quality of our air and water, stopping the destruction caused by a raging forest fire, or producing food on your own land, those interests could lead to a career doing what you like best, in a part of the country you love.

Outdoor careers can be financially rewarding as well. Our society has come to recognize the real importance of protecting our natural resources; it has realized that those charged with nature's utilization and preservation should be well paid for their efforts. Earnings in most outdoor-oriented careers have improved dramatically in recent years, and further improvement can be expected in the years ahead.

This career guide is designed to assist you in getting that all-important first job. But it is also designed to help you plan for the future as your career advances—knowing where you are going is as important as getting a good start. Each chapter explains the professional and nonprofessional openings in every field—from the entry level through the top management. If your interest is in outdoor recreation, for example, you could start as a seasonal aide, advance to a permanent technician, and eventually become a park ranger.

If you are just beginning to think about a career, you will find here where to apply, what job best suits your background, and what to expect for future employment. If you are already working outdoors, this book will show you the wealth of opportunities open to those with outdoor experience.

In the past, it was possible to earn an outdoor living with little or no preparation. Most jobs required only enough physical strength to do demanding work, and an unyielding desire to do it. Today, just like our way of life, most of these occupations have become more complicated and specialized. Society is willing to pay those working with our natural resources, but it quite properly demands that this work be done by qualified individuals—thus a certain amount of preparation is needed by anyone seeking a meaningful job.

Basic to this preparation is a clear understanding of each job or profession; what its training requirements are and how these are met; what work it involves and how this work is rewarded; what are some of its less pleasant features as well as its attractions; where the jobs exist, how are they gained, and what the future offers for those who fill them.

In this book I have tried to present a clear and realistic picture of a broad range of outdoor careers and business opportunities. I have sought information from the best possible sources; universities, colleges, and technical schools; federal, state and local agencies; and business, professional, and trade organizations. Aside from information about pay, working conditions, and career opportunities, I have made a special effort to include tips on getting started in your chosen career, tips that come from the real experts: those who have successfully sought out a better way of life doing exactly what they want, where they want, in the great outdoors. These experts are an invaluable source of information and advice; when you finish reading, get to know someone working in your field of interest. Listen and learn.

As is the case in most other fields, special training is usually required if you are to qualify for a better-paying professional position. Such training is readily available today, with more and more schools, colleges, and universities offering courses that prepare students for outdoor careers. In addition to professional schools, there are two-year technical schools in all parts of the country that teach needed skills. Examples of these schools are mentioned throughout the book, but a complete list of those offering courses on any subject may be obtained without cost by writing the Division of Education,

Department of Health, Education, and Welfare, Washington, DC 20210.

Higher education is not always necessary for an outdoor job, however. Public agencies and private employers are often willing to provide on-the-job training, and they may supplement this training by sending a promising employee to a specialized school to further his or her education.

An important way to prepare for an outdoor career is through volunteer work. Volunteer workers are always welcome in national, state, and local parks, at wildlife refuges, and by private conservation organizations such as the Audubon Society. Such programs allow you to make a real contribution while working alongside experts in a variety of fields—and they provide experience that greatly enhances your chances for the career of your choice. A highly placed official with the National Park Service told me, "To anyone seriously interested in a career in the National Park System, I would strongly suggest they consider our Volunteers in Parks Service Program as a means of gaining experience and knowledge about the operation of an individual park."

Young people between the ages of sixteen and twenty-five should also consider spending a summer or two as a member of the Youth Conservation Corps. The YCC is built along the lines of the Civilian Conservation Corps of the 1930s, and is being greatly expanded as its success becomes evident. Its members spend approximately eight weeks during the summer engaged in important conservation work on public lands such as the national parks. They are paid for this work, provided with food and living allowances, and are given a real chance to experience the actual working and living conditions of an outdoor career. Information about enrollment can be obtained by writing the Youth Conservation Corps, Department of the Interior, Washington, DC 20240.

The Student Conservation Association offers high-school and college students a wonderful opportunity to gain experience while savoring a real taste of the outdoor life. Supported entirely by donations, this organization places interested students in a wide variety of work situations during the summer months. Its young members receive no actual salary, only a stipend for food, travel, lodging, and other expenses, but they acquire on-the-job training that will vastly improve their job chances after graduation. At one national park alone I found SCA members working toward careers in recreation management, fish and wildlife management, forestry, botany, and soil conservation. I also talked with a young premed student who, having seen the intangible benefits offered by an outdoor career, was seriously thinking of changing her course of study, perhaps to marine biology or oceanography. More information about this program can be had by writing The Student Conservation Association, Box 902, Vashon, WA 98070.

Because they almost always live in rural or remote areas, outdoor workers have a better opportunity than most to engage in agriculture, often as a part-time activity. For many, farming is the ideal full-time job or business, and plenty of help is available for those whose interests lie in this direction.

The 4-H and Future Farmers of America have chapters in nearly every county in the United States. In these programs, interested youngsters are given expert help and encouragement in their farming endeavors, often from agricultural scientists holding advanced degrees. Adult participation in these programs is also encouraged.

The United States Department of Agriculture maintains about three thousand County Extension offices throughout the country. These offices frequently offer free courses on specialized aspects of farming, and their staff can put you in touch with experts on any agricultural subject, or provide a wealth of printed material on that subject. They may also be able to direct you to local farmers needing help, where you can gain actual farming experience. Farm work is often seasonal and low-paid, but agriculture is one field where experience remains at least as important as education, and such on-the-job training could pave the way to one of the better farming careers available.

State universities in farming areas usually offer extension courses in various forms of agriculture; such courses are usually inexpensive, and taking one or more might tip the balance in your favor when and if you apply for a loan with which to buy your own farm.

If you are of an age where military service is a possibility, don't overlook it as a source of training. Each branch of the military controls vast tracts of land and the accompanying natural resources, which require care and management. It is possible to choose your field of training and work before enlistment, and also possible to have the government pay for your specialized education at a school of your choice.

Military service offers another advantage: A very large percentage of the better outdoor jobs are filled through the Civil Service Commission, where veterans are given preference points in taking the examination required by law. Competition for many of these positions is very keen. The extra points given the veteran often determine who gets the job; thus military service can not only provide training that will help you prepare for an outdoor career, it can also provide you with a strong advantage when it is time to put that training to use.

Courses in writing and public speaking will be invaluable in many of these fields, as would any training in human relations. Public awareness is increasingly important to the success of outdoor programs, and those working in these programs are frequently called upon to explain them, either through lectures and presentations, or with written pamphlets and brochures. Many outdoor workers are able to supplement their incomes enormously by writing or lecturing about their work.

Training in police science or some experience with a police department could be helpful in many outdoor fields. As public use of our parks, forests, wetlands, wilderness areas, and other recreational areas continues to increase, rangers, foresters, wildlife managers, and others are increasingly confronted by "people problems." To handle these problems, more emphasis is being placed on hiring those with police experience, and many agencies now provide this training for certain employees. For a few outdoor occupations such as game warden or park police officer, where the duties consist almost entirely of enforcement, such training or experience may be an absolute requirement.

Skills and training you already possess may open the door to an outdoor career. Most parks and wildlife refuges actually have difficulty finding people to fill their secretarial and clerical needs. They also have a need for unskilled labor. While such positions may not be outdoor careers in the strictest meaning of the term, or may involve no outdoor work at all, they frequently provide the easiest way of entering the system. By putting yourself in the right spot at the right time, and by acquiring valuable job seniority, it will be easier for you to finally get the job you really want.

At a state park in Maryland I met a youngster on his way to success. He had entered the Park System as a summertime lifeguard—an interesting and worthwhile temporary job but certainly not one he would want to follow as a career. During his second summer as lifeguard, however, the naturalist was taken ill and the young lifeguard was allowed to assume many of his duties. This young man was preparing to enroll in a nearby college offering resource management courses at the time I spoke with him, and next year he will be returning to the same park as assistant park naturalist. His future as a well-paid naturalist seems ensured.

Many of the jobs discussed here are interrelated. For example, foresters often end up working as park rangers, though not all of the latter, by any means, have studied forestry. Your skills may make it possible for you to find meaningful employment and good earnings in several fields. Because this is so, I hope you'll take the time to read the entire book, not just the chapter or chapters that are of particular interest at the moment.

I hope, too, that someday we'll meet and that I will have helped you join the hundreds of thousands who are living the good life in the great outdoors.

PART ONE

1

INDEPENDENT FARMING

Farming in America has undergone many changes in recent years, but the family farm continues to be the dominant unit in American agriculture. Independent farming remains a viable career for those with the courage to tackle it.

The skills for farming are quite different from in the past. In 1940, the average farmer owned 174 acres of land and had a total capital investment of only $6,200. By 1972, the average size of the farm had increased to 450 acres and the capital investment to more than $125,000—both figures are still rising. New technology has made it possible for the farmer to work more land, and economics has made it necessary.

The farmer needs a high degree of technical skill and knowledge to produce food efficiently, and a good deal of business sense to make his production pay. Successful handling of large investments in the face of rising costs, uncertain crop prices, unpredictable weather, and other risks require understanding of the principles of financial management. Farmers also must be familiar with government farm programs, including allotments, subsidies, and marketing quotas. They should know where to obtain and how to use credit.

Renting or Leasing a Farm

Because the capital investment can be so huge, many beginners get started by renting. This can be done under a crop-share arrangement—both the costs and the profits are shared by the owner. This greatly reduces the costs and risks to the tenant, but it provides less freedom in choosing crops and making farming decisions, as well as reducing the potential for profit. A cash-lease agreement, if you can negotiate one, is preferable.

Several years ago, my husband and I signed such a lease with the owner of a small farm in Ohio. The owner had bought it as a real-estate investment and had little interest in farming. The cash rent was high, but we felt we could make the farm pay—and we did. This had once been a dairy farm and most of the fields were planted with alfalfa. We had no money to invest in dairy cattle, and no real knowledge of dairy farming, but we did realize that those alfalfa fields represented a cash crop. But how to cut and bale the hay?

A nearby farmer agreed to do this for half the hay produced, an arrangement that is becoming common. Our share of the profits paid our rent for the entire year, leaving us, in effect, with a farm that cost us nothing. With the alfalfa off, we rented those fields as pasture, producing a tidy profit, and were also able to pocket the income from other small-scale farming operations. But no matter what type of lease you negotiate, be sure that it spells out, in specific detail, the rights, duties, and obligations of all concerned.

Even if you are intent on buying and owning your own farm, remember that such a leasing arrangement may frequently be used to help make your farm pay. Many farmers find themselves in possession of tracts of land that—for one reason or another—they do not wish to farm, or cannot farm profitably. Other farmers in the region may be eager to farm that same tract of land. Instead of allowing the land to lie fallow, the owner may allow another farmer to work it—perhaps on a crop-share basis, perhaps in exchange for a cash rent—and both will profit from the arrangement.

Wilson Gerry, who owns and operates a successful poultry farm in Maryland, provides an example of how such arrangements work. Years ago, when Mr. Gerry bought the farm on which he wanted to establish poultry houses, he had to buy far more land than he needed for his objectives. The farm came without the equipment for planting crops—he had no money or interest in buying such equipment.

A neighbor did have this equipment. He also had an interest in farming these acres, and the two worked out an equitable agreement that continues to this day. The neighbor works this land as if it were his own, paying Mr. Gerry a share of the profits. Mr. Gerry maintains ownership of a beautiful farm, successful poultry houses to keep him busy and provide a good income, and derives an income from land he admits he could not have farmed on his own. Such arrangements have helped many farmers get started.

Advertisements in farm journals and local newspapers provide the most common means of finding a farm to rent, as do contacts with real-estate brokers. County extension agents frequently know of farms for rent, and the local office of the Farmers Home Administration may also guide you. But no matter how you find it, the experience gained on a rented farm will prove invaluable as you begin looking for a farm to buy.

Homesteading

In searching for land to buy, many would-be farmers hope to reduce their investment by finding land that can be obtained from the government under the old Homestead Act. It is a fine hope but seldom realized.

Although these laws do remain on the books, very little public land suitable for farming remains available. When tracts do become available—as about one hundred do each year—they are likely to be found either in Alaska or in one of the western states. Before you could earn a living by farming such a tract, the Department of Agriculture warns, you would have to do a lot of hard work and invest considerable sums of money. If you do want to explore the possibility of homesteading, buying or leasing public land, detailed information (including a periodical listing of the tracts available) may be obtained by sending a request to the Bureau of Land Management, Department of the Interior, Washington, D.C. 20240.

More likely than not, you will have to buy one of the eighty thousand privately owned farms offered for sale each year, and even here—as more farmland is lost with each passing year—the competition for good land is keen. As technology and economics force other farmers to work more land, you must compete with both new and established farmers for the land that appears on the market. This reduces your options.

Specialty Farming

"Beginning farmers who wish to grow crops such as grain and cotton or raise cattle, which are usually profitably produced on farms of a thousand acres or larger, will find extremely limited opportunities, since farms of this size rarely are available for purchase, and those that are cost a great deal," advises the Department of Agriculture. "The beginner should find a better opportunity to get started in a type of specialty farming that requires less land, and in which he or she has an expertise. For example, a successful dairy farm may require only a hundred acres or so; and crops such as tomatoes, strawberries, or melons may be profitably grown on even smaller farms, using intensified farming methods."

No one can tell you how much you can expect to earn with any farm crop, but there are certain crops that are less risky than others, and that may be profitably grown on smaller parcels of land. Many of these may be grown only in limited areas of the country. Listed by the Department of Agriculture as the major specialty crops for small farms are: potatoes, sugar beets, sugar cane, peanuts, rice, tobacco, and dry beans. Few farms can produce all of these, so try a variation.

Poultry operations require less land and thus a smaller capital investment, but because of the limited amount of credit available, the general farm is the type most likely to be within financial reach of the beginner. These, too, require only relatively small amounts of land to be profitably operated.

General Farming

While certain types of farms are found only in clearly defined parts of the country—such as the cotton farms of the South—general farms exist in all areas. Your chances of finding and obtaining one, according to the Department of Agriculture, are best in the rural areas of the East and the South, where there are many small farms. Many small farms also exist on the fringes of most towns and industrial centers, but the price of land is far higher in these regions, and many of the farms are too small to be profitable.

On most of these general farms the acreage that can be cultivated is somewhat limited. On the part of the land that cannot be cultivated intensively and thus used for growing one of the specialty crops, livestock usually becomes important as a means of using pasture and other forage. Most general farms produce several classes of livestock and several types of crops. Poultry houses are common on these farms, and some have small dairy herds. This provides an income that, while not always spectacular, is usually fairly stable because it is derived from several sources.

The crops you grow on any farm are, of course, going to depend greatly on your knowledge of those crops and your experience in growing them—but they are also going to be determined by the area in which you intend to farm.

Financing a Farm

Once you have decided to try farming in a certain state, you should send a letter to the State Director of Extension Service at the land-grant university and another to the county's extension agent. Ask for information about farms and farming in the area. They will provide a wealth of information about farms for sale, soil, and topography—which can vary widely within very short distances—crops suitable to the region, local farming practices, markets, conditions affecting the crops you plan, and the size of farm needed to meet your objectives.

After visiting several farms and carefully selecting one suited to your farming goals, you are faced with the problem of determining how much credit you will need and then obtaining that credit.

This can be a frightening task, but there are many ways by which you can increase your chances of obtaining credit and several sources from which it may be obtained. The first step is to work out a capital budget.

The purpose of this budget is to show how the capital will be used and how it will be repaid. Most lenders will demand that you present one. It should take into account the fact that some of the capital will be needed for operating and living expenses until farm income can be produced, and your estimate of that farm income should be on the conservative side.

Your chances of getting credit are going to be far greater if your capital budget shows income from other sources. The applicant who holds a nonfarm job when applying for a farm loan is generally considered a better risk than the borrower who intends to pay solely from the farm's earnings. To continue to hold such a job may be difficult and will require that you work your way gradually into full-time farming, but it also vastly increases your chances of getting started at all.

Contract Farming

Another way to increase your chances of obtaining credit is through contract farming. This is a type of arrangement that is extremely common in poultry and rabbit production, but which is found in other types of farming as well. Under such an arrangement, a feed dealer, supplier of young stock, or food processor supplies almost everything needed for production. You provide the labor, feeding the young stock to the firm's specifications, and you provide existing facilities or land on which the firm may establish facilities. In most instances you are left to pursue your own interests on all but a small portion of the farm, with just part of your day devoted to the contract farming, and the assured income from the contract may tip the scales in your favor when the lender makes a credit decision.

Your county extension agent will know of any contract farming opportunities available, or you may be able to create such opportunities by talking with farmers, feed and grain dealers, poultry firms, and others in the area. Such contracts not only provide a cash income that will make it easier for you to arrange financing, they also allow you to learn by drawing on the experience and knowledge of the other party to the contract. Check this out before you apply for the loan.

Obtaining a farm loan through a commercial lending institution can be extremely difficult, especially for the beginner. A down payment of as much as 40 or 50 percent may be required, and many commercial institutions refuse to consider the farm's potential earnings in making a credit decision. Loans for operating expenses are also more difficult to obtain at commercial banks.

For those reasons, you will do better to approach one of the 650 Federal Land Bank Associations. Their loans are based on the farm's earning potential, as well as its sale price, a smaller down payment is required, and the loan may be repaid over a longer period of time—up to 40 years. These banks also make loans for such purposes as buying livestock, equipment and supplies, and for operating and living expenses. The address of the nearest one may be obtained from the Farm Credit Association, Washington, DC 20578.

If you are unable to obtain credit elsewhere, you meet the first requirement for obtaining a loan from the best source of all: the Farmers Home Administration of the U. S. Department of Agriculture.

This agency, through more than 1,600 offices across the country, makes low-interest loans to farmers unable to obtain adequate credit from other sources at reasonable rates. As of 1978, they were charging only 5 percent interest on their loans, about half the national average for interest charged on borrowed money, and no down payment was required of the borrower. Veterans and experienced farmers are given preference, but no one is excluded from the program.

Loans are available to both full-time and part-time farmers. The agency works closely with each borrower to develop a plan that, when followed, will provide enough income from the farm and other sources to provide for a reasonable standard of living while making payments on the loan as they are due.

The county supervisor will assist you in filling out your loan application and in preparing a farming plan. This plan will be reviewed by a panel of local farmers, who apply their own experience in deciding if the plan is feasible. They may even suggest changes that will make it work.

You might also inquire about the loans made by the FHA for development of rural businesses and farm recreational businesses. By converting a patch of woodland into a campground, a lake into a pay-for-fishing pond, or a barn into a riding stable, you might do much to increase the potential of your farm. Loans are available for all these purposes, and more. Further information, as well as the address of the agency office nearest to you, may be obtained by writing to the Farmers Home Administration, Washington, DC 20250

The Farm as an Investment

In buying that farm you have bought much more than land, building, and equipment; you have bought a way of life. And like it or not, you have made a long-term investment in real estate. When the modern farmer claims to be "land rich and cash poor," he may be speaking the truth.

Farmers are not only faced with rising costs of production, they are also confronted with many problems caused by the rising value of the very land they farm. If it becomes necessary, for economic reasons, to add more land to the operation, the farmer must compete with others who want this land. Sometimes he cannot afford to do so. Yet to lose out may endanger his farming operation.

As the value of the land soars, so, too, do the taxes—and just meeting these taxes has become a major problem for every farmer. If he adds more land, as his farming knowledge says he ought to do under certain conditions, then he automatically increases a tax burden that may already be staggering. If the land holdings are not increased, on the other hand, the farm may begin to operate at a loss. This poses a real dilemma—making it difficult to keep what is already owned.

One obvious answer to the problem is to obtain higher prices for the farm production, thus solving the economic problems without adding more land. Many farmers, such as those who raise fruit and vegetables, are able to do this by selling directly to the consumer. Some sell from a produce stand on the farm or at the roadside, from a produce truck making home delivery, or through one of the farmers' markets found in most major cities. But for many farmers, such as those producing dairy products, direct sales are not possible, not even for a small amount of the production.

The alternative, then, is to obtain maximum use of the available land and to add crops that can be produced without buying more land and thus increasing the tax burden. This is possible on the vast majority of farms in America.

Most farms, no matter what the major crop they produce, have some land or facilities that go unused, often because, for one reason or another, they are unsuited to production of the major crop. Yet such land and facilities can have great potential for other profit-producing ventures. Most farming operations have peak seasons and slack seasons; this means both farmer and land may be idle for months at a time. By obtaining maximum use of time, as well as of land, the potential for profit again increases.

Fish Farming

An outstanding example of this is catfish farming in the South, where, some years back, rice growers began raising catfish in the rice beds as a supplementary crop. Today, on many of these farms, catfish provides most of the income, and rice is the supplementary crop.

Many farms have one or more shallow ponds, used to water stock or for other purposes, that could be used for fish farming, often without interfering with other farm uses of the pond. Few working farms lack a site where such a pond could be dug.

Ponds for fish farming must have some means of draining them, and they are usually equipped with automatic feeders. Your county agent can provide several books on the subject, and he will assist you in finding stock, pelleted food, and a market. A single worker can care for several acres of fish farm in his or her spare time, except when the fish are being harvested, and the profits are among the best in farming; most estimates place them just over $1,000 annually for each acre of water.

Maple Syrup Production

If your farm lies within the eastern maple-producing region, which extends from Maine to Maryland and as far west as Minnesota, you should take a close look at the possibility of entering the very lucrative maple syrup industry. No matter where your farm is located, you should keep this industry in mind, for several universities are said to be close to the development of fast-growing, high-yield trees that will be made available to farmers for planting alongside fencerows, roadsides, and in similar areas, either for immediate production of syrup or as a long-term investment. And what an investment!

Surveys by the U. S. Department of Agriculture have shown that earnings from the production of maple syrup are among the highest in farming, with profits averaging about seven dollars per hour for time spent in the syrup-making process. Good maple groves yield several hundred dollars per acre. Profits go soaring when part of the production is converted to candies, creams, and other confections, or when the syrup is sold directly to the consumer—yet only about 5 percent of our tappable maples are utilized.

The potential of a maple grove is judged not by the number of trees but by the number of tapholes it will accept. To accurately judge the number of tapholes in a maple grove, the diameter of each tree must be measured at breast height. A tree with a diameter of 10 inches will accept 1 taphole, and an additional taphole can be made for each additional 4 inches in diameter, up to a maximum of 4 taps per tree. Greatest profits are achieved at 160 tapholes per acre, in groves with 30 or 40 large trees per acre, and for maximum returns the grove should be able to accept at least 500 tapholes.

In checking the possibility of adding maple syrup to your farm's production, remember that these must be the so-called sugar maples, *Acer saccharum* or *A. nigrum,* and not any of the dozen or so other maples found in North America, which will produce a fairly good syrup for home consumption but which cannot be profitably tapped.

Remember, too, that it is not absolutely necessary that these trees be on your own land. You may be able to negotiate sugaring rights from other farmers, tapping their trees and paying with a part of the profits. Similar rights are sometimes available on public land, and a quick check with the state forestry office will tell you if this is so. Many syrup producers operate in just this manner, tapping the trees in several groves and transporting the sap to a central collection point.

The period for tapping the trees normally lasts only about ten weeks, and it arrives during a slack period for most farmers, so this is especially attractive as a means of increasing the farm income.

New techniques have also made it far more profitable. No longer is the sap collected in buckets hung from spiles driven into the trees, then transported by hand, truck, or sleigh to the processing plant. Today, plastic tubing is used to convey the sap from the trees to a central collection point, thus enabling one or two farmers to tap groves that once required dozens of workers.

It is not necessary that you convert the sap into syrup—though not doing so will cost you a chance at more profits. Central evaporator plants, some of them owned by farmers' cooperatives, are found in all the maple syrup producing regions, and these will gladly pay good prices for the sap from your trees, the price varying with its sugar content.

Tapping the trees is a simple process that can be learned in minutes. The equipment for doing it costs very little and will pay for itself quickly. Converting the sap into syrup or confections, however, is an entirely different matter.

Not that the process is all that complicated; it is simply a matter of removing the water from the sap, which can be easily mastered by most. The problem, in explaining the process, is that it varies with conditions of weather, altitude, and sugar content of the sap. Each step of the process must be done according to standards set forth by the government. The Department of Agriculture has a free book, obtainable through your county agent, *Maple Syrup Production in the United States*, which provides detailed instructions for tapping the trees, converting the sap to syrup, and making creams and other confections.

The cost of an evaporator house and other equipment will vary according to its capacity, but is less than a farmer might invest in a new barn or a modern tractor. For those who tap a large number of maple trees, the greater profits through processing make the investment almost always worthwhile; but those tapping a small number of trees should consider the economics of the industry before entering this end of the business.

The amount of sap required to produce a gallon of syrup—and the quality of the syrup—vary from grove to grove, but 30 gallons of sap for each gallon of finished syrup is the accepted average. A grove with 500 tapholes will usually yield 5,000 gallons of sap, which would boil down to between 160 and 170 gallons of syrup. If sold in bulk, this would easily bring $10 per gallon, but if marketed directly to the consumer in smaller quantities, or converted into confections, the product would bring at least double that amount—or $3,200 in revenue for each 500 tapholes (a conservative estimate).

For those with enough maples to justify the building of an evaporator house, this can be an incredibly lucrative part of the farm operation. I obtained data on a plant in Wisconsin, built in the early 60s at a cost of less than $25,000—a figure that includes the cost of the land and the grading of a road, in addition to the evaporator. This plant produces nearly 9,000 gallons of syrup each season, which should, according to industry statistics, yield a minimum profit of about $45,000 annually for what is, essentially, a part-time operation.

Beekeeping

Every farmer should consider keeping honey bees as a profitable sideline, or as a major producer of cash revenue. The business requires only a small initial investment, no additional land, and can be learned by anyone.

A single hive and its colony of bees will cost about $20. The tools and protective equipment required by the beekeeper will cost another $40 or so. This single hive, properly managed, should yield no less than 65 pounds of marketable honey each season, but many beekeepers are able to coax as much as 500 pounds annually from a single colony. Honey prices vary widely, usually according to the nectar from which they are produced, but 500 pounds would produce a minimum annual profit of about $250—from a hive costing about one tenth that much and requiring only a few minutes' labor each week. You should also know that, according to the Department of Agriculture, "The demand for fresh honey almost always exceeds the supply."

The labor requirements in beekeeping are so low that an apiary of a dozen or so hives producing about $2,500 in annual income can be handled on a part-time basis, and full-time apiarists commonly handle thousands of hives, adding part-time help during peak seasons. An apiary may also be expanded almost at will; one California beekeeper, for instance, began as a hobbyist with a single hive and now, several years later, heads a corporation that owns more than half a million hives.

It is possible to keep bees without owning even a single acre of land. Because of the valuable services bees perform in pollinating crops, other farmers and orchard owners will actually pay you to place hives on their land. Such arrangements are common to the industry, and your county extension agent can direct you to farmers needing this service.

The extension agent can also provide you with a wealth of free pamphlets and books that give you information to get you started in beekeeping. They will help you recognize the better nectar-producing plants of your region. He or she can also provide contacts with suppliers of bees and beekeeping equipment.

One source of help you should contact is the Apiculture Research Branch of the Entomology Research Division, Agricultural Research Service, Beltsville, Maryland 20705. This agency maintains the world's largest collection of beekeeping literature, most of which is available at little or no cost, and their experts will answer any question you send their way.

Springtime is the best time to order the equipment and get started, for then the bees will have no trouble locating plants rich in nectar and pollen. In looking for sites where beehives might be placed, remember that the hives should be shaded from extremely hot sun and have some protection from bitter winter winds. If a natural supply of clean water is not available it will have to be provided.

Your bees will manage to produce some honey no matter where they are placed, but for maximum production—and profit—each colony of bees should be able to roam over at least five acres rich in nectar-producing plants such as alfalfa, clover, dandelion, fruit trees, berry bushes, or vegetable plants.

Marketing your honey is easy. Of the more than $50 million worth of honey sold in this country each year, more than half goes directly from the beekeeper to the consumer. At least in the beginning you should be able to sell all of your production directly off the farm, either through a roadside stand where other farm products are sold, or just by placing a few signs along your road frontage. Later, as the apiary grows, you may want to wholesale it under your own label, or convert some into granulated honey and other specialty products. The potential for beekeepers today appears almost limitless, and the need for them is such that the Department of Agriculture will help you every step of the way.

Raising Rabbits and Earthworms

Almost every farm in America has facilities that could be put to profitable use by developing them into a combination rabbitry and worm farm—two enterprises that go together like a hand in a glove, require only a nominal cash investment, and offer great potential for expansion.

Well over 10 million rabbits are sold for meat each year in this country, at prices the Department of Agriculture describes as "very stable," and they are among the easiest of all livestock to raise. Anyone capable of operating a farm at all can easily learn the techniques of rabbit herd management. Again, the Department of Agriculture can provide you with bountiful information that will acquaint you with every phase of rabbitry management.

For many reasons, all having to do with profit, either New Zealand or California rabbits are preferable breeds for the meat-producing rabbit herd. In selecting foundation stock, it is essential that you buy healthy, vigorous, fertile bucks and does with a good record of reproduction, and you should make the seller produce those records. As with many other farm businesses, good bookkeeping is the key to success in raising rabbits, and the seller with poor records likely has stock to match.

Start small, buying one buck for each dozen does, and you will be able to learn the basics of rabbit husbandry without risking large sums of money. Initial costs will average about $20 for each rabbit and hutch, but even this can be halved by buying used equipment. The hutches can be placed in just about any available building that offers protection from bitter winter winds and good ventilation during the summer. Only later, if the herd begins to grow large, will you want to consider giving the rabbits a special building.

The largest rabbitry in the world is owned by a producer of pelleted rabbit food, and almost all of these food companies have experimental rabbitries. Eager for your business and familiar with every aspect of rabbit husbandry, these companies will help you with every phase of herd management, even providing free advertising aids. The contact is made through your local feed and grain dealer.

If you prefer to avoid the work of slaughtering and marketing the rabbits, you may want to sell your herd's production to a broker or processor. These are commonly found in New York, California, the Ozarks, and the Midwest, but they are rapidly spreading to other areas, and your county extension agent can help locate the nearest one.

The price obtained from these brokers is somewhat lower than might be had through direct sales to the consumer, but there are many advantages to working with such a firm. Most of them, for example, can provide food and equipment at a savings to you. They also offer a great deal of free advice and technical assistance, and will help you build your herd by providing prime breeding stock and accepting their young as payment. But the greatest advantage in dealing with them is that they offer a steady market for a large number of rabbits, usually at prices arranged in advance.

Each doe in your herd should annually produce a minimum of 125 pounds of marketable meat. This means that a herd of 40 does—which would require only a few hours of care each week—would produce at least 5,000 pounds of meat each year. According to the American Rabbit Breeders Association and the USDA, a herd of about 400 will provide full-time employment for one man. Such a herd would produce an astonishing 50,000 pounds of meat, worth at least $55,000 at current prices.

How much of that would be profit? The answer to that depends on many factors. A study done in 1962 set the average hourly wages earned by rabbit breeders at just under $5. But that study was done well before worm farming made such an enormous impact on the rabbit industry.

As in any livestock operation, the cost of feeding the rabbits accounts for almost all of the expense of raising them.

According to the American Rabbit Breeders Association, which strongly urges its members to raise earthworms along with their rabbits, "Even the *least successful* worm farming operation will yield enough profit to meet the costs of feeding the rabbits." In many rabbitries, however, the worm farming operation hands up profits that match or exceed those gained from the rabbits.

The New Zealand and California breeds are chosen not only because they are the best meat-producing rabbits, but also because they are of a size and weight that allow them to be raised in self-cleaning, wire-bottomed cages. These cages allow the manure to drop through, thus reducing the labor involved in cleaning the cage. Odor in the rabbitry was a problem until it was discovered that earthworms thrive in these droppings and did away with the odor problem. That was the first reason for placing worm beds under the rabbit cages; today it is done as part of a booming industry.

The wormbeds can be made from anything that is handy. But since the beds must be watered regularly, the design should allow for good drainage. They should be just large enough to catch all the droppings from the cages above, but need not be huge. One grower claims that a bed 3 feet wide and 14 feet long yields 40,000 worms per week!

Red hybrid earthworms are offered for sale in the classified advertising section of most outdoor magazines. Stock should cost you no more than $4 per thousand, and your investment for stock should not exceed $150, even for a very large operation. If placed in the beds and left unharvested for 6 months or so, this amount of stock would produce a staggering number of worms.

The manure should fill the beds to a depth of 6 inches before the worms are added, but, if necessary, peat moss, rotting leaves, or other organic matter can be added to achieve this depth. The breeder worms are added at a rate of about 200 to the square foot.

After that, the only labor is in watering the beds to keep them wet but not soggy, turning them with a fork every two weeks or so, and harvesting the worms. If the beds are outside they should also be covered during heavy rains.

Marketing worms is fairly easy. A few signs in front of the farm, a few ads in local papers, and perhaps some promotional offers to sporting goods stores and bait shops will get the business under way. But don't overlook the chance for mail-order sales. Millions of worms are shipped through the mails each year, most sold as the result of ads placed in outdoor and gardening magazines, and these sales are the backbone of the fast-growing worm industry.

At least once a year the wormbeds must be cleaned and fresh manure allowed to accumulate, and the old manure, enriched by the worm castings, provides yet another product—potting soil—that can be bagged and sold to nurseries, greenhouses, and organic gardeners. With the demand for rabbit meat growing steadily, with earthworms that cost nothing to raise bringing at least $4 per thousand wholesale and many times that amount at retail, and with valuable potting soil as another marketable commodity produced at no extra cost, this is a business every farmer should investigate.

Herb Culture

Shortly before I began the writing of this chapter, the Associated Press sent out the story of a man in the Washington, D.C., area who began raising catnip as a hobby and, in about two years, became the largest commercial grower of catnip in the country and the owner of a business grossing millions of dollars each year. His catnip is grown on less than thirty acres of land.

The *Philadelphia Inquirer,* not to be outdone, followed with its own account of a woman from that area who grows tarragon, dill, sorrel, woodruff, and other herbs for sale to chefs in the finer restaurants. She began with a small plot outside her kitchen window, expanded her business steadily for half a dozen years, and today employs a dozen workers on several acres of land—yet she is unable to meet the demand for her fresh herbs. Tales of success are common in this extremely lucrative business.

According to the Department of Agriculture, "Herbs will grow well in any garden where vegetables thrive, in the garden rows or around the edges . . . in flower beds, in borders, among ornamental shrubs and roses, just so there is good drainage and six or more hours of sun." This indicates how easily herbs may be grown on the small patches of land that go unused on virtually every farm, but it does little to reveal just how spectacularly profitable herb culture can be, offering what may well be the greatest per-acre profits in all of farming.

With most of the common herbs, as many as 15,000 plants may be grown on a single acre of land. Each cutting of a single plant will yield about 1 ounce of the herb, and with some species it is possible to make 2 or even 3 cuttings in a single season. As I write this, most herbs, properly marketed, are bringing $1.00 to $1.50 per ounce—for an incredible minimum gross of $15,000 per acre per year!

As I have indicated, growing the herbs is no problem. It can easily be done by anyone with even the most basic gardening or farming skills. Your county agent can provide you with many pamphlets containing detailed information about growing most of the popular varieties, but the following will give you some idea of what is involved.

As a general rule, herbs do best in an alkaline soil, with a pH of 6.5 to 7.5. Have the soil tested by the county extension service, and if the test indicates acidity, just work ground limestone into the soil, according to the instructions that will come with the soil analysis.

After that, the soil can be handled like that in vegetable growing—fertilized with manure or compost, and mulched with leaves, straw, or hulls to keep the foliage clean.

Herbs are particularly resistant to most insects and diseases, and therefore require little time in caring for them. On most herb farms, more time is spent harvesting and marketing the crop than in caring for it.

Dozens and dozens of species are available, each with its own special requirements of growing and harvesting, as well as its own special uses. Seed companies can supplement the information given to you by the county extension agent, and the many uses of the herbs can be learned by studying the cookbooks and herbals available at your local library.

Knowing these uses will help you to determine the local demand for herbs. You will find that certain species predominate in French cuisine, others in the Italian, and so on, while others prevail in herb teas or as regional favorites. It is essential that you know the local market before the herbs are planted.

Chefs at better restaurants represent a major market for fresh herbs. Supermarkets, small grocery stores, health food dealers, and specialty food shops are other markets, though, of course, these establishments must be given a discount and the herbs must be packaged in small amounts.

Various herbs may also be potted and discounted to these same outlets or sold directly off the farm to housewives who like the beauty, fragrance, and utility of fresh herbs growing in their own kitchen. And most herb farms offer special products such as herb teas, vinegars, jellies, and sachets. The number of ways in which fresh herbs may be marketed is limited only by the imagination of the grower.

Recipes for many herbs products are found in the material offered by the Department of Agriculture, as well as in cookbooks, but for some especially good tips on making and marketing such specialties, I would suggest you order the booklet *Profitable Herb Growing*, which is available for $1 from Nichols Garden Nursery, Albany, OR 97321.

In talking about herb farming I have carefully avoided any mention of ginseng, not because it cannot be extremely profitable for some, but because it is a highly specialized crop with its own needs and problems. Unlike the farming of the common herbs used in cooking, initial costs for growing ginseng can be high, the plant is somewhat susceptible to attack by pests and disease, and the market tends to fluctuate. Farming of it should be approached conservatively.

Purveyors of ginseng seed and cuttings like to point out that as much as a ton of ginseng can be harvested from a single acre, and that this would bring $25,000 or more on the open market—but they sometimes fail to mention that the crop will not be ready for harvesting until at least its fifth year. The Department of Agriculture, in contrast to the claims sometimes made by those in the business of selling seeds and cuttings, estimates the profits to the grower at about $1,500 per acre per year—which is more than you might earn with many conventional crops but far less than can be realized by planting the more common, faster-growing herbs used in cooking.

If, however, you are in possession of some wooded land unsuitable for other farming purposes, and if you are interested in making a long-term, somewhat speculative investment, ginseng does offer a way to put that land to use. Just remember that growing it requires a little luck and a lot of patience. The plant requires shade, which is the reason wooded land is the ideal place for growing it. Where no natural shade exists, the farmer must supply this protection, once again increasing costs for materials and labor.

Another reason for planting ginseng in woodlands is that in such areas the soil is likely to be ideal for growing it. The plant will grow in nearly any type of soil, but the black loam found in wooded areas is by far the best for this purpose. But if the soil has a high content of sand or clay, it should be improved, prior to planting, by adding rotten leaves, wood or sawdust, or richer topsoil from another area.

Maine, Kentucky, Tennessee, Massachusetts, New Hampshire, Vermont, Connecticut, Rhode Island, Pennsylvania, and Ohio are the leading producers of ginseng, although this botanical has been successfully cultivated in every state but Florida, where it absolutely defies cultivation. And as with any root crop, ginseng is susceptible to attack by rodents, which must be discouraged by surrounding the beds with traps, and close wire mesh netting set 12 to 18 inches in the ground on all sides.

If such a long-term crop does appeal to you, it is extremely important that you shop around to obtain the seeds or cuttings for planting at the lowest possible price. Buy them from a nursery you already know. More than any other cultivated crop, ginseng has attracted unscrupulous people who earn *their* profits selling start-up stock at inflated prices, usually to people who are lured by false promises and visions of instant wealth.

Once again, your county extension agent can provide several booklets that will acquaint you with the problems of growing ginseng, as well as the solutions to those problems. Study that material before investing—and then, at the end of seven years or so, it may well be that you will find that patch of woodland yielding a cash crop that will go far in paying off the mortage on your farm.

These are not "get rich quick" methods of farming, for no such methods exist. They require the same study, knowledge, attention, and hard work that you, as a farmer, would apply to your major crops. But they do represent some of the very best ways to increase the cash income of the farm without adding land and thus increasing the tax obligation, and for that reason alone they deserve investigation by every person interested in farming.

2
AGRICULTURE AND AGRIBUSINESS

Our national heritage ties us so closely to the soil. Millions of Americans dream of leaving behind the congestion of the city and finding a healthier, more rewarding way of life on the farm. It is possible to earn a decent living through honest labor and applied knowledge, but only for those who understand the enormous changes taking place in agriculture.

Until recently, the word agriculture referred only to agricultural production or farming—an old American industry that provided more than 3 million jobs as of 1976. But today this word has come to encompass much more than just farm work. Agriculture is now closely linked to many other parts of the economy—food and fiber processing, marketing and distribution industries, farm equipment producers and dealers, and feed and fertilizer manufacturers. The modern farmer is a highly trained individual, who knows where to go for expert help in solving any problem.

Ownership of an independent farm is the ultimate goal of many who enter the field of agriculture; farming is a complex business that requires a unique combination of training and experience in order to operate successfully. Most farmers, no matter what their educational background, also have the experience of growing up on a family farm and participating in farming programs for young people such as the Future Farmers of America or the 4-H clubs. For those who have an urban background, however, jobs with other farmers offer the best way to gain the actual experience. Many of these jobs can lead to worthwhile careers that do not involve the ownership of land.

During the last two decades, employment on U.S. farms and ranches has declined to about half its former level—largely due to improvements in farm technology. Nevertheless, about 2 million workers still will be needed in basic agricultural production in the year 1985.

Some farming, according to the United States Department of Agriculture, is done in nearly every county in the nation. More than one third of all farms are found in Texas, Missouri, Iowa, North Carolina, Illinois, Kentucky, and Tennessee, and the largest farms are concentrated in California, Iowa, Texas, Illinois, and Kansas—thus most agricultural jobs will be available in those states.

The topography of the land and the climate of the area often determine the type of farming that is done, which, in turn, determines the type and number of jobs available. For instance, wheat, oats, corn, and other grain crops are best grown on large, flat farms suitable for the use of large and sophisticated machinery. Such crops are ideal for the Plains States of Nebraska, Kansas, Iowa, and Illinois. Family workers frequently provide most of the labor on farms such as these, where the crops can be harvested and packaged by machine. Only a small number of hired farm laborers and almost no labor supervisors are employed in regions that produce such crops.

Raising fruits and vegetables, which must be picked and packaged by hand, generally requires a very large number of employees during the harvest season. Many hired laborers work on these farms on a seasonal basis. About half of all commercial vegetables grown in the United States are produced in California, and Texas and Florida are other leaders in the production of fruits and vegetables; about two fifths of all farm labor supervisors and more than one third of all hired farm laborers are employed in these three states.

Much of the work on farms that produce animals and dairy products is scheduled on a day-to-day basis with few peak periods requiring extra labor. These farms are often able to rely on the farm owner and family members to do most of the work. Only the largest farms of this type will have employment available. Even so, about 40 percent of all farm workers are employed by farms that raise cattle, hogs, sheep, and poultry, while the remainder work for farms that raise crops.

Farm Laborers

More than 975,000 hired laborers and 340,000 labor supervisors are employed on the nation's farms. The position of farm laborer sounds like a menial, dead-end job, yet it provides the easiest means of entry and access to the experience necessary for a career in farming. You might want to consider it as a starting point.

In contrast to the training and experience needed to operate an independent farm, most farm laborers, such as field hands and livestock workers, learn their jobs in a few hours of on-the-farm training. No special background is required. Many perform specialized jobs, such as operating farm machinery, but even these jobs are quickly learned, and previous experience and training are not necessary.

Physical strength and stamina are essential requirements of almost all jobs in farming. Farm workers must often spend long hours on their feet, or stooped over under the hot sun. They may be required to lift and carry hay bales and other heavy objects, and to restrain strong animals.

In considering this job, you should remember that most jobs in farming may be extremely hazardous. Each year many farm workers suffer crippling injuries from farm machinery or animals, and others are affected by illnesses and diseases from handling and breathing in dangerous pesticides and insecticides. These problems are sometimes made worse by the inadequate health care available in rural areas.

Farm laborers are also among the lowest-paid workers in the country. Workers paid on a piece-rate basis were frequently able to earn more, but even so their wages were well *below* those paid to workers in other parts of the economy. In addition to hourly wages, some farm laborers receive free room and board, but other benefits, such as hospitalization, sick leave, and paid vacations are virtually nonexistent.

Many types of agriculture are seasonal in nature, and farm laborers on certain farms may have to work from sunup to sundown during the planting and harvesting season. After half a year or so of such long hours, when the need for labor dwindles, many laborers are forced to seek off-farm employment. The job outlook for laborers is not bright. As machinery continues to replace workers in the field, employment of unskilled help will continue its sharp decline. To understand this decline, one has only to consider the example of the hybrid tomato. It has a hard skin and can be machine-harvested with no damage to the crop. This development allows a single machine to do harvesting that once required many farm laborers.

But this is the gloomy side of the picture. Many people find that living and working in a rural area presents an attractive alternative to the fast-paced life of the city dweller, and for some it is the *only* way to gain experience for independent farming. The knowledge accumulated here may help to qualify you for other outdoor jobs described throughout this book, and the advancement to better-paying farm positions is also possible. According to the Department of Agriculture:

"Opportunities for advancement for farm laborers are somewhat limited; however, such opportunities do exist. The most likely opportunity for advancement is to a position as labor supervisor, and a few may have the opportunity to become farm managers, tenant farmers, or to one day own their own farms."

On many farms, especially the smaller ones with only a few workers, the farm laborer may be called on to perform a variety of duties. On farms devoted to diversified agriculture, for instance, the laborer may drive a truck, operate other equipment, and care for livestock and crops as well as maintain structures and machinery.

On farms devoted to livestock, the work of the farm hand often remains the same from day to day. The laborers must mix feed and additives, and supply feed and water to the animals. Barns and pens must be cleaned on a regular basis, and livestock must be inspected for signs of disease or illness. Some farm workers are expected to vaccinate livestock against diseases, or spray them with insecticides to provide protection against harmful parasites. Helpers on dairy farms are expected to clean and milk the herd twice each day.

Workers on farms that grow crops, on the other hand, will have duties that vary widely with the seasons. Before planting, these workers must prepare the soil by plowing, disking, and fertilizing. When the young plants are partially grown, they cultivate the fields to loosen soil and control weeds. The crops are then sprayed to provide further weed control to destroy harmful insects and fungi, and for plant nutrition. The worker may later assist in harvesting, storing, packing, and transporting crops.

Much of the labor performed requires the use of machinery—milking machines, tractors, combines, hay balers, and picking devices. Hands must be able to set up, operate, clean, and repair this machinery, so some mechanical aptitude is helpful. As laborers also maintain and repair barns, fences, irrigation systems, and other farm structures, a basic knowledge of carpentry and other maintenance skills comes in handy.

Certain types of crops require special attention, and those who provide it sometimes receive special training and slightly higher pay. Most orchards, for example, will have one or more workers who set out young seedlings, prune older trees, thin immature blossoms and fruit to improve crop quality, work at preventing damage by frost, etc. In areas where the water supply causes problems, trained workers are sometimes assigned the job of controlling the water flow from irrigation ditches, through gates or ports, or of placing and operating portable sprinkling systems.

Large farming operations may also employ other specialized workers, such as full-time maintenance workers, machinery operators, fruit and vegetable packers, and truck drivers. Many of these workers receive higher pay for their skills, but the pay is frequently lower than in most other parts of the economy.

Farm Labor Supervisors

The pay gap narrows, however, with the next step up the ladder—to the job of farm labor supervisor. Salaries in this job can vary widely, depending on the nature of the farming operation and the number of laborers supervised. Farm labor supervisors earn an average hourly wage of $4.39, much closer to the average wage of $4.87 an hour paid to production workers in private nonagricultural industries.

The farm labor supervisor must coordinate the work of the laborers in planting, cultivating, and harvesting. He or she schedules the work of crews and must find and hire additional hands as they are needed during peak seasons. Supervisors also teach new employees how to use machinery and tools, and are expected to keep records of crop conditions and production. Most supervisors should be able to do any job performed by those on their crews.

State employment agencies, farmers' and ranchers' associations, county extension offices, and rural newspapers are the best sources to check for information about employment on this level. However, more and more farm laborers and labor supervisors, especially those in California and Florida, are seeking to upgrade their wages and working conditions through membership in unions such as the International Brotherhood of Teamsters and the United Farm Workers. These union halls may be able to direct you to farms with job openings and give you a good idea of what to expect in the fields. The experience you gain on that first job could open the door to a very bright career in agriculture—if not as an independent farmer then in a well-paid position as farm manager.

Farm Managers

Ted Bowen is a manager of a medium-sized farm in lower Delaware. Early on in life Ted decided he wanted to be a farmer, but circumstances beyond his control caused him to leave the University of Delaware after little more than a year of agricultural school. His dream seemed to be over.

Ted had done seasonal work on several farms during previous summers, however, and now he took a job as a labor supervisor on a large produce farm in New Jersey, where he remained until he was offered a more lucrative supervisory position with a large poultry processor near Maryland's Eastern Shore. This job offered few opportunities for outdoor work, but it did keep Ted in close contact with the many farmers who raised poultry for sale to this firm, and it was by one of these contacts that Ted was offered the chance to take over the management of a farm.

The several hundred acres he manages represent only part of the holdings of a corporation formed by several partners. The land is planted in melons, vegetables, and orchard crops, with a small part devoted to soybeans. Several automated poultry houses are another part of the operation. Ted draws a salary against a percentage of the annual profits, which, according to him, "usually means earnings of just over $20,000."

Ted and his helpers had just finished harvesting the soybean crop the November day I talked with him. What advice could he offer?

"You've just said it—'management,'" he answered without hesitation. "It goes without saying that a farmer has to know all that can be known about agriculture, but a lot of good farmers go broke because they know next to nothing about business management. Kids with a real interest in farming should also take courses in bookkeeping, financial management, and accounting, especially tax accounting. A company can almost always find a farmer to hire, but they find it a lot tougher getting a farmer who really knows business management." Ted met these last requirements by taking extension courses, a means he has also used—and still uses—to increase his knowledge of agriculture. His own farm is not very far in the future.

Government agencies are unable to provide an estimate of the average earnings of farm managers. This is due to the fact that many of them have partnership or profit-sharing arrangements with the corporations that employ them, and it is impossible to accurately estimate the average earnings of American farms.

The requirements for a position as farm manager are essentially the same as those needed for success as an independent farmer. If you grew up on a farm and have been fortunate enough to have participated in 4-H and similar youth programs, that training gives you a head start on others. But even with such a background, in order to have a realistic chance at being hired as farm manager by a corporation, you will need some additional training at a recognized agricultural college. A degree may not be required, but a year or two of scientific training will always be expected. For those who have not had the advantage of living and working on a farm in their youth, a degree in agriculture is essential.

Most agricultural schools offer major programs of study in dairy science, crop science, agricultural economies, animal science, horticulture, and agronomy. Most offer special programs of study concerning types of agriculture that are regionally important, such as grain science programs at universities situated in the Plains States.

In addition to this agricultural knowledge, as Ted Bowen points out, the farm manager should have a solid knowledge of business management. Mechanical skills, the ability to work with tools of all kinds, carpentry, welding, and other forms of maintenance skills are important. Like the independent farmer, the manager must be a jack-of-all-trades.

A manager must be able to make the many management decisions required in modern farm production. These decisions can be made or influenced by the actual owners of the farm, but more often they are left solely to the manager. Crop selection is an example. Crops are usually planted in carefully chosen combinations. If the price of one crop goes down, the farm will have sufficient income from another crop to make up at least part of the loss. At such times, the manager may be required to decide whether or not to store and hold crops with the hope that prices will improve.

The manager must also determine when to plant, fertilize, cultivate, and harvest, and see that harvested crops are packaged, loaded, and sent quickly off to market. He or she may take an active part in securing loans for the operation of the farm, and will certainly be required to keep accurate financial records. Last but not least, farm managers must see that hired workers are properly trained for the work they will be doing.

A farm manager is someone with all the skills and training of a successful farmer: He performs the same duties as an independent farmer, and he enjoys the life that makes farming so attractive. But he does it without making the huge financial investment or taking the subsequent risks that prevent many from finding a better life on the farm. More than one fourth of all American farms are operated by such managers, and even that percentage is expected to rise sharply in the next decade. For those with all the qualifications except the financial, these managerial jobs offer an increasingly good way to earn a living in agriculture.

But not the only way.

Agricultural Service Industries

Jobs requiring farming skills or knowledge are also available in off-farm locations. Such jobs have long been available, but their number and variety have increased dramatically in recent years, and this is where most of the future growth in agricultural employment will occur.

The booming agricultural services industry offers career opportunities in hundreds of occupations, many of which require specialized training, farming experience, or the ability to operate heavy farm equipment. More than 250,000 people work to provide crop and animal services to farmers, ranchers, and farm cooperatives. About half of these workers are employed as laborers, while the rest are professional or technical workers such as veterinarians, agricultural scientists, agricultural technicians, mechanics, machine operators, and crop dusters. Most work for small companies or are self-employed, so earnings in these jobs can vary widely.

Individuals who enjoy working with animals will find they are well suited to many jobs in this industry. The skill requirements vary greatly, from professions requiring advanced degrees to jobs that may be learned in a few days, to trades not associated with farming but that provide services increasingly needed in agriculture. Remember that every highly trained professional—such as a vet—who works in agriculture is likely to need one or more aids or technicians to assist in the work.

Vets who work in agriculture not only provide health care to livestock and pets, but also inspect livestock at stockyards and other points to prevent the spread of disease. They also test for sickness, provide shots for disease eradication, and assist the farmer with other problems. There is a real shortage of vets in the country today, so many vets must ease their workload by entrusting some of the simpler tasks, such as administering prescribed inoculations, to an aide or technician. Most of these assistants will have some advanced technical or agricultural training, but many receive their training on the job; the requirements will vary with the needs of the veterinarian, as dictated by the nature of the practice he or she has established.

Animal breeding associations frequently employ those with a knowledge of genetics or animal management to help them develop improved, more productive breeds of livestock. These animal breeders conduct tests to determine potential growth rates for new breeds of beef cattle and the potential milk production of new dairy breeds. They may also provide artificial insemination services; and where this is so they hire technicians to collect semen from male livestock, and artificially impregnate the females. Most of these technicians learn their jobs through training provided by the breeders.

Other jobs in the livestock service industry are just as easily learned. For example, dairy associations hire and train testers to travel from farm to farm on a regular basis and conduct simple tests on the milk from each cow in the herds, recording the acidity and butterfat content of each as shown by the tests. The job can be learned in hours, and pay is almost always based on the size and number of herds tested.

Dairy and ranch associations employ traveling cattle dehorners to remove the horns from livestock and thus prevent injuries to other animals in the herds, and these employees are frequently trained to provide castration services as well. The job requires only a little farming experience, or it can be learned by anyone with an aptitude for working with animals. Pay is on a piece-rate basis.

In addition to workers to provide animal services such as these, there is an increasing need for custom or general crop services, frequently on a contract basis. Most crop services are offered by self-employed individuals or small companies, but larger companies, which often employ trained scientists and professionals, are becoming more common.

The crop-dusting industry is one of many providing such services. The application of insecticides and pesticides has become very complicated in recent years, so more farmers are contracting with specialists to do this work. Many of the occupations in this field require specialized skills and knowledge, yet these can be acquired through technical training, on-the-job training, or training in other lines of work.

Pilots of crop-dusting planes, for example, generally find their way into the profession because of a love of flying, not out of an initial interest in agriculture. That love of flying is what led Joe Hudson into the profession he prefers to call aerial application.

While still in high school Joe took a job "sweeping up," as he remembers it, at a small airport near Rehoboth Beach, Delaware. He traded working time for flying lessons, and by his senior year in high school had both a commercial pilot's license and a contract to spray mosquitoes for the state of Delaware. He also earned money by running charter flights and doing fish spotting for the commercial fishermen on Delaware Bay.

After graduation from high school, he turned down a college scholarship to enter flying: He borrowed the money to buy two World

War II-vintage aircraft and modify them for agricultural purposes. His second day out, because of inexperience and a ground marker he "kind of miscalculated," Joe wrecked one of the planes. He was back on the job in less than two weeks, and today, operating out of Five Points, Delaware, he owns a small fleet of sleek modern aircraft and provides jobs for pilots, assistants to help in mixing chemicals, and ground mechanics to keep the fleet flying.

"It's a science," says Joe Hudson today. "It's not the kind of glamor thing you see in the air shows." But that was hard to believe as I watched one of his pilots make more than a dozen passes over a wheat field one evening, the racy craft swooping down to within inches of the ground, expelling its cloud of spray, then banking sharply away to go skimming over trees and power lines. It looked very much like aerial acrobatics.

But this is, as Joe Hudson points out, a serious business, with the goal of helping produce higher yields of food at a greater profit to farmers and at lower prices to consumers. From the air today, crops are being planted and fertilized as well as protectively sprayed, so Joe and others like him will offer an increasingly large number of well-paid positions for agricultural pilots and those who assist them.

The assistants need a certain amount of knowledge about the proper use of plant chemicals. The usage of these chemicals, in most instances, must follow certain standards set by law. In most parts of the country the United States Department of Agriculture, through its extension offices, offers free training in mixing and applying insecticides and pesticides. This training would certainly qualify you for a job as assistant in the crop-dusting industry.

Other service industries are far less glamorous, yet they often provide excellent earnings for those who work in them. Often these service businesses are one-man operations, started by enterprising individuals who recognized a need and stepped in to fill it. Many involve skills only remotely related to agriculture, such as the welding service operated by Mike Roberts.

Mike learned to weld as an apprentice ironworker. But a few years ago, after a visit to the region, he decided he wanted to live and work on the Delmarva Peninsula, which consists of Delaware, Eastern Maryland, and a small part of Virginia—an area with only a few factories, not a great deal of major construction, and not too many other businesses that hire welders.

Most residents are fishermen or farmers; others depend on the tourists for a living.

Mike realized, however, that all farms have a large investment in machinery, with many parts that break under stress and require welding. As many of these parts are too large to be transported for repairs, the welding must often be done on the farm; thus Mike knew he had a skill that was needed in agriculture.

With a pickup truck, a portable welder, a few other tools, and a small amount of cash in his pocket, Mike moved to Ocean View, Delaware, and began offering his services to area farmers. He had soon established a welding route, calling on farmers on a regular basis, and almost always he found them waiting with one or more metal pieces in need of repair. By taking his services to the farmer he found that he was also given the smaller jobs that might otherwise have gone to shops in town, and today he owns a thriving business, with plans to hire a second welder and add another truck. He raises vegetables and chickens on a small farm of his own.

"I could name dozens of services needed by farmers," he told me the day he made a call at the farm managed by Ted Bowen. "Most folks forget this is an industry, with the same service needs as any other. Just think of farming in those terms—as industry—and you'll see how any number of skills can be sold to the farmer."

Agricultural Extension Agents

Other, less physical, types of service are provided to farmers by workers in the cooperative extension service. The extension agents, as they are generally called, work with rural residents in areas of agriculture, home economics, youth activities, and local resource development. They are the link between the farmer and the U. S. Department of Agriculture, by whom they are employed jointly in cooperation with state land-grant universities.

Extension agents must hold a degree in agriculture—training in journalism and other communications is extremely helpful. Young graduates also receive specific instruction in extension work through special training programs on a continuing basis, and many are employed seasonally or part-time while earning advanced degrees in agriculture.

The nature of this job makes it ideal for those who like working with people and helping them. The extension agent must work with groups of people. He conducts 4-H meetings, day camps, and seminars, and holds group meetings on topics of special interest to local farmers. Such educational duties mean that good skills in public speaking are a basic requirement of the job.

Agents also work with farmers on an individual basis. When a farmer is having problems with a crop, the extension worker will visit the farm, analyze the problem, and suggest a remedy. The agent may also offer advice on crop selection, rotation, or marketing. When the problem falls outside the agent's own area of training, he or she must know where to go for expert help.

The need for skills in writing cannot be given too much emphasis. The extension agent has no duty more important than that of providing information to the local community. Most write articles for publication in local newspapers, often as regular columns that appear once a week. Others provide marketing reports for the media, sometimes appearing on radio or television to personally present these reports, and a few agents write scripts for documentary films that educate the public.

Skills in writing will become even more essential in the years just ahead. According to the Department of Agriculture, "As agricultural technology becomes more complicated, more extension workers trained in education and communications will be needed to disseminate information concerning advances in agricultural research and technology to the farm population. Also, modern farmers are college educated and, thus, more likely to use innovative farming practices. This will increase the demand for extension agents able to relay advances in farming practices from researchers to farmers."

More than 16,000 extension workers are employed—most of them working out of the more than 3,000 county extension offices found across the country. Depending on the population of the county, the size of the local staff ranges from a single agent (who serves a wide variety of clientele interests) to a dozen or more agents, each with special training, and perhaps that many nonprofessional aides. The amount of time spent by an agent in outdoor work is equally variable, but most spend at least part of each day in the field.

The salary paid to an extension agent also varies by locality, but, by and large, earnings are competitive with those of other municipal and county professional employees, such as schoolteachers. In addition to their salaries, since most extension offices are located in rural areas, many agents find it possible to own and operate small farms that can be run on a part-time basis. Few career combinations are better suited to one another.

Agricultural Extension Aides

A degree in agriculture is needed by anyone hoping to work as an extension agent, but opportunities also exist for those without higher education. Depending on the population of the county, the extent of its farming activity, and the subsequent size of the staff, a local office may hire aides to ease the workload of agents. Farming experience would certainly be helpful to anyone seeking a job as agricultural extension aide, but even that may not be an absolute requirement.

On a visit to the post office I came across a bulletin informing the public that the local county extension office was looking for a person to be trained as an aide. A high-school education or its equivalent was the only requirement set forth, though the bulletin added that some typing skills would be a plus.

In checking into this, I learned that the person selected for this job would be trained to call on local farmers, collect data about their problems, and prepare reports for agents. The training period would last for several months, after which the aid would be provided with a car and sent out to work independently. Half the day would be spent in the field, collecting data, and the rest would be spent preparing reports and compiling information to answer questions farmers raised. Starting salary was just over $8,000, which, I was told, "may be a little lower than in other parts of the country, because this is considered an economically depressed area, and local wages are not as high as the national average."

While the pay for such workers may not be great, the experience gained could be critical to your chances of financing a farm of your own. Those who enjoy living and working in a rural setting may find extension work the ideal career. If such work appeals to you, information about job openings is available from county extension offices, the state director of the Cooperative Extension Service located at each land-grant university, or by writing the Extension Service, U. S. Department of Agriculture, Washington, DC 20250.

3
OUTDOOR RECREATION

John Feather was the best fishing guide I met in Ontario. An Algonquin Indian, he worked out of the tiny village of Killarney, where he also served on the Village Council, and his clientele included such notables as Bing Crosby and Branch Rickey, both of whom maintained fishing cottages near Killarney. They hired John not only because he knew exactly where to take the largest bass, perch, pike, and muskies from the brilliantly clear waters of Lake Huron, but also because fishing with him was an enjoyable experience one never forgot. For his services as a fishing guide, he charged $20 per day, plus expenses, which included at least one case of cold Canadian beer.

My first trip out with John began in a disappointing manner. Our party of three had gone to Killarney hoping to battle some of the giant muskies, or at least to set our hooks in some bragging-size northern pike. But our first hour of casting had brought not a single fish to the boat, and we were beginning to wonder about this guide we had hired.

John then rigged his own line with the oddest lure I have ever seen. It was a set of treble hooks fixed to a beer opener—the kind of opener you used before the invention of the pop-top can. Without a word or a glance, he gave the contraption a toss, slowly turned the handle of his reel, and watched his rod bend under the strike of a northern. He repeated the process half a dozen times in the next few minutes, until the three of us were catching fish on identical lures we begged him to sell us.

At the end of a day, when we had all the fish we could legally keep, John told me that he got the openers without cost from a beer distributor and that selling them as fishing lures had turned into a lucrative little sideline. His lures show that folks are willing to pay those who will help them find more enjoyment in the outdoors. With a little creativity, you can make a living from the simplest things.

The field of outdoor recreation was already a booming industry when I went fishing with John Feather, but few could have predicted how big it was going to become. Almost any outdoor skill can now be turned into a major source of income, and outdoor recreation management has a future that looks more promising than almost any career field one can name.

Lots of people have had success in the great outdoors.

For example, I met Jim Power in the spring of 1978, when I visited Boyne City, Michigan, to do a magazine article about the mushroom festivals held in that region. Mushroom hunting in Michigan has become enormously popular in recent years, drawing many thousands of visitors from all parts of the country. Most of them come in April and May, when the mushrooms known as morels are found. During that short season, Jim acts as guide for mushroom hunters. He charges $12 per person a day, taking his customers out in groups, and he locates business by offering his services through area hotels. In asking Jim about this unusual business, I learned that he works as a fishing guide during the summer, as a hunting guide during the fall and early winter, and as a ski instructor later on.

"I won't try to tell you I'm getting rich," he told me with a laugh. "But I'm certainly not starving, I'm not getting ulcers, and one of my biggest problems is trying to remember what it was like working for a living."

Jerry Yingling is another person who earns good money doing what he likes best. After retiring from his job as a machinist in New Jersey and settling near Bethany Beach, Delaware, Jerry quickly found that the upkeep on his fishing boat was costing more than he had anticipated. He decided to help cover those costs by chartering the boat to fishermen one or two days a week. Word quickly spread that Jerry's customers were bringing in fine catches of sea trout, flounder, and bluefish, and today his biggest complaint is, "Seems I never get to go fishing alone." He charges $60 a day for a party of four—which sounds like a high price until one considers the $150 my husband and I paid for a day of shark fishing in 1978, or the $300 per day charged by white-marlin boats out of Ocean City, Maryland.

As I was gathering material for this book, I came across a newspaper account of one fellow who runs a jogging school for visitors to a luxury hotel in Puerto Rico, with reported earnings of $600 weekly. Another account tells of a young man who leads cross-country ski excursions for a resort hotel in Minnesota. Yet another describes the business operation of an imaginative Australian who earns his living providing instruction in the art of boomerang throwing. (Yes, I realize there is no great boomerang craze in America yet. But look at the money we spend on frisbees, and I'd almost bet that somebody, somewhere, will find a way to take advantage of that fad.)

The opportunities I have just described are by and large self-created ones. They are actually small businesses, requiring the same management skills as any business. No one can predict how well they will pay—it depends on how well they are run and how successfully the operator attracts customers. But if you prefer the security of a salary to the adventure of owning your own small business, you should also know that jobs similar to these (and many more) are available in the private sector. Because of the development of public outdoor recreational facilities, there has been an increase in privately owned recreational businesses. This in turn has created thousands and thousands of jobs for those with the necessary outdoor skills.

Each time a large impoundment of water is created by the Army Corps of Engineers, for example, many new businesses develop that cater to outdoor enthusiasts. In a single year, on one particular lake, for instance, private citizens, commercial enterprises, and quasipublic agencies invested more than $40 million in improvements and recreation facilities. Private developers today almost always match the public funds expended for development in recreational areas.

For example, resort hotels need lifeguards; they need people qualified to guide hunting and fishing parties or to lead wilderness backpacking trips. Marinas need workers who have the skills to keep equipment in top working order. Instructors in every outdoor sport are almost always in demand.

Other opportunities are found with the private concessionaires. Such concessionaires are found in both state and national parks. They may rent canoes or horses, outfit mountain climbers, offer guided raft trips down a whitewater river, or almost any other outdoor service you can name.

A ranger with the National Park Service, in mentioning the concessionaires as a good source of training and experience, advised, "Though a list of concessionaires is available from the Park Service, the best way to get started is to apply in person. Visit a national park and see what the concessionaires are offering, what skills are needed. Get acquainted with the manager or owner. Let him know of your interest. Chances are better than good one of them will offer you at least a part-time job to start with, leading to full-time work as you gain experience. I could tell you about several part-timers who went on to develop businesses of their own."

Other groups with outdoor interests need your services. Local museums of natural history and groups such as the Audubon Society and the National Geographic Society sometimes offer guided nature expeditions to their members, and there are many specialized travel agencies who do the same. The Smithsonian Institution, for example, through ads in *The Smithsonian* magazine, offers foreign and domestic study tours. Here are a few of the domestic tours offered in a recent ad:

Yellowstone in Snow—Explore Jackson, Wyoming, in the shadows of the magnificent Tetons; discover Yellowstone in the peace of the winter season; learn about the wildlife of the park and the surrounding region.

Big Bend National Park—A guided nature tour of this Chihuahuan Desert wilderness park in southwest Texas.

Victorian Washington—A fascinating program of lectures and neighborhood walking tours to learn about the city's 19th-century history.

If you have a real knowledge of the natural history of your region, chances are good that you can find a job guiding tours such as these. As a matter of fact, local knowledge is often the key to getting any of the jobs just mentioned. Your skills in mountaineering might be needed in Alaska, for instance, but they would not be so valuable in a state like Delaware, where the highest point is a sand dune with an elevation of about 400 feet; and your knowledge of sand dune ecology would lose much—but not all—of its value in a region with no dunes. Your chances of getting one of these jobs are far better if you apply in an area with which you are intimately familiar, carefully matching your skills to the needs of an employer.

Most of these jobs are seasonal, like the activities with which they are associated. Pay is not the highest. For those reasons, they are too often spurned by those planning professional careers in the field of outdoor recreation. Yet a few seasons spent working in one or more of these jobs could prove to be the most worthwhile time you will ever spend.

Not only will such a job test your aptitude for the work and perhaps help to pay for your education, it will also give you the opportunity to improve your outdoor skills while learning to work with a variety of people—some of them highly competent outdoorsmen. It will provide you with work experience that will be considered important if you decide to apply for a full-time, professional job in outdoor recreation. This point cannot be stressed too strongly. Even if you hold a degree related to outdoor recreation, or if you are working to obtain one, your past experience in an outdoor job could be critical to reaching your career goal.

Employers in this field, far more than in most others, tend to look at the over-all qualifications of the applicant, not just at his or her education. Experience can frequently be substituted for at least part of the education. The National Park Service lists "scuba diving, horsemanship, boating, crafts, mountaineering, etc.," as a few of the skills it considers in reviewing applications—and what better way to prove these skills than by showing past experience on a job where they were put to use?

You should also realize that if you apply for a career job without being able to list such credentials, you are almost certainly handing the opening to another applicant. The field of outdoor recreation is booming but the competition for these highly desirable jobs is very, very keen. The National Park Service receives about 100 applications for each job opening, and the ratio is about the same at other public agencies. This means that the holder of a degree with honors may lose the job to one with similar education and experience.

So get all the actual on-the-job training possible, even if it means working as a volunteer. By adding experience to your other qualifications you will have a good headstart on the job you want in the future.

Entry-level Jobs

Because the competition for outside jobs is so great, you might also consider working your way outdoors from indoors. While most of the agencies offering jobs in this field are swamped by applications from people wanting to work as rangers, aides, guides, or technicians, they sometimes have great difficulty filling other positions. Tom Wilson of the National Park Service tells me, "Clerks, secretaries, and various management assistants of nonprofessional level are almost always needed," and he adds that these jobs not only provide a means of entry into the Civil Service system but also give workers inside knowledge of vacancies and the needs of the parks. It is a situation that exists in many public agencies, and at Assateague Island National Seashore I talked with one young lady who was taking advantage of it.

Although Linda Brooks holds a degree in marine biology from the University of Delaware, she had been unable to find a summer job in her specialty. However, she was able to find work as a clerk-typist at Assateague—and only a few weeks after accepting that job she was made assistant to the park naturalist. It is outdoor work she loves, better suited to her training, and it is a job she would have missed if she had been unwilling to make the sacrifice.

Recreation Planners

Recreation planner is another indoor job that might be used as a springboard toward outdoor work, though it is a professional job requiring a degree. Recreation planners are hired by all agencies in the field, and the competition for available openings is not so great. Some time on this job could make it far easier to step into a meaningful outdoor job.

Wendy Brand is one recreation planner who could do just that. Ms. Brand works for the Heritage Conservation and Recreation Service of the U. S. Department of the Interior. After obtaining her degree in recreation and going to work for the Interior in 1970, she quickly became their first female grants project officer with field responsibility. She reviewed applications for grants, performed onsite inspections, met with state and local officials to discuss problems and solutions, and generally served as a source of information about the agency. She is currently working on a recreation study for the city of Seattle, Washington.

"One of the rewards of my job," she writes, "is the chance to see a vacant lot turned into a useful recreation facility within a short period of time, knowing that I had a small part in making it happen."

It is worth noting here that the Heritage Conservation and Recreation Service, created in 1978 by President Carter to replace the old Bureau of Outdoor Recreation, is largely a planning agency, responsible for channeling federal funds to state and local governments. When funding is approved by Congress, "several thousand jobs in at least 800 categories will be created on the state and local level." Only a few of these jobs will be found within Heritage itself, and relatively few of those will be outdoor-oriented. I point this out because the old Bureau of Outdoor Recreation received thousands of inquiries annually about jobs as ranger, even though it had not a single ranger on its staff. Virtually every agency involved in outdoor recreation reports a similar situation—a flood of inquiries about jobs that do not exist within that agency. You can save a lot of time and trouble by doing a little preliminary research before you start sending out letters of inquiry. Federal Job Information Centers can tell you what positions exist in which agencies.

Recreation Resource Specialist

The job of recreation resource specialist (although it is often called something else) is another professional job that exists in most agencies. Like the recreation planner, the resource specialist devotes only a little time to outside work, though most are qualified. But while the planner concentrates on the utilization of resources, the resource specialist pays attention to the economics.

Jean Kujawa, a former high-school teacher of economics, who also holds a masters degree in business administration, is one who looks at recreation from this point of view. Now with the Bureau of Reclamation, she deals with the overall funding of future projects, with an eye toward determining how these will relate to other public and private recreational projects. She also represents Reclamation in its dealings with other federal agencies such as the Park Service. Beginners in this job, like those starting as recreation planners, start at a salary of $13,014 with most federal agencies, but the pay can go as high as $38,160. Perhaps more important to those interested in outdoor work, though, is the fact that some time spent here can help qualify one for almost any job in outdoor recreation.

Ms. Kujawa notes that while "more and more women are studying fields related to recreation, still a small percentage actually hold jobs in the profession. So, to obtain 'that cutting edge,' one should receive training in management as well as recreation, and it is always well to take *any* job that provides some experience in the field." It is advice that both sexes would do well to follow.

Virtually every employer in the field offers inside employment that can provide entry and experience that will make it easier to reach your real goal, and these often involve skills not normally associated with outdoor work. Here are a few positions found in the National Park Service, any of which might lead, eventually, to a well-paid job in outdoor recreation: accountant; administrative assistant or officer; budgetary assistant; curator; information specialist; management and systems analyst; paralegal specialist; photographer; procurement officer; writer and editor.

Maintenance Workers

No matter what your true career goal may be, you should not overlook the possibility of using a job in park maintenance as a means of reaching it. In almost every park or recreation area in the country, there is at least one maintenance worker, and in some parks the carpenters, electricians, plumbers, painters, janitors, general maintenance workers, and motor-vehicle operators account for more than half the payroll. Competition for these jobs is usually not so great as for those in management, and many have worked at them for a while and then gone on to other careers within the system. For others, however, this becomes a rewarding career in itself: They assist in maintaining the natural environment, in fighting forest fires, in building conservation projects, constructing nature trails, planting trees and wildlife cover, and a variety of other duties that make their jobs interesting and worthwhile.

Leroy Ross, chief of maintenance at Assateague Island National Seashore, found a very satisfying way of life in this important work, though it was not his original choice as a career.

Mr. Ross took his degree in ornamental horticulture, which he supplemented with additional training in landscape architecture. He put this training to good use on his first job, which was with the Urban Parks Division of the National Park Service, but he says he was only biding time until he could go to work in a more rural environment.

His chance came when he was offered a job at Everglades National Park, as supervisor of road maintenance. He remained in that position until another promotion brought him to Assateague, where he supervises a permanent staff of about a dozen workers. He lives with his wife and children near the tiny community of Berlin, Maryland, a mile or so from Assateague, and his only complaint is that promotions have reduced the amount of time he can spend doing outdoor work.

His employees, like all other maintenance workers with the National Park Service and most of those with other federal agencies, are hired on the local level and their wages are based on wages paid in the private sector of the region. "Usually, there is no written exam," says the Park Service. "Applicants are rated according to their training and experience." I asked Leroy to describe the training and experience he seeks when adding to his staff.

"The 'jack-of-all-trades' has the best chance with us," he told me. "Somebody who can do a little electrical work, a little plumbing, a little carpentry, and who has all-around mechanical ability. A broad background in civil engineering is what I'm really describing, and some experience with the Army Corps of Engineers is the best way I know of getting that background; applicants who have spent some time working for the Corps often have the ideal qualifications for these jobs."

Seasonal Jobs

Even with the National Park Service or other large-scale employers in the field of outdoor recreation, the odds are good that your first job—no matter what your training and no matter what your ultimate goal—will be a seasonal one. This is true simply because park work, like all jobs in outdoor recreation, is irrevocably linked to the seasons of the year, with far more workers needed during peak periods than at other times. The National Park Service, for instance, has a permanent staff of about 10,000, less than 3,500 of whom actually work outdoors on a regular basis. But it hires about 7,000 seasonal workers each year, and more than half of these are placed on outdoor jobs. A similar ratio exists in most park systems.

These jobs not only pay reasonably well and provide extremely important training and work experience for the future, but are also essential to your chances of filling a professional position with any large public recreation system. Talk to almost any professional worker in the field of outdoor recreation and you will learn that he or she worked at one or more seasonal jobs before being hired on a full-time basis: *Advancement almost always comes from within the system.* By taking a temporary job, you give the employer a chance to evaluate your skills and aptitudes and you increase your chances of stepping into the first full-time vacancy that occurs.

Not that these temporary jobs are menial or dull. If anything, the exact opposite is true. During my research visit to Assateague Island, for instance, I observed seasonal workers acting not only as lifeguards, receptionists, and guides, but also sharing the duties of the full-time professional staff. One young girl led a daily canoe excursion on Chincoteague Bay. Another worker demonstrated how to dig the quahog clams that thrive in these waters, while another was demonstrating the art of crabbing. At the campgrounds, a seasonal employee taught visitors how to prepare a seaside clambake, and others gave daily presentations on the natural history of the region.

Competition for these jobs is understandably keen. To have any real chance of getting one, you should pay *at least* one or two visits to the park where you want to work, find out what jobs exist at that park, and then *inquire and/or apply well in advance of the peak season.* With the National Park Service such early application is mandatory, and with other systems it is good common sense. If you want a summer job, go after it in the autumn or winter, and look for winter jobs during the summer. *Seasonal jobs will be filled before the season begins.*

The National Park Service is the largest single employer of seasonal employees in outdoor recreation; however, the individual states, when taken in combination, provide a larger number of jobs, so almost any job found with the NPS will also exist on the state or local level. The pay, the requirements, and the duties may vary on these other levels, but the standards of the National Park Service provide the best guidelines in planning your search for a seasonal job.

Seasonal lifeguards are employed at many parks. Among the national parks using them are Assateague Island, Cape Cod, Cape Hatteras, Coulee Dam, Delaware Water Gap, Fire Island, Gateway, Golden Gate, Gulf Islands, Lake Mead, Padre Islands, and Point Reyes. To qualify, you must be at least 18 years of age, possess a current Red Cross life saver's certificate or water safety instructor's certificate, and have at least 3 months' lifeguard or water safety instructor experience. You may also be required to pass a performance test and complete additional training courses in rescue work. As of 1978, starting wages for a lifeguard were $4.02 per hour.

Students majoring in history, science, engineering, and landscape architecture are also hired as trainees during the summer months. They work out of the National Park Service headquarters in Washington, D.C., or the Denver Service Center in Colorado, though a few are assigned to work in individual parks. They gain on-the-job training while assisting professionals in science, history, and engineering projects. To be eligible, you must have completed your first year of study at an accredited college and be actively pursuing a degree related to one of these professional fields. Student trainees earn the same wages paid lifeguards.

Seasonal Aides and Technicians

A large number of park aides and technicians are hired on a seasonal basis. They share many of the same duties, but the technicians work with less supervision and earn slightly higher wages. As of 1978, technicians began at $4.51 an hour, while aides started at $3.57 or $4.02, depending on their background.

To be hired as an aide you will need 6 months' experience of a general nature that is related to park operations, or a high school diploma or certificate of equivalency. A valid driver's license may also be required.

To be accepted as a technician the Service requires "1½ years of experience of a general nature and 6 months of specialized experience directly related to park operations, recreation or conservation work which provides a good knowledge of standard practices required in park operations. Successful completion of at least 2 years of college study may be substituted for the required experience if course work includes any field-oriented natural science, social science, history, archaeology, police science, park and recreation management, community outdoor recreation, or other disciplines related to park management." Since technicians sometimes perform as lifeguards, having the necessary certificate for that will improve your chances, and a driver's license will almost certainly be helpful here also.

Duties assigned to aides and technicians include fee collection, conservation and restoration work, firefighting, nature interpretation, and assistance in law enforcement. They also serve as guides, dispatchers, and receptionists, as well as seeing to the public safety and providing information to park visitors. Their varied duties provide training that enables many to find full-time positions.

To apply for one of these seasonal jobs you should first contact the nearest office of the Civil Service Commission and establish your eligibility. Then write the nearest regional office of the National Park Service and request an application for seasonal employment. An application for a summer job must be returned between December 1 and January 15. Applications for seasonal jobs in parks where heavy visitation occurs during the winter months should be submitted as soon as possible after June 1, and in no event later than July 15. On this application you will be allowed to list no more than two parks at which you desire consideration, and two types of job you would like. It is imperative, therefore, that you make an effort to find out which parks might need the skills you possess, and apply accordingly. The

Park Service publishes many pamphlets and brochures about the individual parks that can be of help, and these can be obtained from the parks or regional offices. If you are a student, you may also increase your chances by including a transcript or a list of courses you will have completed by the time your employment begins.

Permanent Aides and Technicians

After gaining some experience on a seasonal basis, many of the park aides and technicians are selected for full-time employment. Most aides are quickly promoted to technician—and experienced technicians can earn an annual salary of as much as $20,699. The pay is good because these technicians are capable of assuming many of the duties of the park ranger—the key member of all park operations. And opportunity does not end here, for many technicians do go on to fill jobs as rangers, and some are promoted to higher management positions.

Seasonal work makes good sense: To qualify for full-time employment the applicant must have 6 months of technical specialized experience *actually gained in park operations,* perhaps as park guide, tour leader, or guard. Some applicants are hired solely on the basis of education, but competition for these jobs is so great that the experience should be thought of by applicants as an absolute requirement.

Simply because they have this experience, technicians on the permanent staff are likely to be found performing many duties once the prerogative of the rangers and other professionals. Following the directions of these professionals, they work at preserving and restoring buildings and sites in historic and archaeological areas. They may assume nearly complete control of campground operations, assigning campsites, replenishing firewood, performing safety inspections, and being of general assistance to the public.

Technicians also lead guided tours and give talks to groups of visitors. They operate projectors and sound equipment for slide shows and movies. They direct traffic, go on road patrols, and perform many other duties designed to make a park visit more enjoyable for the visitor.

"Our real job—in fact, our only job—is helping Americans enjoy

America," I was told by one technician. "And that means you've got to enjoy working with people. I mean really enjoy it. I'd say half of each working day is spent in some kind of communication, even if that means only giving directions on how to reach a campground. This is no job for the born grouch, or for the guy who can't leave his personal troubles at home, or for the one who's somehow always too busy to answer a question. We work for our visitors and they have a right to go away liking the people they've hired."

A real liking for people, that warmth of personality and spirit of friendliness, is never listed by the employers as a job prerequisite, yet it is a quality found in almost all who are successful in this field. This is especially true of those who fill one of the most visible and exciting jobs in outdoor recreation—that of park ranger.

Park Rangers

The park ranger's job is by far the most popular in outdoor recreation, yet the nature of the job is widely misunderstood. It is often confused with the job of forester, but as the Park Service points out, while some park rangers are qualified foresters, not all foresters are rangers. The job involves more than one discipline.

A ranger today includes such former career designations as park historians, naturalists, and archaeologists. A large park may employ one or more rangers with specialized training in each of these fields, but at smaller parks a single ranger may be required to have a working knowledge of each, and much more.

Rangers are responsible for planning and carrying out conservation efforts designed to protect plant and animal life from fire, disease, and the bad effects of heavy visitor usage. They conduct programs of public safety, including law enforcement and rescue efforts. They design and put together interpretive programs such as lectures, nature walks, and dramatic presentations, all carefully planned to make visitors more aware of the natural and historic significance of the park.

Recreation activity planning, park organization, financial management, supervision of aides, technicians and other employees—these are more of the duties the ranger must handle within the park. Other duties, such as environmental education programs, are frequently performed beyond the boundaries of the park, but even then the ranger is found wearing the familiar uniform.

Because of the growing problems with crime and vandalism within the parks, the Park Service looks for applicants with adequate training in the social and behavioral sciences, and the welcome mat is usually out for those with actual police experience.

To qualify for the job of park ranger on the entry level you must have completed a full 4-year course in an accredited college or university leading to a degree with at least 24 semester hours in one or not more than two of the following: park and recreation management, any field-oriented natural science, history, archaeology, police science, sociology, business administration, the behavioral sciences, or closely related subjects applicable to parks management. Three years of actual experience in park or conservation work may be substituted for the degree. In combining education with experience, an academic year of study (35 semester hours or 45 quarter hours) is considered equivalent to 9 months' experience. Most successful applicants have the degree *and* some actual experience, the latter usually obtained through seasonal employment while in school.

To apply for the job, check with your nearest post office and take the Civil Service entrance exam. On the application you will be asked to specify one region of your choice, so you would do well to make an effort to match your qualifications to the region where they are most likely to be needed. A historian, for instance, should apply in a region with a large number of monuments, landmarks, and historical sites, such as Washington, D.C.

The competition for this job is so keen that you may not be hired immediately upon applying. It is extremely important, therefore, that you stay in touch with the Civil Service and keep your name on its list of eligibles. Persistence is essential.

Malcolm Ross, chief ranger at Assateague Island, is one who knows that persistence is rewarded. It gave him the job he holds today.

Early in life Malcolm had set this goal for himself, so he prepared for it, while still in high school, by finding seasonal work with various concessionaires at Grand Teton and other parks. While at the University of Miami, where he took a degree in geology with a minor in botany, he added more experience as a maintenance worker during the summers at Everglades National Park. He felt fully qualified to work as a ranger by the time of his graduation, but his first application brought no response from the Park Service.

Over the next three years Chief Ranger Ross worked at a number of jobs, but each summer he managed to add to his experience by working at a private lodge in Jackson Hole, Wyoming. Throughout this period, he stayed in touch with the Park Service and had himself retested to maintain his Civil Service eligibility—and finally, after taking the test for the fifth time and just as he was about to lose hope, he was hired as a full-time ranger with the National Park Service.

Like all new rangers, Ross spent most of his first year in developmental assignments, including enrollment in the course "Introduction to Park Operations" at the Horace M. Albright Training Center at Grand Canyon, Arizona. This is a period of critical evaluation, a probation period carefully designed to weed out those who do not have the aptitude and temperament for this line of work.

After leaving Grand Canyon, Chief Ranger Ross worked at Shenandoah for a brief period, was transferred to Lake Mead, which sprawls along the border between Nevada and Arizona, sent to the Park Police Training Center in Georgia, and again assigned to Shenandoah. After three more years as ranger there, he was promoted and transferred to his present position at Assateague.

Looking back on it all, Chief Ranger Ross feels the path might have been much easier had he earned his degree in police science. "We deal with all kinds of people, most of whom are fine folks. But because we have to deal with so many people, it's very important for those who want to become rangers to study the social sciences. I can't emphasize that enough." But no matter what your course of study may be, Chief Ranger Ross has some additional advice that deserves attention. He says, "When starting out in your career, you've got to find a way—by hook or by crook—of breaking into the system. This means take any job you can get—typing, sweeping floors, even volunteer work or a job in the concessions. If you can't get even one of these jobs at first, then visit the parks and talk to the rangers until you do. If they see that you're really interested and dedicated, most will go out of their way to help. Sooner or later, you'll get a foot in the door, and you'll find you move through the ranks pretty quickly."

Joe Fisher, the ranger who serves as chief naturalist and interpretive specialist on the staff at Assateague, provides another example of the persistence that is sometimes needed. After receiving his earth science degree with a major in biology from the University of Pennsylvania, Joe found that he was being offered plenty of desk jobs with other agencies, but nothing from the Park Service. He made his résumé more attractive by returning to school, this time with a major in history and minors in journalism and communications. He was hired before another year was out.

The additional education has served him well. Today, after a dozen years with the Park Service, he supervises a staff of six technicians that has the responsibility for the exhibits, environmental education, guided tours, and daily lectures at Assateague, as well as for writing and publishing the free brochures handed out to the public. The job involves a little more financial management and paperwork than Joe would like, but he loves it. The chance to meet people, pursue his outdoor interests, and live in a part of the country he likes has been very rewarding.

Ranger Martha Aikens, who serves as staff interpretive specialist at Everglades National Park, is another who puts her summers to good use and found a career in outdoor recreation. While majoring in parks management at the University of Virginia she did seasonal work as a technician at Assateague and Chincoteague. Immediately upon graduation she was hired and sent to Grand Canyon as a ranger trainee, and then to a special training session in environmental education at George Williams College in Wisconsin.

Following this special training Ranger Aikens was assigned to the Capital Parks in Washington, D.C., where she worked in several pilot programs in environmental education, and then she was given her present assignment at Everglades.

Her duties there involve inspecting interpretive facilities and devices; assisting in selecting and training both temporary and permanent employees; working with the public, conservation groups, community officials, and educators; and assisting in the development of annual work schedules and financial budgets.

Even with these many duties as part of her job, Ranger Aikens performs most of her work outdoors—walking, wading, canoeing, and operating a boat. "The most important quality for this job," she feels, "is a strong, personal commitment to the environment because one must encourage the development of an environmental consciousness in employees and visitors."

As of 1978, most new rangers were paid a starting salary of $13,014, but advancement is quick and most earn an annual wage in excess of $20,000. Promotion to district ranger, park manager, and other upper-level management jobs can lead to wages at the very top of the governmental scale—$50,000 or more. Almost all of these jobs are filled by former rangers.

As you may have noticed by now, during their careers most rangers can expect to be assigned to several different parts of the country, perhaps even to urban areas. And you may be surprised to learn, as I was, that more than half work in areas east of the Mississippi.

"We try to take account of each employee's preferences," says the Park Service, "but we cannot guarantee that a ranger will remain stationed in only one area."

"I don't know why they apologize for *that!*" laughed one ranger when I mentioned it to him. "What other job gives you the chance to become intimately acquainted with one fantastically beautiful part of America after another? To me, it's the best fringe benefit the job has to offer."

Park Guards

The National Park Service, like all other park systems, also hires a large number of guards to patrol and protect the public's property. Most are hired on a permanent, full-time basis, because that property must be protected throughout the year.

There are no special educational requirements for guards, but the Service does look for qualifying experience, and the more of this you have, the better your chances—and your starting salary—will be. Desirable experience listed by the Park Service includes: "service in the armed forces, Coast Guard, federal, state, local government or private protection agency, which involved guard duties such as protecting lives, property from theft, damage, etc., maintaining law and order, or performing similar duties." Applicants must also have emotional and mental stability, be in good physical health, and be able to stand moderate to arduous physical exertion.

No written test is required for this job. If it appeals to you, you must first contact the Civil Service office with jurisdiction over the region in which you wish to work. Ask to take the guard examination. If you pass and are accepted, your starting salary (as of 1978) will be between $8,366 and $10,507, depending upon your experience, and you will have many opportunities for advancement, perhaps later becoming a member of the Park Police.

Park Police

Although many members of the U. S. Park Police are assigned to duty in areas throughout the nation, all are hired by the National Capital Region of the National Park Service and most are assigned to operations within that region.

Within the District of Columbia the Park Police have the same powers of arrest as the D.C. Metropolitan Police—but they also act as hosts to millions of visitors annually, serving as guides and information specialists, and providing police services for many civic events in the D.C. area. The duties often require irregular, unscheduled hours and sometimes involve personal risks, exposure to all kinds of weather, and arduous physical exertion under rigorous and unusual environmental conditions. But it is highly rewarding work to most who have chosen it as a career.

Private Karen Lee, who graduated from George Washington University with a B.S. degree in special elementary education and worked briefly as an elementary-school teacher, finds this an interesting and challenging profession.

Ms. Lee works in the Communications Section at Park Police Headquarters in Washington, D.C. After a brief stint as desk officer, where she received incoming complaints and dispatched officers, she was assigned to act as relief desk sergeant—spending 3 days in the office and 3 days on patrol. Her desk duties included compiling reports and recording tickets, but like most officers, she preferred the patrol duties and the days of outside work. This included controlling traffic and crowds, assisting pedestrians, opening and closing park areas, helping visitors obtain information and data, and coordinating activities.

Private Lee does little desk work these days. In addition to her patrol duties, she now helps the Park Police promote community relations and conducts environmental education classes for mentally retarded children. Few tasks could be more rewarding than that.

The salary paid members of the Park Police is excellent. As of 1978, most recruits began at $14,415, with even higher wages paid to those with outstanding experience or training. After some time on the job most officers earn a salary in excess of $20,000.

To qualify you must be between the ages of 21 and 31 at the time of appointment, with 2 years of academic study above high school or 2 years of experience "demonstrating the ability to learn and apply detailed and complex regulations and be able to effectively communicate with people individually and in groups," or have a combination of education and experience totaling 2 years. You must also possess a valid driver's license, have good vision, have height in proportion to weight, and, needless to say, be of good moral character. You will also be required to pass a Civil Service exam.

Competition for these jobs is keen—the Civil Service frequently suspends the receipt of new applications under the Park Police exam, due to an overabundance of qualified applicants. To learn if applications are presently being accepted, and for further information about this particular job, direct your inquiry to the National Capital Region of the National Park Service.

Snow Rangers, Ski Patrol Officers, and Wilderness Rangers

With well over 31 million acres set aside for the use and enjoyment of the American people and placed under its care, the National Park Service is the agency that attracts most specialists in the field of outdoor recreation. In recent years, however, certain other agencies have begun to compete for the services of those with the skills needed to help Americans enjoy America. One such agency is the Forest Service of the U. S. Department of Agriculture.

While recreation is a secondary interest of the Service, the 187 million acres, with more than 7,000 camp and picnic grounds and 200 winter sports areas, under the care of this agency may well be the largest playground in the world. They contain the greatest amount of wilderness in America, and also provide Americans with boat-launching ramps, swimming beaches, hiking trails, interpretive centers, and many other recreational facilities.

Every ranger district in the system of national forests has employees with duties similar to those of workers with the National Park Service, with the same qualifications and comparable pay. But the Forest Service also has a few opportunities not found with the National Park Service. Good examples of these are jobs as snow ranger, ski patrol officer, and wilderness ranger, frequently combined under one job heading.

Because the national forests are so popular for outdoor sports, especially in the winter, these jobs have come into being to provide protection for those who participate in these sports—especially protection against the killer avalanche. The Forest Service now has its own avalanche training school, which is used by its employees and by recreation people from across the nation.

To qualify for one of these jobs the candidate must be in excellent physical condition. He or she must be a highly qualified skier and an accomplished mountaineer, for most of the jobs are found in rugged areas of the West. A high-school education or its equivalent is needed, with a thorough understanding of geology, physics, and other natural sciences. In order to forecast avalanches and guard against them, he or she must also know about wind, snow, weather, and terrain. This knowledge, coupled with the special training given these workers, enables them to keep our forests safe for recreational purposes.

Snow rangers have the primary duty of protecting the public from the hazards of deep snow on steep terrain. They do this by identifying hazardous areas and posting warning signs, and by using dynamite or other means to trigger avalanches and render an area safe. They also lead ski patrols and rescue teams, searching out stranded visitors and rendering first aid when necessary. After the snow season is over they perform similar rescue work as it relates to hunters, horseback riders, and backpackers. They are rated as technicians, with starting salaries in 1978 ranging from $8,366 to $11,712, and they are hired according to the Forest Service procedures described in the chapter on forestry.

The Fish and Wildlife Service is another agency that has recently begun to expand its outdoor recreation projects—and understandably so, with annual visitation to its refuges now well beyond the 25 million mark and continuing to climb.

Most of our wildlife refuges are large enough to accommodate a great number of visitors without unduly disturbing the birds and wildlife. Recognizing this, the Service has recently begun to add recreation specialists to resident staffs at some of the more popular refuges, hiring them through procedures described in the chapter on fish and wildlife management.

The recreation on these refuges tends to be somewhat specialized; most visitors are there for the purpose of viewing or photographing the wildlife. But more varied forms of recreation are being offered—such as hunting, swimming, boating, hiking, and camping—and the Fish and Wildlife Service is likely to increase its recreation budget in the years just ahead.

The Tennessee Valley Authority is another employer not to be overlooked by anyone hoping for a career in the field of outdoor recreation. Hiring is done through its Recreation Services Section at Norris, Tennessee, and the Authority provides employment for a wide range of recreation workers, with pay scales ranging from as low as $3 an hour to well over $20,000 a year.

The TVA has one program of special interest to students enrolled in recreation programs. This continuing program is held at Land Between the Lakes, the huge 170,000-acre isthmus in western Kentucky and Tennessee that lies between Kentucky Lake and Lake Barclay, two of the largest man-made lakes in the nation.

The Authority has partially completed a major outdoor recreation and conservation project that has already begun to demonstrate how terrain with limited mineral, agricultural, and forestry assets can be developed as an asset to the economy of the surrounding region. The area's 300 miles of shoreline will eventually have facilities to serve 10 million visitors annually. It has become the region's largest outdoor playground, and has done much to bolster the local economy.

College students from about a dozen southern and midwestern universities and colleges have in years past assisted in workshop training programs for teachers and students at the 5,000-acre Environmental Education Center within the park. Other students assist in the Public Information Center, and still others are hired to supervise recreational programs offered to the thousands who visit this park each year. More students help construct new trail systems, run tests on water-supply and sewage-treatment facilities, or do historical research that will guide restoration. All gain experience that will be useful in building their careers.

The individual states and their political subdivisions have long been the major suppliers of outdoor recreation opportunity—but in recent years the job situation with the states has been tight. That situation may shortly be reversed, however, and the states are likely to once again assume their rightful place as leaders in providing outdoor recreation facilities.

Statewide recreation programs exist in all of the 50 states, with more than 36 million acres set aside for this purpose. Visitors to these areas far outnumber those who visit areas administered by the federal government. The problem is that a lot of money is needed—money that has not been forthcoming from the federal government.

The major source of those funds was to have been the Land and Water Conservation Fund, which was created by Congress in 1965 and amended in 1968 to provide federal grants to the states for recreation and conservation work. Revenues from outer continental shelf mineral leasing programs were to be used to guarantee annual funding of at least $200 million. But in 1973 these funds were impounded by the Nixon administration, leaving the states with inadequate financial resources and causing most to clamp down on new hiring. This caused a rippling effect that was felt wherever recreation workers are hired.

But in 1978, when President Carter created the Heritage Conservation and Recreation Service, he immediately released these (and other) funds and rightfully gave control of them to this new agency. He has also called on Congress for additional funding (in amounts not yet established) so the state and local governments will now be able to hire those who are needed if we are to have strong outdoor recreation facilities. This move truly brightens the future for those interested in helping Americans enjoy America.

For more information contact:

National Parks and Conservation Association
1701 18th Street NW
Washington, DC 20009

National Recreation and Park Association
1601 North Kent Street
Arlington, VA 22209

National Wildlife Federation
1412 16th Street NW
Washington, DC 20036

Here are the addresses of the regional offices of the National Park Service:

North Atlantic Region
15 State Street
Boston, MA 02019
(Connecticut, Maine, Massachusetts, New Hampshire, New Jersey, New York, Rhode Island, Vermont)

Southeast Region
1895 Phoenix Boulevard
Atlanta, GA 30349
(Alabama, Florida, Georgia, Kentucky, Mississippi, North and South Carolina, Tennessee, Puerto Rico, Virgin Islands)

Midwest Region
1709 Jackson Street
Omaha, NB 68102
(Illinois, Indiana, Iowa, Kansas, Michigan, Minnesota, Missouri, Nebraska, Ohio, Wisconsin)

Pacific Northwest Region
601 Fourth and Pike Building
Seattle, WA 98101
(Alaska, Idaho, Oregon, Washington)

Washington Office
National Park Service
Interior Building, Room 2328
18th and C Streets NW
Washington, DC 20240

Mid-Atlantic Region
143 South Third Street
Philadelphia, PA 19106
(Delaware, Maryland, Pennsylvania, Virginia, West Virginia)

National Capital Region
1100 Ohio Drive SW
Washington, DC 20240
(Metropolitan Washington, D.C.)

Rocky Mountain Region
655 Perfet Street
P.O. Box 25287
Denver, CO 80225
(Colorado, Montana, North Dakota, South Dakota, Utah, Wyoming)

Western Region
450 Golden Gate Avenue
San Francisco, CA 94102
(Arizona, California, Hawaii, Nevada)

Southwest Region
P.O. Box 728
Santa Fe, NM 87501
(Arkansas, Louisiana, New Mexico, Oklahoma, Texas)

4
SOIL CONSERVATION

Soil science is one of the oldest sciences known to man; yet, in another sense, it is one of the newest. Born thousands of years ago, at the same time as agriculture, soil conservation was practiced in all parts of the world, and a great deal of writing on the subject was done by the early Greeks and Romans. This writing shows a remarkable understanding of the need for conservation and the means by which it is achieved. But the knowledge of centuries was cast aside as Columbus and others enlarged the known world.

America was to become mankind's greatest example of exploitation. The European settlers, as they began farming this rich, productive soil, saw no need to worry about conservation. It was impossible, was it not, for such rich soil to wear out? And even if the soil of one plot should be exhausted, so much land—so much good earth!—was available that they could simply pack up and move to a new farm just over the endless horizon.

The settlers cut forests away without thought. The land produced well for a few years and was abandoned—allowing the unprotected soil to wash away with each subsequent rainfall. Seldom, if ever, were the forests replanted. These early settlers were mining the soil as well as farming it. Upon learning the use of tobacco from the Indians, the farmers allowed it to become a medium of exchange. No matter what the consequences, as much land as possible was planted in tobacco, year after year, thus depleting essential minerals in the soil.

Thomas Jefferson, on his farm in Virginia, was among the first Americans to seek a less destructive way of farming. He rotated crops, applied fertilizers, prevented erosion by the use of contour plowing, and revived his soil by planting legumes. Jefferson swapped information on these better principles of farming with George Washington, who shared his great love of the land. Few heeded their example.

Much of the best farmland had been lost or destroyed by 1881, when Hugh Hammond Bennett, the father of modern-day soil conservation, was born on a farm in North Carolina. While walking the abused, eroded hills of his father's farm, young Bennett decided to dedicate his life to the study of soil science and to share with others the knowledge he would gain.

After completing his formal education, Dr. Bennett went to work for the U. S. Department of Agriculture's Bureau of Soils and began his crusade to stop destructive farming practices and establish standards for soil conservation. He spent years doing soil surveys, putting the results before anyone who would listen, testifying before Congress, and sounding his lonely call. But not until 1928 did the Department of Agriculture publish *Soil Erosion: A National Menace*, coauthored by Bennett; it was the first USDA bulletin on soil conservation.

Bennett finally began to see his dreams fulfilled in 1935, when soil erosion and conservation work was charged to a single new agency: the Soil Conservation Service of the Department of Agriculture. Within a year of its birth, the new agency had established 147 demonstration projects averaging almost 30,000 acres each, 50 soil-conservation nurseries, 22 research stations, and 454 Civilian Conservation Corps camps under its jurisdiction. During that same period of time, more than 50,000 farmers, with the help of the Soil Conservation Service, had accepted and applied conservation techniques to more than 5 million acres of agricultural land.

Laws were passed authorizing farmers and ranchers to organize soil conservation districts in each of the states. The first such district, suitably enough, was established in Anson County, North Carolina, where Hugh Bennett was born. As of 1978, about 3,000 such conservation districts had been established throughout the country, and they led the way in bringing sound principles of good soil conservation to the ranchers and farmers of America.

Soil Conservationist

An estimated 8,000 soil conservationists are at work, most of them employed by the federal government in the Soil Conservation Service or in the Department of the Interior's Bureau of Indian Affairs.

Those employeed by the Bureau of Indian Affairs generally are found working on or near one of the Indian reservations, most of which are located in the western states, while the others are working to conserve soil throughout the country. Soil conservationists and soil scientists are also employed by state and local governments, and others teach at colleges and universities. Still others are employed by rural banks, insurance companies, the lumber and paper industry, and by others with large holdings of land.

Employment of soil conservationists and scientists is expected to increase about as fast as the average for all occupations throughout the 1980s, with many of the new jobs occurring in banks, public utilities, and other organizations that have large holdings of farmlands or ranchlands. Many such organizations are adding conservationists to their staffs to help them protect the value of farmlands on which they hold mortgages or to help them comply with recent conservation and antipollution laws. A number of colleges and universities will be adding soil-conservation majors to their degree programs, thus increasing the number of teaching positions available.

The jobs in soil conservation are attractive not only because of the great satisfaction derived from doing work so enormously important to society, but also because much of the work is done in the field—providing the conservationist with a better opportunity than most others to work under conditions he loves. The Soil Conservation Society of America describes the work of its members as "A system of using and managing land based on the capabilities of the land itself, involving the application of the best measures or practices known, and designed to result in the greatest profitable production without damage to the land." The conservationist must be out there working closely with the farmers, ranchers, foresters, and others who need his or her skills and knowledge.

If, for example, a farmer is experiencing an erosion problem, the conservationist will visit the farm, identify the cause of the problem, and develop a program to combat the erosion. Where the erosion is caused by water runoff on sloped fields, the conservationist would probably suggest ways to terrace the fields, or to construct pathways so the runoff will not wash away soil. Where the erosion is caused by the wind, a conservationist might suggest planting hedges or trees in an arrangement that will provide windbreaks or may suggest improved techniques of farming, such as providing ground cover by leaving the wheat or corn stalks on the field after the harvest is completed.

In many regions—particularly in the West—rainfall is insufficient to permit the profitable growing of crops. But much of this land can be made suitable for other purposes, such as grazing livestock, if proper water-conservation techniques are applied. In these arid regions, soil conservationists inspect rangelands and work with range managers in selecting sites where ponds can be constructed to provide water for livestock. They may also recommend solutions to problems caused by overgrazing, such as a seeding program for grasslands or placing salt licks in certain areas to lure cattle away from areas that have been overgrazed.

If work such as this sounds a little tame for your tastes, you might be more interested in the snow surveys conducted by soil-conservation workers.

Snow Surveyors

How much water will the farmer in the West have for growing his crops? Will enough water be available for industry and power? Will flooding be a problem this year? Answers to these important questions come from measuring the snow on the watersheds—a duty of the Soil Conservation Service since 1939.

In the West much of the streamflow comes from melting snow high in the mountains. The best way to forecast the water supply is to measure the amount of this snow. Since it would not be practical to measure all the snow in a watershed, a series of samples are taken from key locations to measure the depth and water content of the snow.

Places where snow data are collected are called snow courses. Each is about a thousand feet long, and sampling stations are spaced 50 to 100 feet apart. Small meadows high up in the watersheds are selected for this purpose. In such meadows, snow falls directly on the ground with no hindrance from trees. These sites are chosen so that winds cause no drifting that alter the snowfall pattern.

Snow surveyors travel on set schedules to these remote snow courses. They go as far as they can by snowmobile, then use skis or snowshoes for the rest of the trip. More recently, light planes and helicopters have been used in survey work, but the great difficulty in reaching many snow courses requires that most surveyors travel by snow machine or on foot. In a recent snow-survey season, for instance, snow surveyors logged 30,000 miles by snowmobile and 20,000 miles over the snow by skis or showshoes.

At present there are about 1,500 snow courses throughout the western United States, in Alaska, and in western Canada. These courses are visited and measured several times each winter. Since most of them are very high in the mountains, far from civilization, reaching them requires skills not often taught in school. Snow surveyors are trained to avoid avalanches and to survive against the elements in case they are delayed by blizzards, accidents, or other emergencies. They learn not only to take care of themselves, but also to give first aid should there be an accident.

Shelter cabins are provided at some remote sites for overnight stops and emergencies. In areas where deep snow frequently buries the cabins, "Santa Claus chimneys" are built above the roofs. These have ladders and trap doors at different heights so the surveyors can always climb through the first door above the snow and enter the cabin.

A snow surveyor visits these sites with a variety of equipment in his backpack. For sampling the snow, he carries sections of aluminum tubing long enough, when screwed together, to reach the bottom of the snow. Sections are 30 inches long so the surveyor can carry them in his backpack. On the outside of the tube is an inch scale that indicates snow depth. The tip of the bottom section has a serrated steel cutter blade to cut through layers of ice and hard-packed snow.

Also in the backpack is a driving wrench and weighing scale. Where the snow is extremely deep and contains layers of ice, one surveyor stands on the wrench to force the tube down. A snow core is drawn out and weighed, the scale interpreting its weight as inches of water.

Important in predicting streamflow is the amount of water the soil will absorb from melting snow. Some years the soil may be very dry at the time snow begins to fall. As moisture becomes available from melting snow, some will then filter down into the soil.

To measure this moisture, waferlike soil moisture measuring units are inserted in the soil at different depths. Their resistance changes with the amount of moisture in the soil. This change in resistance is then measured with an ohmmeter; the higher the resistance, the drier the soil. Several hundred of these soil-moisture stations must be checked several times each year by surveyors.

Snow surveyors are always needed by the Soil Conservation Service and they are recruited from all walks of life. There are no special educational requirements for the job, but stamina, good physical health, and a real desire for this rugged, frequently lonely way of life are called for.

The outdoor survival skills and training in first aid already mentioned will make it easier for you to get this job, as will any experience in farming or ranching, or any technical-school training in soil conservation, forestry, agronomy, or the related sciences. When the snow season is over, most snow surveyors remain with the SCS as technicians or aids, though others prefer to work as independent farmers or ranchers.

Snow surveyors are hired and trained on the local level. Pay a visit to any Soil Conservation Service office; if no jobs are presently available at that office, your name will be added to a list of applicants and you will be given a list of offices where openings do exist. The local SCS will also advise you on the procedures for applying.

The pay varies widely because it is based on such variables as local wages, cost of living, etc. Those who take full-time positions as aids or technicians, however, can expect to be earning more than $10,000 at the end of the first year. As often as not, these full-time workers are able to earn that much again by part-time farming or ranching.

Soil Surveyors and Scientists

The most valuable work done by professionals and technicians in the field of soil conservation is the soil survey. It provides information that is useful to people in all walks of life. A few examples provided by the Soil Conservation Service clearly demonstrate the importance of this work.

The town of Cohasset, Massachusetts, saved more than a quarter of a million dollars on its sewage system by using information from a soil survey, which revealed that less than 1 percent of the area was suitable for onsite sewage disposal.

A town close to Detroit, Michigan, however, lost nearly the same amount by constructing its new water main over a wide area of deep peat. A soil survey would have revealed the existence of this peat, which settles, and the main could have been placed in mineral soil, which does not.

More than one hundred new homes in Richmond, Virginia, were flooded, causing several hundred thousand dollars in damages, then promptly flooded again in the following year. A soil survey, which shows the boundaries of flood plains, tells where flooding has occurred and where it is likely to recur, and would have caused these homes to be built in another area.

Foresters use soil-survey information to decide what trees will grow best in a particular area and what conservation measures are needed. Wildlife conservationists find soil surveys helpful in locating and establishing wildlife areas; in building ponds and lakes for fish, ducks, and geese; and in selecting sites for hunting, fishing, and recreation areas. Engineers are major users of soil-survey information. The surveys help them select sites for building airports, highways, dams, and buildings.

The list of those needing soil survey information is almost endless. A primary purpose of making the soil survey, however, is to provide for the nation's agricultural future. Most food can come only from the soil; soil must be protected; and protecting it is possible only when it is understood. Only a few soils produce economically just as they are, but most can be made to produce through the farmer's art. Soil surveys guide the farmer in doing his work.

Most of our farmland is privately owned, so our farmers—nearly 4 million of them—are the ones who must do most of the actual work of soil conservation. The job of the soil conservationist is to give them technical advice based, among other things, on soil surveys.

But what is a soil survey? At the start, the one doing the survey needs a set of aerial photographs that completely cover the area to be surveyed. These are taken from an airplane flying at about 12,000 feet.

With each pass over the area, the plane overlaps the ground covered on the previous flight, thus photographing each part of the same landscape from more than one angle. When the soil surveyor looks at two of these overlapping photographs under a stereoscope, he is able to see the land in three dimensions. Differences in elevation are sharply defined, and hills and valleys are easily seen. The presence of shrubs, trees, and small buildings is made obvious, while draws and canyons, too, can be distinguished. With the aid of the stereoscope, the soil conservationist can mark off certain features of the soil, such as steeply sloping areas, before ever actually putting foot on the land.

With his special training and experience, the soil scientist can study the photographs, confer with his associates, take a preliminary look at the area, and thus come to know a great deal about the soils beneath the surface before the actual field work is begun.

For this field work, the conservationist takes along the photographs (known as field sheets), a spade, a hand auger, and several devices for making on-the-spot tests. It is now time to map the soils.

First walking over the area, the conservationist studies it from the surface. This is followed by the boring and digging of several holes, using a power auger where necessary. Often it is possible to take advantage of recent excavations and bare roadbanks. All soil is made up of distinct layers, and at this stage the scientist notes the texture, structure, color, and thickness of each one. Special attention is now given to soil characteristics that cannot be seen from the surface—for instance, hard subsurface layers that might interfere with water movement and the growth of plant roots.

Thousands of different kinds of soil are known, and the conservationist must now measure or estimate the important properties of those he finds, to establish exactly which types he has. An estimate must be made of how much water flows through the soil and how much will stay there. The steepness of sloping land is calculated and an estimate made of the amount of soil that might be lost to erosion. The depth of the rooting zone is measured, as is the amount of organic matter, and tests are made for acidity and alkalinity.

The location of natural land features such as streams, rock outcrops, lakes, ponds, marshes, and tree stands are added to the charts, along with man-made features such as dams, levees, ferries, fords, buildings, quarries, gravel pits, and cemeteries. Such features help users of the survey locate soil boundaries in the field, many of which will not be obvious from the surface. This information is recorded by placing symbols on the field sheets.

Throughout this process, the soil surveyor draws lines on the field sheets as he leaves one type of soil and comes to another. Some of these lines indicate abrupt changes, while others reveal gradual transitions. Where two types of soil merge, special lines on the field sheets are drawn to show the transition.

The finished field sheets resemble jigsaw puzzles. Each piece of the "puzzle" is marked with a special symbol that is used each time a particular type of soil is encountered.

After this essential field work is completed, soil samples go to a laboratory for further study. These studies serve several purposes.

The worker in the field performs several simple tests that the lab now carries a few steps further. For example, the field worker judges texture by rubbing moist soil between his thumb and forefinger; the laboratory will test his judgment by measuring exactly the percent of sand, silt, and clay in typical samples.

This laboratory work helps in classifying the soils by making each description as precise as possible. For example, the lab can learn the distribution of many important minerals by studying thin sections of soil under a microscope. Other samples may go to specialized labs to be tested for their content of valuable plant nutrients, providing information that will assist farmers and gardeners in their efforts to develop efficient fertilizer programs.

As the soil in the field is mapped and described, the surveyor also places each one tentatively in a class with other soils that have already been described, named, and mapped.

Through the National Cooperative Soil Survey, all soils are classified and named according to a nationwide system. About 80,000 types are presently recognized. The field worker must fit each soil properly into this system. When a new soil is discovered, the soil surveyor selects its name; and later on, after these findings are confirmed, the system is expanded to include the new soil. Most new soils are given a local name, one that indicates the region of discovery, such as "York" or "SoCal."

Throughout the course of such a survey, supervisory soil scientists keep a constant check on the findings to assure that they agree with the national system of classification. Specialists in soil classification—known as soil correlators—have the job of studying the evidence compiled by the field worker and of comparing soils in a new survey with similar soils already classified.

While doing the field work, however, the surveyor is as exacting as possible. Standard terms are used for making notes, and these are organized daily so they may be used as an active reference throughout the course of the survey. At any given moment, the information already collected is available to those who want it. When the field work is done, the notes and field sheets are used in writing a soil-survey report for publication.

As you probably realize by now, the conservationists and soil scientists who conduct such surveys are highly trained individuals. Although aides and technicians often assist with this work, the scientific nature of it requires that most of it be done by one with the proper educational background—a trained scientist.

Until quite recently, only a handful of universities offered degrees with a major in soil science; and for this reason many working conservationists hold degrees in agronomy. Others hold degrees in related fields of the natural resource sciences, such as forestry, wildlife biology, range management, or agricultural education. The course of study generally must include 30 semester hours in natural resources or agriculture, with at least 3 hours devoted to soils.

A background in agricultural engineering is very helpful to the soil conservationist, and courses in cartography, or mapmaking, are nearly essential. Soil conservationists must enjoy working with people and have the ability to communicate with them on several levels, so courses in public speaking and human relations will also prove handy.

"But in addition to this training," I was told by Katherine Mergen of the Soil Conservation Service, "today's professional should have good training in written communications—basic skills such as spelling and the ability to put together a mechanically accurate and logically constructed report, news release, or publishable article. Audiovisual skills will also come in handy for dealing with the public and participating in professional meetings. Also important is any training in the social sciences that will enable the professional to assess economic, cultural, historical, and political impacts of resource decisions."

"A real interest in science is a must for anyone planning a career in soil conservation," says Jim Marthon, a former SCS employee who now works as a private consultant. "The training in science should begin as early as possible, at least during high school, and I would never suggest this as a career to anyone who finds science boring. Sure, it's outdoor work, and that's the best part of it—but to the conservationist the field is just a laboratory as large as the world."

"I hope you'll advise your readers to investigate our student work program," suggested an SCS public-relations officer. "It's the best way I know of starting a career—and there are opportunities for those interested in many natural sciences other than those related only to soil."

You may qualify for this outstanding program if you are a college student majoring in soil conservation, soil science, engineering, farm management, animal husbandry, agronomy, biology, forestry, range management, agricultural economics, or any other agricultural science. The training received could really serve as a catapult at the start of your career.

If you meet that first requirement, you should visit the nearest office of the Soil Conservation Service. You will be given an application form and instructions on how to apply. You will then take a written aptitude test and a Civil Service exam.

Those students selected by the SCS are hired to work during nonschool periods after completing the first year of college. They work each summer during the vacation period, go on leave from the job in the fall, and return to college. Trainees become eligible for promotion between the sophomore and junior year, and are usually promoted again at the end of the junior year.

Upon graduation, without further Civil Service examination, trainees become full-time professionals, usually starting at higher wages than those paid to new employees who did not participate in this program; and time spent as a student trainee even counts toward retirement.

Student trainees learn by doing. They gain practical experience by working under the guidance of qualified experts. Each follows a planned training schedule designed to fit his or her individual goals, and supervisors give study assignments that tie in with the job. The experience and training gained on the job also carry over into the classroom, helping trainees make better selection of courses than might otherwise be the case.

As a trainee in this program, you may work alongside soil scientists, range conservationists, engineers, woodland conservationists, economists, or biologists. Whichever specialty you choose, you will be well on your way to a satisfying lifetime career.

Upon graduation, if you decide to continue with the federal government as a soil scientist or soil conservationist, you can expect to earn an annual salary of around $11,500. Those who had an outstanding record in college, or who held a master's degree, were, during 1977, earning $14,000. Salaries of those with several years' experience ranged from $17,000 to just under $29,000 annually.

In preparing yourself for your career in soil conservation it is quite possible that you will find your aptitudes and interests better suited to the work done by another group of professionals in the conservation field—the agronomists. Their work is so closely related to that of the soil scientists' that the jobs are frequently classified as one, and some knowledge of soil science is essential to a career in agronomy; but pure agronomists use a somewhat different approach to conservation, so let's take a look at what they do, how they do it, and the rewards offered by a career in agronomy.

Agronomists

When the United States Gypsum Company's New Braunfels, Texas, office contacted the local Soil Conservation office, they handed it one of the toughest reclamation problems seen in years: They wanted to grow grass on a barren rock quarry.

"We want to repair the ugly scars of mining, clean up the stream nearby, and bring more wildlife back to the area," Delbert George, works manager for the company, told the SCS. "We think it can be done—but it sure doesn't look like it's going to be easy."

The SCS readily agreed with that, but they were also excited by what the company hoped to accomplish: the revegetation of the same amount of land yearly that they disturbed with their quarry operations—about 10 acres. They assigned agronomist R. B. McDonald the job of helping the company achieve its goal.

McDonald and other SCS plant specialists chose an incredibly tough test site for their first try: an 80-foot-high crushed-rock slope that tilted at a 45-degree angle. Knowing there were no proven methods for growing grass on the steep sides and rough bottoms of the limestone rock quarry, McDonald began to experiment.

First, most of the area was bulldozed to a 20-degree angle. What couldn't be altered was left in a steep slope, then covered with a few truckloads of soil. Most of the soil promptly tumbled down the hillside, but enough remained in place to give some hope of rooting.

McDonald ordered 21 varieties of grass seed from an SCS plant materials center, then he and employees of the company spent days planting the grasses in small separate test plots. Some seed was fertilized, some was only mulched, and some plots were both fertilized and mulched.

Spring found a number of plots sprouting grass. Then a torrential May rainstorm devastated the planting. Only a few patches of green survived. But the fact that even some grass survived in this hostile environment was so heartening that the company and SCS decided to give it another try.

More soil was added, more bulldozing done, more seed planted. The results were surprising, even to the specialists. Luxuriant, dark-green, waist-high grasses sprang up to cover what previously had been gray, crushed-rock surface. Natalgrass, a species imported from Africa, thrived where other grasses were unable to grow.

Today, the scars of the quarry are being healed, the creeks of the region run cleaner, and wild deer and turkey roam the area once again—the agronomist knew which grasses had the best chance of recovering the land.

The people of Texas, like those in most other states, clearly recognize the value of maintaining certain tracts of land in their natural condition. In Texas, however, the state's Parks and Wildlife Department, working with agronomists from the SCS, is making an extensive effort to let modern-day Texans see their land as it was before the arrival of the first settlers.

The casual visitor to the rangeland of Texas rarely appreciates how greatly it has changed over the years. Even in areas remote from the cities and towns, the very plants in front of the viewer are often quite different from those that existed only a century ago. When settlers cleared the land and forests and grazed their livestock, they drastically altered many time-tested and nature-proven plant and animal communities unique to the region.

In 1974, as part of a program to restore these natural communities, the Texas Parks and Wildlife Department stationed a full-time biologist at the James E. Smith Plant Materials Center, operated by the SCS, at Knox City, Texas. The biologist would work with—and receive training from—the agronomists and horticulturists at the center; assist in its operation; and work directly with area parks in the application of plant materials and science.

The purpose of this Plant Materials Center is to assemble, select, test, and provide for the commercial production of plants for conservation purposes. It collects, evaluates, and distributes for field testing plant materials throughout Texas and much of Oklahoma. At any given time about 1,400 plant collections are being evaluated on its 70 acres of irrigated cropland. This includes 290 different species, ranging from grasses to woody plants; and in 1974, 8,000 pounds of seed, 8,538 plants, and 30,760 rhizomes were grown for evaluation.

More than 750 pounds of seed, chosen from a wide variety of species once native to the region, were allotted by the center to the Texas Parks and Wildlife Department for use in local parks. About 7,000 rhizomes and more than 800 native trees and shrubs were also made available.

Even while this first allocation was being planted, agronomists from the center were working with Texas officials in a program to reestablish communities of threatened and endangered plant species. The threat to most of these comes chiefly from man's activities, so the lands of the state park system offer an excellent haven.

Using relic sites, historical accounts, and incorporating scientific knowledge of plant production and species distribution, this program is well on its way toward reestablishing many of the native plant communities and making it possible for visitors to see these areas as they were before the first settlers arrived in Texas.

Why would plant scientists pour rock salt around the base of pine seedlings, as plant technician Donald Hamer was doing the day I visited the Cape May Plant Materials Center at Cape May Court House in lower New Jersey?

"It's part of a long search for pines resistant to salt water and salt spray along the seacoast," I was told, and I learned that this search, joined by the Forest Service for obvious reasons, is nearly over.

The tests, using four species of pines, began in 1971, with 4,000 pounds of rock salt per acre spread around the seedlings. All were stunted as a result, but agronomists quickly realized that Japanese black pine was the most salt-tolerant and white pine was the least.

Later plantings confirmed these early findings, so another test was conducted, with rock salt spread around Japanese black pine seedlings at the incredible rate of 16,000 pounds per acre—and only a single seedling survived.

This single "super seedling" was then transplanted to another site, to be grown as a seed source. Agronomists hope that from this small start will eventually be developed a strain of Japanese black pine able to tolerate great amounts of salt either in the soil or in the air, and that it will be useful in combating the costly erosion that occurs along all our seashores.

The list of such projects could go on and on, for the work of the agronomist takes many directions. One may be involved in research on field crops, crop management and rotation, or weed control, while another might be planning field experiments, making field observations, or providing technical assistance to farmers on agronomic phases of soil-conservation programs.

Basic requirements for a position as agronomist are a bachelor's degree from an accredited college or university with a major in agronomy or closely related subjects, including 10 hours in crop production or plant breeding. Because the plant scientist must know the system of soil classification and its symbols, some emphasis should also be placed on training in soils.

"Even more than those who specialize in soils, I think," agronomist Walter Pitts told me, "the agronomist is called on to interpret for the public the meaning of technical information. If a farmer wants to plant alfalfa and I know that for one reason or another it can't be grown, I have to help him understand why this is so. I don't make planting decisions for him—those are his to make, based on many things—but I do help him understand what is possible, what is not, and why. Many farmers today have a great deal of educational background, but others do not, so it's important that the agronomist have the ability to discuss his findings. It's a part of the job some professionals dislike, but one that I find especially enjoyable. I think anyone wanting to become a plant specialist should love people at least as much as he loves growing things."

Agronomists have many opportunities other than those found with the Soil Conservation Service, though they remain the major employer in the field. Many work for other agencies of the Department of Agriculture, such as the Forest Service or the Extension Service; and others work with private industry or in agribusiness. Salaries range from a low of just over $10,000 for beginners holding the bachelor's degree to more than $30,000 for old pros with advanced degrees. The need to produce more food while conserving the soil, along with greater environmental awareness, however, will cause those salaries to soar in the years just ahead—and job opportunities will be greater than ever for those who love working with things grown on the good earth.

Conservation Aides

If you do not intend to go to college, or if you have already completed your education, the field of soil conservation offers many chances to do worthwhile outdoor work while earning a good living. The highly trained soil scientists and agronomists who set the course of soil conservation need a large number of aides to implement their plans, and the job of conservation aide is open to almost anyone.

The conservation aide does the actual work in a conservation program, planting seedlings at a Plant Materials Center, spreading topsoil in a reclamation effort, or cultivating a field where experimental crops are being grown. The aide also helps farmers practice the measures called for in conservation plans.

To qualify as an aide, you should have some experience as a

farmer, rancher, greenhouse worker, or in a plant nursery, though many aides are hired with no experience at all and given on-the-job training. Participation in any volunteer conservation program may be substituted for actual farming experience (in most cases), and 4-H or Future Farmers of America training will almost always do. Extension courses in the type of agriculture practiced in your region would also prepare you.

"The ideal applicant would be one with a good deal of *local* farming experience," I was told at the Soil Conservation Service office nearest my home. "That is because the problems of farming, and their solutions, vary so widely from one region to another. I'd never discourage anyone with any agricultural knowledge, training, or experience—no matter where and how it was acquired—from applying, though. Locally needed skills are easily picked up by anyone with the aptitude for conservation farming."

No written test is required for a job as conservation aide, and the SCS, through its county offices, fills most openings by hiring local residents. Pay varies widely from one office to another, but most aides shortly make it to the five-figure annual-income bracket.

Aides are given an excellent opportunity to improve their own farming skills, so many, like Clifford Bertrurn, operate their own small farms in the areas where they are employed.

"Tourism and farming are the two big industries in this area," says Clifford, an SCS worker who raises poultry and melons on his farm on the Delmarva Peninsula. "I knew I wanted to live and work here, but I also knew the tourist business wasn't for me. My job as aide not only made it possible for me to earn a living, my job experience made it possible for me to get the loan I needed to buy my own farm. Now the farm pays and adds to my income, so I've got the best of two worlds."

Aides have the enormous satisfaction of doing good and useful work in the outdoors, but many move on to better-paying, more demanding jobs by taking the courses usually required for advancement to a position as soil-conservation technician.

Soil Conservation Technicians

To qualify for a position as a soil-conservation technician, you need not take a written test, but you must have successfully completed two academic years of study above the high-school level in a junior or community college, technical school, accredited college, or university. Your program of study must have included courses in such fields as agriculture, soils, agronomy, engineering, biology, meteorology, physical science, forestry, or other subjects pertinent to soil science and conservation.

If you fail to meet the educational requirements, you may substitute two years of technical on-the-job experience, so long as that experience was gained in a closely related field. A combination of two years of training and experience is also acceptable. Your training should include thirty semester hours.

Technicians assist in conducting field tests and carrying out scientific experiments planned by the soil scientists and conservationists. They take instrument readings, record data, and perform other work requiring more technical knowledge than that required of an aide. Chances for advancement are somewhat limited, but many technicians continue their education and go on to find careers as fully qualified soil conservationists.

Pay varies, with adjustments made in accordance with other wages in the area of the job; but after a year or so on the job, most technicians earn a five-figure income—about the same as that paid to a beginning soil scientist with the bachelor's degree. Some find even higher wages with large agricultural enterprises, or with banks and others who hold large tracts of land. You can have the satisfaction of knowing you are helping conserve our soil and increase our production of food.

For more information write:

Soil Conservation Society of America
1715 NE Ankeny Road
Ankeny, IA 50021

National Association of Conservation Districts
1025 Vermont Avenue NW
Washington, DC 20005

5

RANGE MANAGEMENT

Rangelands cover more than a billion acres of the United States. These rangelands, most of them in the West and Alaska, must be preserved and protected, but at the same time fully utilized, if we are to meet our future food requirements. Range managers are the outdoor workers who will enable us to meet these goals.

Range management is an agricultural science, similar in many respects to agronomy and soil science. Range managers (also known as range scientists, range ecologists, or range conservationists), along with the aides and technicians who assist them, bring new skills and knowledge to an industry that goes back many years. A brief history of the American range industry will help you understand why those skills are so desperately needed.

The Spaniards who came with Coronado in 1540 were the first to use these rangelands in a large way, grazing herds of sheep, cattle, and horses on the seemingly endless ranges of the Southwest. Some of their animals escaped or were left behind to be captured and put to use by the Indians of the region. By the time of the great migration westward in the middle of the nineteenth century, horses, sheep, and cattle were established throughout the United States, and already their impact was beginning to show.

Those original grasslands were truly marvelous—a seemingly endless expanse of grass and shrubs for grazing animals, habitats for buffalo and other wildlife, with a natural water supply from vast watersheds. They covered about 40 percent of America and gave sustenance to millions of grazing animals on which those early settlers depended for survival. Few thought such seas of grass could ever be depleted.

Oddly enough, the first recognition of the need for range conservation came about with the creation of the Forest Service of the U. S. Department of Agriculture. Chief Forester Gifford Pinchot saw the grazing of livestock as a legitimate use of the lands he was charged with protecting, but he quickly made it clear that grazing was to be done without abuse to the land.

Albert F. Potter, a conservation-minded cattle rancher from Arizona, was hired as the first range-management specialist to work for the Forest Service, and he and Pinchot began to work out policies and regulations that, while they would continue to allow the grazing of livestock on public lands, would assure that the land would be preserved for future generations.

The policies of these two pioneers were well ahead of their time. The Forest Service now decreed that first grazing rights on our forested land would go to those already using the rangelands, with the new management policies to be invoked gradually to avoid causing hardships on the users; small ranchers would be favored over the large; range use would be in compliance with the new conservation and management work soon to begin; and stockmen would be given a voice in setting policy.

For the first time in history, permits would be required of those wishing to graze stock on public land. The permits not only told the rancher how many head could be grazed in the permit area, but also decreed when they could be turned out on the range in the spring and when they must be removed in the fall. To help implement these new conservation rulers, as well as to assist the smaller ranchers, the two leaders in this new field also helped establish several hundred local stockmen's associations.

Much of our rangeland was not under the control of the Forest Service, however, and that portion of it remained unmanaged until 1934, when the Taylor Grazing Act was signed into law and the new Grazing Service was established. As set forth by Congress, the purpose of this Act was to "stop injury to the public grazing lands by preventing overgrazing and soil deterioration; to provide for their orderly use, improvement, and development; to stabilize the livestock industry dependent upon the public range; and for other purposes." In its mention of "other purposes," this Act established that these lands would continue to be used for public recreation and enjoyment.

This Act of Congress set up grazing districts, using as a model those already established by the Forest Service, with local stockmen serving as advisers in every district, and it issued permits for grazing that followed the guidelines of the Forest Service.

In that same year, Congress also established the Bureau of Indian Affairs, placing both it and the Grazing Service in the Department of the Interior. Among its other duties, the new agency was charged with the conservation and controlled development of the land resources on the many native American reservations—vast tracts that can now be grazed only by permit and by specified numbers of livestock.

States with large amounts of rangeland began to establish grazing rules and regulations, and the new Soil Conservation Service started to serve as an adviser to them and put together its own staff of range-management specialists.

Before the end of the decade, range management had gained recognition as an educational discipline, and many colleges and universities throughout the West were offering degrees with range science as the major course of study.

In 1946, the Grazing Service was merged with the old General Land Office to form the Bureau of Land Management; and what had been known as "Taylor Grazing Lands" became "BLM Lands"—the largest block of public land in the country. An attempt was now being made to see that most of our rangeland was properly managed.

By 1947, professional workers in this field had formed The Society of Range Management "to advance the science and art of grazing land management, promote progress in conservation and sustained use of forage, soil and water resources, to stimulate discussion and understanding of range and pasture problems, to provide a medium of exchange of facts and ideas among members and with allied scientists, and to encourage professional improvement of members." One year later, an estimate of the Soil Conservation Service was that more than 300 million acres of valuable rangeland had been lost since 1880, in spite of our new efforts at conservation.

The decline in acreage for grazing continues. Today we have just over 600 million acres of permanent grassland—with roughly 350 million more in mixed grass and forest, most of which is in high country and can be grazed only briefly during the summer. The rest of our range includes cropland and planted fields that double as pasture for cattle or other livestock.

Most of the rangeland loss is caused by conversion to cropland. The conversion of grazing land to plowed fields for growing cultivated crops will produce desirable results, but not all rangeland can be successfully converted, and most conservationists now agree that we have reached a point where our remaining range must be kept intact. To cultivate more of it could cause grievous land problems, particularly in times of drought.

The increasing need for fossil fuels and the resultant mining of the land have also claimed much of our range, and in the future, reclamation of these mined areas will become an increasingly important part of range management. If we are to meet the constantly growing demand for meat, we must preserve our remaining rangeland. We should reclaim as much land as possible, and we must increase the production of each and every acre to feed future generations.

Range Managers

Range managers restore and improve rangelands through techniques such as controlled burning, reseeding, and biological, chemical, or mechanical control of undesirable plants. For example, selected areas with natural sagebrush vegetation may be plowed and reseeded with a more productive grass. In studies conducted at Manitou Experimental Forest in Colorado, it was found that the meat production of 1 square mile of range could be increased from 7,300 pounds per year to over 11,000 pounds annually simply by planting a proper selection of grasses.

To prevent ecological destruction of the grasslands, a prime duty of the range specialist is to analyze the area and determine the number and kind of animals to be grazed, the grazing system to be used, and the best season for grazing in order to yield the highest possible production of livestock. While performing this basic part of the job, these specialists must conserve the soil and vegetation for other uses such as wildlife habitat, outdoor recreation, and timber production. They must also carry out projects that will provide animal watering facilities, erosion control, and fire prevention.

About 3,000 persons worked as range managers in 1976, assisted by about twice as many nonprofessional aides and technicians. Most of these worked for the federal government—principally for the Forest Service and the Soil Conservation Service of the Department of Agriculture and the Bureau of Land Management of the Department of the Interior. Range managers in state governments are employed in game and fish departments, land agencies, and extension services.

An increasing number of jobs are found in private industry. Coal and oil companies hire range managers to help restore ecological balance to mined-out areas; banks and real-estate firms employ them to help increase the revenue from their landholdings; and large ranchers frequently place range managers on their own payroll. Some specialists in this field work for private consulting firms, while others work overseas with United States and United Nations agencies, or with foreign governments.

Employment in the field of range management is expected to grow faster than the average for all other occupations through the mid-1980s. Job opportunities will be especially good for those with degrees in range management or range science, but many other jobs will continue to be filled by persons with degrees in related fields who have had some range-management courses or experience.

The increasing demand for meat and other products of the rangelands will continue to stimulate the need for more range managers. Since the amount of rangeland is fixed, range managers will be needed to increase the output of those grasslands while protecting their ecology.

The use of rangelands for wildlife refuges and recreation areas is expected to create even more jobs with broader duties for range managers. Especially in Alaska, where enormous expanses are being added to the national parks and other public-land systems, large numbers of new jobs will be opened.

As our explorations for coal and oil continue to accelerate, these industries will certainly require many more range ecologists to rehabilitate areas disturbed by their mining. Many of these new range managers, then, will be involved in reclamation projects such as the one I am about to describe.

The Dave Johnson Plant of the Pacific Power and Light Company is located in Converse County, Wyoming—a part of the northern Great Plains that has low rainfall, high winds, and thin topsoil. The coal strip-mining activities of the company had, by 1971, left more than 500 nearby acres of land rearranged into raw, humped, ugly spoilbanks, worthless for any purpose. The company was determined not to leave it that way.

Calling in range specialists from the La Prele-Glenrock Conservation District, and other advisers from the Soil Conservation Service, the Dave Johnson people sought to develop a program for returning this land to its natural state.

The idea of returning postmined land to a useful state—much less an aesthetically pleasing one—is a relatively recent concept. The techniques for doing this are still experimental in most parts of the country, and they are often expensive. The fragile Wyoming ecology, especially the low recuperative powers of disturbed land, made the problem confronting these experts especially difficult.

The steep soilbanks were first reshaped and covered with layers of good topsoil. The gently rolling slopes were then covered with thick layers of hay and straw mulch, which was disked into the life-giving soil layer to reduce soil erosion and speed plant growth. The area was then seeded with wheatgrass, chosen by the experts as the grass most likely to survive. Other small experimental plots were sown in half a dozen varieties of grasses, including a high-protein shrub with good grazing qualities.

Deer and antelope now graze on land that, just a few years ago could support no animal life. The company estimates that its reclamation effort cost far less than one penny for each ton of coal removed from the land—and now intends to make the same effort at its Jim Bridger Plant in southwestern Wyoming.

Another example of the work done by range managers is at the Los Lunas Plant Materials Center of the Soil Conservation Service, in New Mexico, a region with special problems in conservation.

In this region, "normal" climatic conditions mean low rainfall, drought, high winds, and low humidity. This area also has a rapidly growing population. Since 1964, in a cooperative effort involving the Forest Service, the Soil Conservation Service, the New Mexico and Colorado state universities, and various state agencies, experts from Los Lunas have been working to combat these problems by developing plants especially suited to these conditions.

In an effort typical of this program, workers were sent into the high country of the Cibola National Forest, where, at an elevation of about 7,400 feet and in an area with an annual rainfall of only 16 inches, they collected seed from Rocky Mountain Pentsemon, a native plant whose growth habits make it a good stabilizer for sloping land.

In plantings at the Los Lunas Center it was found that this excellent forage plant would do well under the demanding local conditions, so its seeds now joined the many others distributed by the Center—seeds that will provide superior forage production, windbreaks, wildlife cover, and even ornamental growth on the rangelands throughout the area.

Projects such as this require the range manager to spend considerable time away from home—working and living in remote parts of the range. A real love of the outdoor life is critical to the job, along with good health and physical stamina. But the range manager—unlike the aides and technicians who assist in the work—must also meet certain educational requirements.

The essential courses for a degree in range management are animal husbandry, zoology, botany, plant ecology, plant physiology, soils, chemistry, mathematics, and specialized courses such as identification and classification of range plants, range improvement, and range sampling and inventory techniques. Desirable electives include recreation, fish and wildlife management, police science, statistical methods, physics, geology, meteorology, watershed management, surveying, and forage crops.

The range scientist must meet and deal with the ranchers he serves; thus public-speaking skills are essential. Writing skills are needed for the publication of reports and articles about the work performed.

In the federal government, range managers holding the bachelor's degree start at either $9,303 or $11,523, depending on their college grades. Those having a year of graduate work begin at $11,523; and those who have completed two years of graduate study begin at an annual salary of $14,097. Persons with Ph.D. degrees start at either $14,097 or $17,056. Range managers on the federal payroll average about $20,000 a year; and, based on limited data, the Department of Labor believes these wages to be about the same as those paid to range managers in the private sector and on state payrolls.

"I believe that in addition to the meeting of the educational requirements, extensive local historical research would be of great help to the beginner trying to get started in range management," I was told by one official of the Forest Service, a graduate of the University of Montana School of Forestry with a major in range management, who now works on the rangeland of Montana's Lewis and Clark National Forest. "In many instances, the problems of the present echo the problems of the past, and so do the solutions. I'd also suggest as much training as possible in wildlife management. In the Forest Service in the years ahead, the protection of wildlife resources is likely to be a major part of the range manager's job. Time spent working on a ranch and learning firsthand about the problems peculiar to the rancher would also be excellent training. Decisions in range management have strong economic impact, and I think observation from the other side of the fence is the best way to learn the real meaning of this work."

As of 1977, the Forest Service employed about 700 people with degrees in range management. About 50 more college graduates are expected to be hired each year through the mid-1980s. They will oversee the grazing of about 6 million cattle and sheep owned by 20,000 ranchers and farmers in all the states west of the 100th meridian, and will be charged with the conservation of several million browsing deer, elk, moose, and other wildlife found in these national forests and grasslands.

Careers with the Bureau of Indian Affairs and the Bureau of Land Management

"Preference in hiring is given to native Americans but it is not absolutely necessary that one be an Indian in order to work for this agency," says the Bureau of Indian Affairs, which hires range managers to work on the 39 million acres of tribal lands under its care. "However, any prospective employee should make an effort to know and understand the problems unique to the native Americans, as well as to know and respect their customs. Skills in communication are essential, as employees on all levels must frequently work with the Tribal Councils."

The Bureau of Land Management, with more than 400 million acres of rangeland to manage, hires a number of range management specialists each year. Most opportunities with this agency exist in Arizona, California, Colorado, Idaho, Montana, Nevada, Oregon, Utah, Washington, and Wyoming, but Alaska offers the brightest job prospects for the near future, because of the millions of acres of land in that state being placed in the public domain.

Congressional legislation calls for multiple use of all lands under the control of the Bureau of Land Mangement, so range managers in this agency, like those with the Forest Service, gain experience in the closely related fields of wildlife and watershed management, mineral resources, forestry, recreation, and reclamation. Training in these fields will increase the new range manager's chances with this employer.

As you certainly realize by now, the job of range manager is a combination of several disciplines, yet the work is more closely related to that of the soil scientist than to any other. And while the agencies just mentioned do hire college students to work during the summer months, the Soil Conservation Service of the Department of Agriculture, one of the largest employers of range managers, is the agency that most actively recruits them. The student work program described in Chapter One is also available to those working toward a degree in range management.

Range Technicians

Jobs are also available in these agencies for those who have no college degree. Technicians are needed to help implement the conservation programs designed by the range managers, to assist in compiling data, and to otherwise relieve the workload of the supervising range managers. Growth in employment of range technicians is expected to be faster than the average for all occupations through the mid-1980s.

Starting salaries for technicians in this field range from $7,500 to $10,000 a year, with experienced technicians averaging about $12,300.

Like the skilled scientists with whom they work, range technicians spend time in remote areas with all kinds of weather. Under emergency conditions, such as range or forest fires, or floods, they are required to work long hours without rest. Physical stamina, as well as a love of outdoor work, are essential for success.

Technicians are usually hired on the local level. Preference is given to those with experience in ranching, tree nursery work, fire-fighting, or recreation, and opportunities are best for those with a year or two of postsecondary-school training. About 50 technical colleges, community colleges, and universities offer training that could qualify you for this work.

Technical courses related to this field include the study of biol-ogy and botany, land surveying, soil and plant identification, aerial photograph interpretation, and animal husbandry. But new techni-cians begin work as trainees or in relatively routine positions under the direct supervision of an experienced range manager or technician. As the trainee gains experience, he or she then works directly with range owners, users of the range, survey crews, and workers on con-servation projects.

Range Management Aides

Experience alone may qualify you for a job as aide in the field of range management. Aides carry out much of the actual physical work done in range conservation—building irrigation projects, fighting brush or forest fires, making plantings—and the local offices of the agencies already mentioned are often actively searching for those will-ing to do this work.

A background in construction could qualify you for a job as aide, especially if you have worked with heavy equipment, and ranching experience would be even better. A couple of summers spent with the Youth Conservation Corps, where you would actually be involved in one or more of the conservation projects carried out in cooperation with other federal agencies, would almost automatically qualify you for a job as an aide. Starting pay is low and varies from one part of the country to another, but after a year or so on the job, most aides have gained the training experience necessary for promotion to technician . . . and they have gone a long way toward a wonderful career on the wide American range.

More information about careers in range management can be obtained by contacting:

Society for Range Management
2760 W. 5th Avenue
Denver, CO 80204

For more information on jobs with the federal government, contact:

Bureau of Indian Affairs
U. S. Department of the Interior
Washington, DC 20250

Bureau of Land Management
Denver Service Center
Federal Center Building 50
Denver, CO 80255

Forest Service
U. S. Department of Agriculture
Washington, DC 20250

Soil Conservation Service
U. S. Department of Agriculture
Washington, DC 20250

6

FOREST SERVICE

As the Pilgrims waded ashore they must have felt fascination and fear as they saw the forests crowding the Atlantic Seaboard—forests that, unknown to these settlers, stretched back from the coastline at least 1,500 miles. The forests along the Pacific Coast had a depth of at least 500 miles, and all the forested areas totaled more than 1 *billion* acres. As we move into our third century as a nation, more than 450 years after colonization, 750 million of those acres, covering fully one third of our nation, remain forested. The forest is a special and important resource.

It covers vast areas of nearly every state. While providing habitat for a multitude of wildlife species, it is a source of recreation and relaxation for millions of Americans, and insures a supply of clean air and water. It also serves as the base for industry that provides direct employment for at least 300,000 people.

Most Americans believe that almost all our forests are found in the West. And while it is true that these forests are valuable and are the center of the logging industry, over half of our forest acreage is found east of the Rockies. Even New York and New Jersey, containing some of the most densely populated areas of the country, are each *over half covered with forests!*

Surveys show that most Americans believe the forests are being cut down, that soon we will have no forests to enjoy or to provide useful products. The opposite is true. Through the application of modern forestry, we are actually growing *more* trees than we were three decades ago. This results from the efforts of those who work to protect, manage, and properly harvest this enormous natural resource, and there are opportunities for you to make your own contribution, no matter what the level of your education or training.

Three major areas of employment, each uniquely different, are found in the great American forest. They can be classified as forestry, fire prevention and management, and timber management. Forestry came first, so let's begin there.

Timber Management

Forestry came into being at the turn of this century, after much effort by a conservationist named Gifford Pinchot, who was founder and first chief of the U. S. Forest Service. An ecologist who saw the forest as a community of living things and not just as trees to be harvested, Pinchot created the idea of multiple-use management of forested lands—a concept intended to honor the balance and harmony of that living community. Thus evolved the science of forest management, which deals with much more than timber.

Twenty-five thousand professional foresters are at work in our woodlands, along with about 11,000 forestry technicians and at least that many aides. More than 50 universities offer courses of study leading to a degree in forestry.

Each year The American Forestry Association receives hundreds of letters. Nearly all of the writers express a strong interest in outdoor work and a love of nature, but many fail to realize that the forester is a highly trained professional who possesses many qualifications other than a great love of nature. "About nine out of ten writers have in mind a job as U. S. Forest Service ranger on a national forest, a job that has been glamorized in fiction and in movies," says the Association. "They see in their mind's eye a man on horseback, riding along a trail in the deep woods or pausing on a height to view a vast expanse of timbered hills. A ranger's work may involve many exciting adventures, but foresters have many other things to do besides rescuing lost or injured persons, and they do most of their traveling by auto or truck, rather than on horseback."

Even young graduate foresters do not usually step into the Forest Service as rangers. They usually enter the Forest Service as junior foresters or assistants. Only after several years of experience is it possible to obtain the eagerly sought job of district forest ranger.

A district forest ranger is the administrator and manager of large forest areas. He or she is responsible for protecting its resources from fire, for the growth, management, and sale of its timber, the safeguarding of its watersheds, the development of its wildlife habitat and recreation facilities, the leasing of land for private use, and the management of recreation programs. The ranger generally supervises a staff consisting of assistant rangers, technicians, aides, and office workers, and handles a volume of business larger than that of any other enterprise in the community.

While the job of district ranger is a management position with many indoor duties, the beginning forester is likely to spend most of his or her time working outdoors. The duties vary somewhat with the individual forest and its management plan, but they are always interesting and rewarding to those who perform them.

Most national forests are managed for a variety of uses. Within a single forest certain areas may be devoted to recreation, others to timber growth, others to livestock grazing, mineral production, preservation of unique scenery, or wildlife habitat. Many areas may be devoted to a combination of several of these; if the forest covers hilly or mountainous terrain, most or all of it will be managed in a way designed to protect its watershed value. The staff at such a forest must include specialists in all these fields, with a supervising ranger whose training and experience give him a working knowledge of each.

On multiple-use forestland the young professional forester may be called upon to survey boundary lines, to cruise the forest and inventory timber, to select and mark trees for cutting, and to supervise the logging operation of the purchaser. The work might also include the supervision of tree-planting operations, or the grazing of sheep and cattle under permit. Some time would be devoted to maintaining and improving recreation facilities and supervising their use by the public, and the new forester will work with fire lookouts, smoke chasers, dispatchers, and others in the forest's fire-protection organization. Later the forester may specialize in only one type of work, but since even most privately owned forests today are managed for multiple use, the young forester must be prepared to help manage for all these uses.

A very large percentage of foresters go on to specialize in timber management, although this is a specialty frequently filled by technicians.as well. Timber production was one reason for the creation of our system of national forests, and it continues to be a major goal of their management.

Those who have raised objections to the cutting of timber on public lands by private industry should consider that this is done not only to help the country meet its timber needs, but also to keep our forests healthy and to pay for their proper management. By cutting old, perhaps diseased, trees and replacing them with younger and healthier stock, the forest stand is improved, making it what the professionals call "thrifty"—a healthy forest that is producing vigorously.

Timber sales require a lot of planning. It begins when foresters and technicians survey the country from the ground. A tract that is to be sold is marked off on a map. The boundary lines are marked off, roads are surveyed in, the volume of timber by species is estimated, and logging procedures are set forth. The sale is then opened for bidding by private companies.

After the highest bidder has been selected, the foresters and technicians remain on the job, supervising the work to see that no undue harm is done to the forest. At least some remain on the site until the logging operation is brought to a halt. Some of the courses given at a school for timber-management technicians will give you a better idea of the work done during the course of a timber sale. A catalog from one school lists courses in elementary and advanced surveying, technical drawing, basic forestry, road location and design, forest ecology and silviculture, insect and disease control, forest measurement, forest products, soil science, forestry tools, photo interpretation, forest laws, forest economics, mathematics, and timber harvesting.

Everyone who works in forestry and timber management may be called on, at one time or another, to help fight or control a forest fire, and fire prevention is a daily part of every job. But fire prevention, control, and management is also a highly specialized field that provides many jobs for professionals and nonprofessionals alike.

You will note that I mentioned fire management, not just fire prevention and control. Foresters have recently begun to see fire as an ecological tool that can sometimes be used to improve timber stands and wildlife habitat rather than as a complete enemy. Fire prevention and control remain tremendously important, but only as they are used in an overall program of what the foresters prefer to call fire management.

In the early days of the conservation movement, fire was seen only as an enemy, in spite of the fact that Gifford Pinchot and a few other leaders were already pointing out that some trees, including the western larch and the giant sequoias, actually benefit from fires that burn away other growth. But a quick look at history makes it easy to understand why few realized that fire was an important part of the growth cycle that could sometimes be a friend to ecology.

Since the earliest days of the nation, devastating fires had occurred wherever forest communities were established and where subsequent logging activities left behind piles of slash to act as a fuse. The danger was made evident to all in 1871, when fire roared across 2 million acres in Wisconsin, destroying the entire town of Peshtigo and killing 1,200 people in what may be the worst natural disaster in American history.

Fire prevention was one of the goals when the Forest Service was created, but not until 1910 did the firefighters of that new agency meet what is generally regarded as their first real test. That year, one of the worst fires in American history ran wild over the forests of Montana and Idaho, destroying several million acres of timberland and taking 187 lives. Thanks to the efforts of the firefighters, fire lines were established, millions of acres were saved, and a dozen towns were spared the fate of Peshtigo.

In subsequent years the Forest Service pioneered fire lookout towers for quicker fire detection, with telephone lines strung to range and guard stations; built forest trails, roads, and bridges for transportation of firefighting equipment; and worked constantly to improve its crew organization and firefighting techniques. By the 1930s it was using aircraft to drop firefighters and equipment into areas on fire, and was using aircraft to patrol forested areas.

The average burned acreage on national forests decreased with each passing year, and the fire-control methods of the Forest Service became the standard for most other public agencies. Large forest fires continued to occur when conditions were just right, but the Forest Service was able to take quick action, and most fires were kept small.

But in the 1960s the statistics began to show a dramatic reversal. Suddenly, forest fires began to take a heavier annual toll of timbered acreage, even though firefighting organizations had by then developed scientific methods and tools and placed them in the hands of the most highly trained firefighters the world has ever known. In analyzing the situation and seeking a cause for the reversal, foresters came to realize that they had been *too* effective in fighting fire, and this realization gave birth to the concept of prescribed burning and the new specialty of fire management.

Foresters today realize that wildlife thrives where fire has been. They know that fire adds minerals and other nutrients to the soil, thus creating a favorable seedbed for the desired species of timber; it enhances the growth of the species by reducing the competition for sunlight and moisture. Foresters also know that if the good effects of fire are to outweigh the bad, the fire must come at exactly the right time and under the right conditions; thus the need for prescribed burning.

The new science of fire management, combined with work in fire prevention and control, provides a very large percentage of the jobs related to forestry. Fire-management teams are headed by trained foresters, usually with a strong background in physics, soils, and chemistry. No college yet offers a degree in fire management, but most forestry schools now have courses in the specialty. An excellent textbook on the subject, *Forest Fires—Control and Use*, has been written by Kenneth P. Davis, professor of forestry at Yale and former president of the Society of American Foresters, and should be read by everyone interested in working in this field.

Many other specialties are found in the forest, of course. Some foresters specialize in research. Others work as consultants. Still others choose fields—such as range management—that have been described elsewhere in this book. But the three broad areas just described—forestry, timber management, and fire management—account for almost all of the jobs actually done in the outdoors. Now for a look at some of the specific jobs, where they are, what they pay, and how to get them.

Professional Foresters

The top professional job, in any of these three major employment areas, is, of course, that of forester. It is a job that offers a chance to earn excellent pay while doing outdoor work in some of the most beautiful areas of America. The position has an almost unlimited potential for advancement, but an unusual situation confronts those seeking a career in the field. This situation has been created by the very popularity of the job.

According to the U. S. Department of Labor, "Employment requirements for foresters are expected to grow somewhat faster than average for other occupations through the mid-1980s. In recent years, however, the number of persons earning degrees in forestry has exceeded occupational requirements, creating competition for jobs. If the number of degrees granted each year remains at present levels, competition is expected to persist throughout the period." This means, quite obviously, that the jobs will go to those who are best prepared to fill them.

Forester Charles Randall has some advice for students planning a career in forestry: "In high school, prospective forestry students should get as broad a general background as possible, in order to qualify for college work," he says. "It is not necessary or desirable that you try to specialize in forestry-related subjects here. but you should be sure to take the preparatory work available in chemistry, physics, mathematics, biological sciences, English literature, composition, and public speaking.

"Your first years in college should be devoted to broadening your cultural background and acquiring a foundation in scientific, engineering, economic, and social studies. Only in your junior year, in most schools of forestry, will you begin technical courses in forestry, such as silviculture, forest management, forest protection, forest economics, and forest utilization."

Even while working toward this degree, you can begin to improve your chances of being hired as a forester upon graduation. Many forestry schools conduct summer-school camps, where students are given actual in-the-woods experience. If your school has no such camp, you should seek as much experience as possible through employment in a state or national forest or with a lumber company. According to the American Forestry Association, "The U. S. Forest Service and most other forestry agencies, as a matter of policy, give preference to forestry students over other college students in hiring young people for summer jobs." The U. S. Department of Labor points out: "Opportunities will be better for those who (in addition to a degree) can offer the employer some actual experience."

Any job described later in this chapter will provide experience that will weigh heavily when and if you apply for a job as professional forester. Some time spent working in one or more of them will also allow you to test your aptitude for the specialty and give better direction to your career planning. The experience may also mean that you will start at a higher salary when you are accepted for full-time employment.

The best opportunities for the new forester are found with the U. S. Forest Service of the Department of Agriculture, which has nearly one fourth of all working foresters on its payroll and takes on about 200 new ones each year. About half of all foresters began their working career with this agency—it is an important training ground.

Foresters also are employed by other federal agencies involved in the management of forests and rangelands, including the Bureau of Land Management, the Fish and Wildlife Service, the National Park Service, and the Tennessee Valley Authority. A few other federal agencies do hire foresters but in very limited numbers.

Permanent professional positions as forester with these land-management agencies are Civil Service positions. Entrance exams are given once a year, and those hired are usually placed in positions that provide broad training in the multiple-use concept of forestry. The average starting salary for foresters with these agencies in 1976 (the last year for which statistics are available) was just over $10,000 a year, and experienced foresters with those agencies were, in that same year, earning salaries that averaged just over $18,000 annually. But one advantage of working for these agencies is that all higher positions are filled by promotion from the lower ranks, and it is quite possible for the forester to advance to a management job with an annual salary of more than $40,000.

Nearly one third of our foresters now work for the forest industries and other private owners of timberland, who have ownership of more than 67 million acres of forests. These private owners control 59 percent of all our commercial forestland, and they are expected to increase their employment of foresters in the years just ahead, to meet our growing need for timber, pulpwood, paper, and other products of the forest.

Timber production is the major goal on most privately owned tracts of forest, but foresters in the private sector do many kinds of work—supervising logging or the cutting of pulpwood, tree planting and other reforestation work, laying out roads, timber appraisal, and silviculture. Starting pay is a little higher than with agencies of the federal government, but chances for advancement are more limited.

A number of states have extensive areas of state-owned forest land administered under the multiple-use concept, where the work of the forester is much like that done in the national forests. But in many states the forestry effort is directed almost entirely toward assisting private landowners with timber management and with timber-stand improvement. Fire-control work almost always accounts for much of the state's activity in forestry. Pay with the individual states averages slightly below salaries paid by the federal government or private industry. About 14 percent of all foresters work for the states, with hiring usually done under a system similar to the federal Civil Service system and through the office of the state forestry organization.

Since about 70 percent of all foresters work for federal or state employers, the odds are good that the young professional forester will get his or her start with one of these employers. But you need not be a graduate forester in order to find meaningful employment in the great American forest. As a matter of fact, this is one career field in which opportunities for the nonprofessional are at least as good as those offered the professional.

Loggers

No matter what your ultimate career goal may be, one good way to obtain experience in forestry and timber management is to seek out a job in the logging and timber industry. Over 75,000 workers are employed in logging camps—harvesting trees and removing them from the forests—and another 60,000 individuals have gone on to become self-employed loggers. Because these jobs are hazardous, rigorous, and usually pay slightly less than those in other industries, they are often available to those rugged enough to meet the physical demands.

Loggers must work under unpleasant weather conditions. The forest can be extremely hot and humid in the summer, with swarms of annoying insects, and it may be extremely cold, wet, or muddy at other times. But for many persons, the opportunity to live and work in forest regions away from crowded cities more than offsets the demands and disadvantages of the job.

Although some logging operations are carried on in nearly every state, more than half of all loggers work in the seven states of Oregon, Washington, California, Alabama, North Carolina, Arkansas, and Georgia. Wages are slightly higher in the Northwest, but employment is growing at a faster rate in the South.

Almost all loggers get their first jobs without special training, for the entry-level work is such that it can be learned in a few days or weeks of observing and helping experienced workers. A description of a logging operation will give you a better idea of what the work entails and the possibilities for advancement.

After a forester or technician has selected and marked the trees to be cut, and mapped out the area of the cutting, heavy-equipment operators build access roads and trails to the cutting and loading areas so they can be reached by logging crews.

The initial harvesting task—known as "falling and bucking"—is the process of cutting the tree down and then cutting, or "bucking" it into logs for easier handling and, perhaps, higher value. Fallers, who work singly or in pairs, use power saws to bring down the trees marked for cutting. They are experts with the saw, able to place a fallen tree within inches of where it is wanted, with no injury to the trees nearby.

The moment the tree is down, buckers saw off the limbs and cut the tree into logs. It is then ready to be removed from the cutting area to the landing area.

This is usually done by a method called "skidding." A steel cable is noosed around the log by workers called "choker setters" and then attached to a tractor, which drags the log to the landing area. Other workers, known as "rigging slingers," assist in this part of the operation.

Skidding is not the only method of removal. In areas of extremely rough terrain, power winches often replace the tractors, and in very large, very modern operations, helicopters are being used—a method that greatly reduces the environmental damage of the logging operation.

At the landing area, logs are loaded on a truck trailer by machine, and from there they are transported to the sawmill, where they are stacked on the ground or dumped into a pond to await cutting.

At this storage area workers known as log scalers measure each log, examine it for knots, splits, and other defects, and estimate the amount and quality of lumber it will yield. Other workers sort the logs according to size and type, arranging them so that all of one kind or size will go into the sawmill together.

A beginning logger is usually put to work helping choker setters or buckers. With experience, one of these jobs can be learned and assumed, and these can lead to promotion to log scaler, pond worker, or rigging slinger, among the top jobs in a logging operation. Workers holding these jobs are earning average wages of $7.70 an hour.

Fallers and buckers—or, if you prefer, lumberjacks—are by far the best-paid workers in the logging camps. Those who worked for hourly wages in 1978 earned an average wage of $9.15; however, in many camps, falling and bucking is paid on a piece-work basis, so expert sawyers are able to earn even more.

Wages and earnings aside, these jobs provide an excellent background for other careers in the forest. Loggers sometimes assist surveying crews. In the spring and fall they may help with tree planting and other reforestation work. During the summer they may be called on to fight brush and forest fires. Most important of all, they are given the chance to see modern forestry and timber management in action, to participate in a program worked out according to the principles of good forest conservation.

For some, this road can lead to other careers in the forest, perhaps providing the experience needed for a good job in one of the national forests. For others, like Walter Friend, it may lead to a career as an independent logger.

Mr. Friend was raised on a farm in Kentucky, but like so many others, he migrated to the city to find higher wages and better economic conditions in general. But even though he found a good-paying job on an auto assembly line in Detroit, he soon yearned to get back outdoors. His wife agreed, so they headed West, and they were settled in California by the time my letter caught up with them.

"I was attracted to the logging industry because it offered a chance to work in the woods," he replied to my letter asking about his job. "I had only a high-school education, but I figured I had a few other things going for me. I'd tinkered with machinery all my life, and had an aptitude for mechanical work. That helped me convince my first boss I could handle the power saws and other equipment used in the woods. Then, of course, I'm fairly strong and not afraid of an honest day's work.

"My first job was helping set choker cables, then I worked in a landing area, stacking and loading logs. After a year or so of that, I was set to work bucking—trimming limbs and such. A year later I began felling, and I've been at it ever since."

Walter now works on a free-lance basis, providing his own equipment and moving from one camp to another as he is needed, much as lumberjacks have done for years. He has worked in Oregon, Washington, Idaho, and Wyoming, as well as in California, sawing trees that range in size from the small lodgepole pines of Wyoming to the giant sequoias of California. He has averaged about $90 a day in earnings, but on some jobs has made as much as $125 a day. He works long hours during the winter, but does little cutting during the summer, devoting that time to the small farm he now owns. Near the close of his letter he adds, ". . . I'm thinking about borrowing the money to set up my own logging and sawmill operation," and the chances are good he'll be able to do just that.

Forestry Aides and Technicians

"No organization can exist without people who know how to get the basic job done," says the U. S. Forest Service. "Our agency is no exception. It has always been fortunate in having hard-working aides and technicians who not only get the job done, but enjoy doing it." This sentiment is but one indication of the very real opportunities that exist for nonprofessionals in the field of forestry.

Another indicator is the fact that while foresters must compete for the jobs available, technical schools report that about 75 percent of their students find work in forestry immediately upon graduation, a percentage that would be even higher except that many of these graduates switch to other fields or decide to seek higher education.

Even graduation from technical school is not an absolute requirement for placement in a well-paying job in forestry. To qualify as an aide with the U. S. Forest Service, for example, you need only 6 months of general experience. Then after 18 months of experience as an aide you would become eligible for promotion to technician. You may also be hired as a technician if you have already acquired the same amount of experience with other employers in the field of forestry.

Starting aides with the U. S. Forest Service in 1978 were earning an annual salary of $8,366, and most first-year technicians were being paid $10,507. But these are not dead-end jobs; far from it. It is possible for the salary of a technician with the Forest Service to go as high as $30,000—which greatly exceeds the wages earned by many professional foresters.

About 12,000 forestry technicians are employed on a year-round basis, with that many more finding temporary employment during the spring, summer, and fall, the peak seasons in forestry. About half of these work in private industry. The U. S. Forest Service is the major employer among public agencies, with state and local governments combining to be next in line. Wages paid by these other employers are comparable to those earned by employees of the U. S. Forest Service, providing an average salary of just over $13,000.

The chances are good that, as a beginner, you will be hired on a seasonal basis. Remembering that most forestry work is done in the spring, summer, and fall, before many forests are made inaccessible by snow, you should inquire about these jobs well in advance of the peak seasons. Federal Job Information Centers can provide you with information about openings with the Forest Service or other federal agencies.

A written test is not always required as part of the Civil Service qualification procedure; a good background in mathematics, biology, and botany will improve your chances of being hired as a forestry worker and will prove helpful on the job.

In the spring and fall of the year, it is likely that, as a newly hired aide, you will spend at least some of your time in tree-planting work. This sounds like menial work, but it is one of the most important jobs in the forest, and almost every forester has done it at one time or another.

Natural reproduction often fails to restock the forest, so planting must be done. Logging often removes all the standing trees from a given area, and natural disasters—fire, insects, or disease—may also wipe out all the trees in a forest, thus creating the need for planting.

Hundreds of millions of seedlings from nurseries are planted each year in the forested areas of our nation. Many of these have been planted in areas—such as the Great Plains—where only a few trees once existed, and Nebraska now has a national forest in which every tree was planted by man!

Most tree planting, however, is done in the South, where the pulpwood industry is extremely important and where seedlings may attain harvestable size in only a few years. In the Northwest, where the magnificent Douglas fir is the most important lumber tree, a method of harvesting called "clear cutting" has been developed. After this method has been used to completely clear a forested tract, the tract is then replanted with Douglas seedlings, which require a lot of sunlight and are now able to obtain it.

Tree-planting machines are being used where possible, but most of the work continues to be done by hand. The work is hard and requires a strong back, but the jobs are fairly easy to get and they provide a good way to start learning about timber-stand improvement.

Known to foresters as TSI, timber-stand improvement is a program designed to keep the forest healthy and growing vigorously. If done following a timber harvest, as it frequently is, it is referred to as SAB—sale-area betterment.

Timber-stand improvement involves not only the planting of new trees to replace those harvested, but also includes thinning the forest, removing less desirable trees, and giving the desirable ones adequate room for growth; pruning trees so they will produce a more valuable crop of timber, and implementing sanitation measures to combat attacks by insects and disease. Through timber-stand improvement foresters give their trees care equal to that which a farmer gives his crops.

Most timber-stand-improvement work must be done by those able to use the tools of the trade—the ax, the power saw, and the pruning saw. A knowledge of silviculture (the study and cultivation of trees for timber) is required of the technicians who head crews doing this work, but many obtain that knowledge on the job.

Bud Jones (not his real name) is one technician who gained his knowledge on the job, as a profile provided by the U. S. Forest Service reveals:

"Bud began with the Service doing general labor and fire-control work. He later advanced to fire dispatcher during the fire season, and worked in TSI (timber-stand improvement) programs at other times of the year. During this same period, he was active in working with members of the Job Corps program, helping disadvantaged youngsters learn basic forest skills. Less than ten years after he came to the Forest Service, he assumed his present position as principal timber-management technician in an important ranger district."

Slash disposal is another important task that requires a lot of labor and provides many jobs for beginning workers. These jobs provide an excellent way to learn to use the tools of the trade while becoming acquainted with some of the basic principles of forestry.

Slash is what foresters call the debris left after timber has been harvested: the smaller limbs and unsalable trees. If left in place, this debris becomes a fire hazard. Some of the worst forest fires in history sprang from slash left after the cutting of timber, so it is extremely important that a harvested area be ridded of slash as soon as possible.

In some areas bulldozers are used to heap the slash into great piles; and then, under constant supervision, it is burned. But in scenic areas and in forests where the fire hazard is great, the slash is gathered by hand for burning.

A newer method of slash disposal—known as "lopping and scattering"—is gaining favor among foresters. This method requires workers who are skilled with axes and power saws. They go into the area that has been logged, saw away the limbs of the small trees left behind, cut up the trash timber, and spread these cuttings evenly over the forest floor. This greatly reduces the danger of fire because it places the foliage close to the ground, where it deteriorates quickly. In deteriorating, the foliage returns vital nutrients to the soil, thus strengthening the ecosystem of the forest.

New aides also may be set to work scaling logs, marking specific trees, and collecting and recording such data as tree heights, tree diameters, and tree mortality; installing, maintaining and collecting records from rain gauges, streamflow recorders, and soil-moisture measuring instruments on watershed improvement projects; or they may serve as rodmen or chainmen, notekeepers, or instrument readers on survey teams.

During this training period most will begin to show an aptitude for one or more phases of the work, and will settle into a specialty before experience makes them eligible for promotion to technician. Some will become timber and forestry technicians, some range technicians, some recreation specialists, some engineering and surveying technicians. However, almost every forestry aide gains some experience in fire control, fire prevention, and fire management, and many will go on to specialize in this critically needed part of forestry.

Smokejumpers

If you are ready for some excitement and no small amount of danger, and if you are truly dedicated to the preservation of our wilderness areas, you might be interested in becoming a smokejumper for the U. S. Forest Service. A letter from Robert Montoya, parachute loft foreman for the Forest Service in Boise, Idaho, provides some idea of the courage and dedication this job requires:

> I have been with the Boise National Forest Smokejumper Unit for eighteen years [he writes], and have been injured to the point it is advisable I quit jumping, which I have. I am now in charge of the parachute loft.
>
> The majority of our smokejumpers are summer employees only, mainly because they are either school teachers or students. For teachers it is a nice break in the teaching routine and for the students it means money for school. Smokejumping is a bit like farming because our fire seasons are dominated by the weather; so if we have plenty of lightning fires in primitive, inaccessible areas, it could be a very lucrative season because of the overtime, hazardous duty pay, per diem, and travel. If we have wet summers there is little fire activity and we are earning our regular daily wages like we would on any other job.
>
> Smokejumpers not only parachute into forests to fight

forest fires, they are members of highly trained and highly organized crews, ready to be flown to California or any other Western state and fight fires as part of organized crews. We also use helicopters to reach remote areas; our main objective is to fight fires, no matter how we reach them, and parachuting is only one specialty we use when conditions warrant.

Our men are hired [in 1978] at $5.05 an hour, earn $5.63 an hour after the first year, and $6.26 an hour after that. Most earn considerably more, depending on their seniority and other factors. Overtime wages of time and a half are paid for all over forty hours per week, and hazardous duty pay is 25 percent of your total daily hours. We get this hazardous duty pay for low-level parachute delivery of air cargo and for being on the fire line of a fire that is out of control. Hazard pay ends when the fire is brought under control. We get no extra pay for parachuting because we knew that was expected of us when we signed on—and besides, that's the only fun part of the job!

We do work standby hours when conditions warrant, say, when a lightning storm is predicted. This is one of the reasons you cannot hold two jobs during the fire season. Smokejumping is pretty unpredictable work, so you might be called at two in the morning to fly to Alaska and be gone a month or more. You must be available all summer.

You asked about the men I work with. We have a great many who do nothing but smokejumping for a living. These work six months and take six months off to travel or whatever, or they work as ski instructors or do rescue work to get them through the winter. Most of our men have a degree or two in various fields from theology to biological science, with the ability to teach in any university in the country—but they prefer the freedom and adventure of an exciting job like this.

You will never run into a more tightly woven concoction of personalities than in our unit. We live in a survival-of-the-fittest type world, but in smokejumping it is turned around a bit. We need each other to survive, so the jumper behind you is constantly watching out for you and checking your equipment, and you are doing the same for the guy in front of you. This goes on and on. Sometimes during a flight to a fire they remind me of a bunch of baboons preening each other.

How dangerous is the work? Well, I'll say this: If you remain on the active jumping list you are eventually going to get a bad or crippling injury. You will get bruises and bumps so often they come to be expected. The more you jump, the higher the odds become against you. I have seen countless numbers of people injured. Some recover, but all too many never return.

For that reason, my advice to rookie jumpers is to jump four years, use the money to pay for an education, and then pursue their academic careers, as most do. Or they might use the experience to get started in another forestry job.

But for all the dangers, the work is important enough that we have been in business since about 1932. Where we are really valuable is in saving millions of acres of timber and watershed, especially in the primitive forested areas where there are no roads and the quickest way to get there is by aircraft and the fastest way to deliver manpower is by parachute. Someday I guess we will suffer cutbacks, due to the shrinking forests, and there will be fewer jumpers. Civilization seems to be taking over now and there are roads where there were no roads before. . . .

During the fire season, most forestry agencies double or even triple the number of their employees, and the job of smokejumper is only one of many exciting entry-level positions that become available at that time. The U. S. Forest Service employs about 500 of these jumpers each season, about 90 percent of whom are temporary, with the permanent positions going to experienced firefighters who show exceptional qualities of leadership.

Smokejumpers are selected each spring from among those applicants who have applied before February 15. They are hired through

U.S. Forest Service offices in Missoula, Montana; McCall, Idaho; Boise, Idaho; Winthrop, Washington; Redmund, Oregon; Cave Junction, Oregon; and Redding, California.

Emphasis is placed on good health and physical condition, though any experience in fighting forest fires will give a candidate an edge, and forestry experience will be helpful. Jumpers must weigh from 130 to 190 pounds; have a height of 5 feet, 5 inches to 6 feet, 3 inches; have minimum vision of 20/40 in one eye and 20/70 in the other without glasses; unimpaired hearing; no heart disease, hernia, or other physical defect; and must be able to pass tests of stamina and endurance.

Jumping experience may be helpful, but it is not a requirement. New smokejumpers are given several weeks of training in parachute jumping, firefighting techniques, first aid, woodsmanship, communications, aircraft procedures, and equipment use. Some also learn parachute packing. After training they may be assigned to any part of the national forest system to stand ready for fire duty.

It is not absolutely necessary that you learn parachute jumping in order to become a member of a firefighting team. As Robert Montoya mentions, helicopters are seeing more and more use as a means of delivering firefighters to threatened areas. These large helicopters deliver entire crews of trained men exactly where they are needed, and take them out when the fire is under control. These firefighters greatly outnumber the smokejumpers, their pay is about the same, and they must meet the same physical requirements. Applicants are hired and trained through the same Forest Service offices, and under the same procedures as for smokejumpers.

Fire-control Aides, Fire Lookouts, and Fire Dispatchers

Fire-control aides are also hired during the fire season by every forestry agency in forest districts. Unlike the highly trained firefighting teams just described, these aides receive on-the-job training in the use and maintenance of fire tools and equipment, as well as in safety methods and practices. Their job is to prevent or contain fires in their area, and to assist the mobile fire teams when they arrive.

When not performing fire-control duties, these aides help maintain roads, trails, and other improvements, work on general forestry projects, and often participate in planned burning operations. After gaining experience and advancing to the technician level, they may be given responsibility for such fire-management projects.

But fire-control work requires many other workers in addition to those who actually fight the devastating flames. Since early detection is one key to reducing the destruction caused by fire, many beginners find employment in this phase of fire management.

Local residents, because they are likely to be familiar with the topography, roads, and weather conditions, are given some preference for positions as fire lookout, but these jobs are also available to students and others with an interest in forestry.

Fire lookouts are assigned to lookout stations—often in remote parts of the forest—to detect and report fires, fire behavior, and conditions related to fire occurrence, and to perform other work related to fire control. Although many lookout towers have been phased out due to the increasing reliance on aircraft, in many forests the stationary lookout is still considered essential. There are times when planes assigned to carry aerial observers are grounded, often during the most dangerous days of the fire season. Too, the stationary lookout may be able to see hard-to-detect fires that aerial observers miss, and he is essential to radio communications—the stationary fire lookouts will be with us for a long time to come.

More and more, however, fire detection is becoming the job of the aerial observer. As with the stationary lookout, there are no special qualities—except good eyesight and the ability to read maps—needed to fill this job. Nor is a pilot's license required, for this is strictly observation work, flying alongside the pilot of a helicopter or light plane, spotting fires and reporting them to the nearest fire dispatcher. Women seem to have a special aptitude for this observation work, which may be one reason the U. S. Forest Service frequently hires husband-and-wife teams as either stationary lookouts or aerial observers.

Observers are hired and paid as aides, but after gaining experience they are advanced to the technician level, and a few are assigned to more specialized jobs. One important job on this level is that of fire dispatcher.

Dispatchers are assigned to forest, district, and regional offices throughout the National Forest System. They are required to have good background knowledge of forest fires, the techniques used in fighting them, and the local terrain where they are to be fought. The job also requires the ability to make quick decisions, and make them correctly, on the bases of training and experience, for fire does not wait. This is a job with heavy responsibilities, for it is the fire dispatcher who makes the first move in responding to a fire reported by observers. The decision made by the dispatcher, in calling for firefighters and equipment, may determine whether a fire is quickly controlled or gets out of hand.

Because of those responsibilities and the knowledge required, most dispatchers obtain their jobs only after gaining lengthy experience in every phase of fire-control work. It is a job with excellent pay. As of 1978, district dispatchers with the Forest Service were generally paid on the GS-7 level, which provides a salary between $13,014 and $16,920; dispatchers in forest offices earned GS-9 wages, from $15,920 to $20,699; and regional dispatchers were rated GS-11, with a salary ranging from $19,263 to as much as $25,041. All dispatchers are year-round employees, who assume other duties during seasons when fire is not a threat.

Fire-control Officers

The job of fire-control officer is another position that becomes available to those who qualify for advancement to the technician level. The position is found in every national forest, and even though it pays a salary of not less than $15,920 (as of 1978), and sometimes much higher, a college education is not required. What is required is the kind of experience one gains only through long years of working in the forest.

Despite the fact that they are called fire-control officers, they are more than that title implies. Fire control is a prime responsibility, but this officer must also be an all-round woodsman, able to assume most of the duties of forester or ranger. As a matter of fact, the duties are so varied that until recently the job title was "alternate ranger."

Fire-control officers must have a wide assortment of skills and abilities that enable them to plan and direct such fire-management jobs as prescribed burning, fire-prevention projects, and the construction and maintenance of fire-control improvements. They must also have the leadership abilities needed to head firefighting teams, and the communications skills necessary for teaching others. Almost every young forester who begins a career with the Forest Service receives training from a fire-control officer.

Forest-fire Staff Officers

Forest-fire staff officers are usually graduate foresters, but again, a degree is not an absolute requirement of the job. They are found in all national forests, and most worked as firefighters, dispatchers, or fire-control officers at some point in their career.

This is a management job, not allowing as much outdoor time as many others. The staff officer heads up the fire-management team in the forest, with the basic duty of seeing that the districts in the forest are in compliance with fire-control standards. He or she, however, like all other forestry workers, may be called on to actively participate in fighting a major fire. Most are rated as GS-12, with earnings that (in 1978) range from $23,087 to $30,017.

Not everyone is suited for fire-management work, of course. But for those who are, it may provide the best route to a meaningful career in forestry, if only because it is a new and developing science.

Though the science of fire management is new, foresters have already recognized its importance—they know that certain endangered species of wildlife, such as the Kirtland's warbler of Michigan, can only survive in a habitat created by fire, just as fire is needed for the propagation of many species of trees. Prescribed burning will see increasing use in the future, on both public and private lands, and more fire-management specialists will be needed. Combined with the jobs already existing in forestry and timber management, these should assure a bright future for those who want to work in the great American forest.

For more information contact:

American Forest Institute
1619 Massachusetts Avenue NW
Washington, DC 20036

American Forestry Association
1319 18th Street NW
Washington, DC 20036

Society of American Foresters
1010 16th Street NW
Washington, DC 20036

Southern Forest Institute
Suite 280
One Corporate Square NE
Atlanta, GA 30329

Western Forestry and Conservation Association
1326 American Bank Building
Portland, OR 97205

For information about jobs in the logging industry:

International Woodworkers of America
1622 N. Lombard Street
Portland, OR 97217

National Forest Products Association
1619 Massachusetts Avenue NW
Washington, DC 20036

PART TWO

7
WATER CONSERVATION

What can be done about a continuous flow of thousands of gallons of water per minute containing high caustic soda and tons of potato peelings? In 1964, when the J. R. Simplot Company began operations at their Caldwell, Idaho, plant, they were faced with the problem of disposing of huge amounts of treatment water in a manner that would not be destructive to the environment. But their plant, like many others of that era, had not been designed with conservation as a primary goal.

Five large earth reservoirs covering 30 acres were used to hold the vast amounts of water required for processing raw potatoes into french fries for distribution nationwide. After treatment, the only outlet for the caustic water was into the nearby Boise River—which soon began to suffer from this pollution. It was evident that some steps had to be taken to clean up the problem.

This company, like many other large firms in that region, owned a large tract of land—in this instance, 850 acres that they used to grow feed crops for their cattle feedlot. Would it be possible to recycle the water and use it to irrigate this land? Jim Oates, director of environmental affairs for the firm, decided to find out.

Working with the general manager of the feedlot and farm operation, Oates began a pilot program to test the idea. He also launched a search for suitable crops that would tolerate such water. For help he turned to Don Fulton, a range conservationist with the state, and to Glen Nielson, a soil conservationist with the local SCS.

"Our real problem was to balance the water and crops on a year-round basis. A farmer doesn't irrigate in the winter, but we have to use all the water twenty-four hours each day, every day of the year, and maintain total retention on our land," says Oates.

After the specialists called in by Oates had studied the soil and determined which types of forage would be best adapted, trial plots of various grasses and legumes were planted. After it had been determined which of these would do best in this situation, an extensive improvement program was started.

The entire 850 acres of land was leveled and planted. With the SCS acting as consultants, a private engineering firm designed and constructed a system for irrigating the land. This system required the lining of 25,000 feet of canal with concrete, installing 4,200 feet of underground pipeline, building 2 water-recovery systems, constructing hundreds of feet of new drain, and improving roughly 3 miles of old open drains.

Today, from 10 to 12 feet of recycled water irrigates each acre every year—this is more than twice the average used on nearby farms. Fields receive water every 6 to 8 hours during the hottest part of the summer, and all the water is retained on company-owned land.

Water leaves the plant at a temperature of 75 degrees and is very rich in nitrogen—an unexpected bonus for the company. The enriched water makes it possible to harvest around 8 tons of dry forage from each acre a year. An average hay crop in the area is about half that much.

The harvested hay, which is rich in protein, is chopped and mixed with other rations, including the waste potato. The mixture provides partial rations for 26,000 yearling steers. "Our operation now has what you might call a self-contained recycling system," explains Oates. "The wastes from the processing plant either feed the steers directly or supply nutrients for grass, which then feeds livestock. In turn, wastes from the livestock feeding pens are applied to the fields to produce more forage."

Oates notes, "Getting established the way we are today has been very expensive, but we feel that every dollar spent will pay in the long run. Last year, for example, a single pipeline cost us $100,000, but it allowed us to use our wastes to irrigate an additional 350 acres." More and more leaders in industry are recognizing that conservation is practical and successful. Water conservation and soil conservation can work hand in hand; they will not only improve our natural resources but also maintain them. If mankind is to survive, conservation is imperative.

Water conservation is one of the oldest sciences, like soil conservation and agriculture. The remains of ancient aqueducts and irrigation works are to be found in the oldest civilized regions of earth—evidence that man long ago learned to guide and store water, and proof, too, that it has long been recognized as our most valuable natural resource. Humanity could linger far longer without food than without water: it sustains all life.

The need for water conservation is clearly written in history. The collapse of more than one civilization has been a direct result of lack of attention to this need. The great empire known as Mesopotamia collapsed after heavy siltation of its canals converted highly productive agricultural land into desert, and the Sahara Desert, which once provided much of the food of the Roman Empire, became wasteland for much the same reason.

Too much water can be as bad as too little. Floods do more damage than any other kind of natural disaster. So the field of water management must be considered a part of water conservation—the two are inseparable. Aside from that of controlling floods water management exists for another very good reason. Our earth has plenty of water to fill the needs of mankind—now and in the foreseeable future—but the problem is in *getting* the water where it is needed. Because our water resources were so vast and gave the appearance of being unlimited, the earliest settlers did little to preserve or protect them. Like our land and forests, the lakes, rivers, and streams of America were abused in many ways—and still are.

The first American to recognize the need for conservation and control of our water resources was George Perkins Marsh. In 1864 he published a book entitled *Man and Nature.* This book correctly pointed out that a well-forested watershed was one means of conserving water, and that it was necessary to study an *entire* watershed before instituting measures to prevent erosion and to control floods. His call for study and research was largely ignored, however, and the abuse of our water supply continued.

Wisconsin and New York were exceptions to this rule. Following the advice given by Marsh in his book, Wisconsin established a commission to study the relation between forest cover and stream flow in 1867; a year later New York appointed a group of scientists to study and report on water pollution. The New York study led to the creation of the State Park Commission, which was chartered to study forest conditions in the Adirondacks, with the hope that such a study would benefit the Erie Canal, the Hudson River, and other silt-threatened waterways in the state. Eventually this led to the establishment of the Adirondack Forest Preserve—the first such preserve in the country.

Other preserves in various states soon followed. Massachusetts began to acquire and protect forests as a means of protecting its watersheds and thus helping maintain adequate water supplies for its cities and towns. Such actions quickly gained the backing of foresters and other early conservationists.

An important step forward was taken on June 4, 1897, when Congress passed the Organic Act for Forestry; it provided for the acquisition, protection, and administration of huge tracts of forested lands. It contained a clause stating that one reason for acquiring these lands would be "for the purpose of securing favorable conditions of water flows. . . ."

The election of Theodore Roosevelt as President gave new impetus to the conservation movement. A champion of many environmental causes, he was largely responsible for the establishment of two new government agencies that became leaders in the field of water conservation and management: the Forest Service and the Bureau of Reclamation.

These two agencies continue to rank high on the list of employers in the field of water conservation, but they are joined by a long list of other agencies and private employers, making this one of the most promising fields for the future. Thousands of professional and non-professional workers will be urgently needed in the years just ahead—at top wages. Let's take a look at the qualifications needed to fill those jobs, as well as at the type of work they actually involve.

Engineers and Hydrologists

Engineers are the key workers in any water-conservation program. They hold important roles in every phase of conservation, and though many of them specialize, they may also work across the board—taking part in all phases of the work. For example, on a small project, an engineer might do a mix of things, from design through actual construction. On major building projects that same professional might work as a specialist in only one engineering field. The word to remember is "engineering." Although other specialists may contribute to a water-conservation project, virtually all such projects are the work of engineers. Even the untrained aides and semiprofessional technicians who assist in these projects—and there are thousands—should be oriented toward engineering.

Hydrologists are especially needed by the agencies heavily involved in water-conservation projects. Their duties involve studying any or all phases of the hydrologic cycle—precipitation, including all types, amounts, and frequencies of occurrence; streamflow, including flood flows and monthly, seasonal, and annual yields; and watershed influences, including effects of soil, cover, land use, land treatment, and channel hydraulics. Hydrologists also work in flood routing to determine the effects of retarding dams, floodways, and other control systems on flood flows. Their work requires that they be able to use the latest electronic computer techniques and equipment. In hydrologic studies and in formulating programs for water management and flood control, a knowledge of the appropriate technology is important.

Engineers who specialize in hydraulics are called on to assemble the basic data and to prepare detailed hydraulic designs for flood prevention and water-storage dams, spillways, channels, siphons, flumes, chutes, energy dissipators, culverts. They must also work toward solving problems of waterflow in reservoirs, determining the capacity of water-holding structures and the relationships of structures.

Structural-design engineers must work in the field to assemble the basic data for, and then design, irrigation and drainage systems, spillways, drop structures, chutes, culverts, and dams for flood prevention, water diversion, and water storage. They must also understand the loads on these structures, compute stresses, and supervise the preparation of detailed construction drawings.

Engineers must also work on the site to supervise the construction of dams, irrigation systems, water-disposal and water-control systems, and various streambank stabilization projects. Other irrigation projects such as farm and ranch ponds, and storage reservoirs require that they work closely with the public.

In the West, where most water for irrigation comes from snow melting high in the mountains, engineers may be called on to travel into remote parts of the watershed to establish the snow-course networks used to predict the supply of water. Engineers who work with the snow courses must also develop forecast formulas and parameters, develop critical water-supply forecasts, and be able to use automatic data-processing equipment for these purposes. The engineers must also be able to use automatic radiotelemetry systems.

Engineers interested in doing water-conservation work with any of the agencies described on the following pages may find opportunities in thousands of locations across the United States—including Puerto Rico and the Virgin Islands. Detailed information about job openings in a specific area can be obtained from the postmaster in that area, or by contacting the nearest office of the agency involved.

If you are a student working toward a degree in engineering, remember that most of these federal agencies have excellent student-training and placement programs. As a student worker or as a graduate fresh out of college, you will find that these programs offer great opportunities for intensive and specialized training. Some of this training is given on the job, but some agencies also maintain group training centers. Your college placement officer, postmaster, or the nearest office of the agency involved can provide detailed information about the programs currently available, as well as application blanks.

The pay varies with the engineering specialty, but it is never less than adequate. As of 1976, the last year for which figures are available, engineers with a year of experience had average earnings in excess of $23,000, when working for the agencies described on the following pages. Engineers with long experience can, of course, earn a great deal more, and the sky is the limit for those who open consulting firms to work with private industry.

Engineering Aides and Technicians

For every engineer who designs a water-conservation project there must be many others to carry out the actual work. Building a small pond for watering stock in a forest might require only three or four workers, while the construction of a huge dam creates thousands of long-lasting jobs. On very large building projects, much of the work is done by private contracters, but even their employees will be working alongside aides and technicians from the agency in charge of the conservation project.

If you are in reasonably good health, have plenty of stamina, and think you would find fulfillment in doing hard but worthwhile work in the field of water conservation, the job of aide may be just what you are seeking. It is an essential job that exists in every agency doing water-conservation work, and it is one that offers the chance to work in a variety of situations, performing a variety of tasks that must be done if we are to preserve this vital resource. As an aide you might help a farmer construct the pond needed for watering his stock, you might go into the high country to build a shelter for use by snow surveyors, or you might assist in damming a small stream to create a better habitat for waterfowl.

No special education is required of those interested in becoming aides. Most agencies require the applicant to have at least six months of experience directly related to the type of work the aide would perform if hired. Ranching, farming, or forestry experience would be acceptable to most agencies, but far better would be some experience in construction. If you have ever been actively involved with construction—poured concrete, laid pipe, driven nails, worked with heavy equipment—chances are good that you can find outdoor work as an aide.

Young people interested in gaining the experience to qualify them for a position as aide should consider spending a summer or two working for the Young Adult Conservation Corps. Funded by the Department of the Interior, the Forest Service, and to a lesser extent by various other agencies, this program offers the chance to be paid while learning.

"We've already placed quite a few former YACC workers in permanent jobs," I was told by one official of the Bureau of Reclamation. "With the YACC they've been active in exactly the sort of work they would be doing with us, so, all other things being equal, I would say the ideal applicant is one with this experience."

Job openings for aides are filled on the local level, based on work experience, with no written exam required. Pay is set according to local wages for comparable work and can vary widely. In recent years, starting wages in a typical office of the Bureau of Reclamation were $7,198, but even then most aides quickly advanced to earnings in excess of $10,000. Many of them have the opportunity to acquire on-the-job training that eventually qualifies them for the better-paying job of technician.

Most technicians, however, start on their work after completing one or two years of technical schooling directly related to the field of engineering—drafting, surveying, soil mechanics, instruments, etc.

Technicians new to the job typically perform as aides to trained engineers, scientists, or technicians with longer experience. But after some time on the job, technicians frequently assume tasks comparable to those of the professionals, even though they are not required to hold a degree.

Pay for this job can vary. In a typical agency, annual salaries paid to technicians just out of school range from $7,198 to $17,397, but many experienced technicians draw salaries of more than $20,000. Few careers offer better chances for advancement, and Pauline Wong is living proof of that.

In 1948, Ms. Wong went to work for the Bureau of Reclamation as a clerk-typist—a good way to enter the Civil Service system. She was first promoted to a position as an engineering aide, and later worked as a hydraulic engineering technician and civil engineering technician. She finally advanced to her present position as hydrologic technician.

Ms. Wong is responsible for the direct daily control of the water operations of the Central Valley Project facilities of the Bureau of Reclamation in California. This includes water releases from Millerton Lake to the Friant-Kern Canal, Madera Canal, and San Joaquin River. She is also responsible for the ordering of water from Delta-Mendota Canal to meet demands in the Mendota Pool. It provides water for about 1,265,000 acres of cropland. To accomplish this, she collects daily water-supply information from various field branches, and keeps a daily record of water deliveries, thus enabling her to apprise the local districts of approaching water shortages. Her additional duties include summarizing and preparing a weekly statement of water requirements, determining and incorporating necessary adjustments during flood-control operations to assure daily operations, and contacting other irrigation districts for hydrologic and various other data. About half her work is done outdoors, the remainder in lab or office.

"Being a hydrologic technician is hard work," warns Ms. Wong. "Anyone seeking a career in this field should be enthusiastic and energetic and should try to learn every aspect of the job. I enjoy my work. I think that is important."

Careers with the U.S. Government

Ms. Wong's employer, the Bureau of Reclamation, hires all types of engineers, technicians, and aides, but most of their work involves water conservation and management. This agency is charged with administering the federal program in western states for the use and development of that area's water resources. Best known for the huge dams it has planned and constructed, the Bureau also involves itself in fish and wildlife protection, recreation, and providing water for farm and industrial use.

Young engineers and technicians who work for the Bureau of Reclamation are placed in an orientation program. During this period of familiarization and advanced training, they are introduced to half a dozen or so regional offices, where they are given the chance to learn about the variety of work the Bureau does. After completion of this orientation program, most go on to specialize in one type of water-conservation engineering.

After the Bureau has completed a dam, power plant, reservoir, water-distribution system, or whatever, the facility is often placed in the hands of others for management. However, the Bureau must protect the huge investment made in these projects, so it frequently assigns engineers to advise and guide the water users after they have assumed control. Many of its newer engineers are placed in these advisory positions. Others in the Bureau quickly become involved in flood-control or irrigation projects, in hydrology or hydraulics, or even in weather modification and in evaporation control. The Bureau is constantly at work on many projects and is one of the better employers for those seeking variety.

The Forest Service of the Department of Agriculture continues to be very active in the fields of water conservation and water management. There are conservation specialists, technicians, and aides on the staff of every regional forester. At the numerous forest and range experiment stations operated by this agency a great deal of research relating to water conservation in the national forests is done, which often leads to projects to test the results of that research.

More than one third of the land area of the continental United States is forested land, and that land yields more than 60 percent of our streamflow. For that reason alone, the Forest Service is certain to remain very active in water conservation during the years ahead.

The Bureau of Land Management, which manages hundreds of millions of acres in the West, has a watershed-management program that provides outdoor employment for thousands of professionals, technicians, and aides.

The program is directed primarily toward conservation efforts on more than 120 million acres in 11 western states, with intensive work on about 40 million acres that are frail and deteriorating.

Conservation efforts include water spreading, modern tillage, and other land-treatment practices that help conserve water; the building of check and detention dams, diversion and drop structures, and the installation of other water-control structures.

Because the work of the water conservationist is so closely linked to the soil scientist, the Soil Conservation Service of the Department of Agriculture will certainly continue to be one of the major employers in this field.

Until fairly recent times, irrigation of farmland in America was commonly practiced only in the arid and semi-arid lands of the West. But in the last few decades farmers east of the 100th meridian, especially in the prairie states and the semihumid zones of the Midwest, have come to realize that irrigation assures more stable crop production and higher yields. Each year more and more land is placed under irrigation. The Soil Conservation Service must involve itself in many of the problems connected with the establishment and maintenance of such irrigation systems. It must also help solve the problems connected with the disposal of excess irrigation waters, as well as the problems of purifying runoff water that might be contaminated by

pesticides or insecticides. Added to its extensive work in helping forecast the natural water supply (as described in the chapter on soil
conservation), there are plenty of jobs with this agency in the field of
water conservation.

The Fish and Wildlife Service, in the Fish and Wildlife Coordina-
tion Act of Congress, was ordered to: "Investigate and report on water
resource development projects prior to their construction or license by
the Federal Government; to determine the probable effects of such
projects on fish and wildlife habitats; and to recommend measures for
preventing or reducing damage to, and improving conditions for,
these resources." This agency is very active in water conservation, and
though its specialists are hired for the purpose of advising and consulting on the environmental impacts of the projects of others, the
Service itself diverts and impounds water for its numerous wildlife-
refuge and fish-propagation programs.

The Geological Survey of the Department of the Interior, in cooperation with other federal, state, and local agencies, conducts water
studies for planning the safe use and the maximum development of
the nation's water resources. About 1,700 research and data projects
are under way, with hydrologists, technicians, and aides measuring
the quantity and quality of water at more than 50,000 sites—streams,
rivers, lakes, ponds, wells, and even springs—across the nation. These
studies have a wide range of purposes, but they are largely directed
toward finding solutions to various hydrological problems, and the
greatest opportunities are for those with experience in that specialty.
If you feel qualified, further information about specific job openings
can be obtained by writing the Geological Survey National Center (see
end of this chapter).

The Army Corps of Engineers, which has nearly 45,000 civilian
employees engaged in water conservation and management in every
state of the union and a dozen foreign countries, may be the best place
of all to turn for employment in this field. Since the Revolutionary
War it has been charged with the internal improvement of the nation,
and must manage about 700 of its already completed projects, which
are valued at about $20 billion. Maintaining these requires skilled
help, and with more than $1 billion annually being appropriated for

new projects, job opportunities will continue to exist within the Corps.

The water-conservation programs of the Corps are extraordinarily diverse. Hydrologists are especially needed, and they are often given the opportunity to become involved in other types of water-related engineering. This is the largest engineering organization in the world, with operating responsibility for more than 20,000 miles of navigable waterways. The Corps studies every major river basin, as well as many other water areas, and is responsible for giving out the permits that must be acquired for any work done in these waterways. The Corps also issues discharge permits, a responsibility it was given under the Refuse Act, to control what is discharged into our rivers and streams. In addition to all this, it is the Corps that is called upon to do rescue and rehabilitation work in times of flood or other natural disaster.

Those interested in working as aide or technician for other agencies would do well to consider using the Corps of Engineers as a stepping-stone. Aides and technicians of all types are hired by the Corps through its hundreds of regional offices, and they receive training and experience that make it easier for them to enter other agencies. Maintenance workers of all types are used in forests, wildlife areas, and national parks, and when I asked a forester, a park maintenance chief, and a refuge manager where one could best obtain the training or experience required of their maintenance workers, the answer was unanimous: "The Army Corps of Engineers."

The Tennessee Valley Authority (which has built or acquired twenty-eight dams on the Tennessee and Cumberland rivers and assists private enterprise in the management of nearly a dozen others) is a major employer of foresters, recreation experts, fish and wildlife-management specialists, and many other kinds of outdoor professionals. The TVA, however, is primarily a water-management agency, and its greatest need is for those with skills in water management.

Early on, the TVA began encouraging the states in its region to establish effective pollution control and water-management programs, and its efforts were vastly increased in the 1960s. Today, working with dozens of state and local agencies, the TVA prevents water pollution through an extensive program of monitoring and research. It also sets standards for waste treatment from commercial and industrial developments along the lakeshores, as well as for disposal by floating craft on the lakes.

As of 1978, among its many other research and planning projects, the TVA was engaged in experiments to find beneficial ways of using heated water from its power plants—for field and greenhouse production of crops, for commercial fish farming, and for heating poultry sheds and livestock barns. In another project, as a joint effort with the Environmental Protection Agency, the Authority that year began a study to learn more about the effects of heated water on aquatic life.

The TVA also conducts studies of the effects on water quality of insecticides and pesticides washed into streams and lakes by rainfall or dissolved into groundwater from farms where they have been applied. These studies are complex and require a large number of trained workers to carry them out. The TVA will continue to offer opportunity for those interested in water conservation.

The Environmental Protection Agency, which began operation in 1970, now has more than 10,000 employees and an annual budget of more than half a billion dollars. It also administers an $18 billion program for the construction of sewage-treatment plants. The central task of the EPA is to protect the health and welfare of the American people by controlling pollution hazards. To do so, it sets and enforces both air-pollution and water-pollution standards, monitors pollution, controls pesticides, sets standards for noise and radiation, works on waste management, conducts research and demonstration projects, and assists state and local environmental efforts.

The Agency has established regional offices—which it describes as "the cutting edge of major EPA programs"—in Boston, New York, Philadelphia, Atlanta, Chicago, Dallas, Kansas City, Denver, San Francisco, and Seattle. Its research programs are centered at environmental research stations in Las Vegas, Nevada; Cincinnati, Ohio; Research Triangle Park, North Carolina; and Corvallis, Oregon; but it also operates a large number of smaller research centers throughout the nation.

Summer jobs are usually available with the Environmental Protection Agency, and information about these can be obtained from the agency itself or from the nearest Federal Job Information Center. "Application for summer employment," advises the EPA, "should be made very early in the year."

"Part-time and temporary positions also exist at most EPA installations," the EPA adds, "but opportunities for such employment vary from installation to installation." Information about such openings may be obtained from the EPA or from the nearest Federal Job Information Center.

"Generally," continues the EPA, "there is a continuing need, on a full-time basis, for engineers, physical scientists, life scientists, biological technicians, physical science technicians, engineering technicians, and environmental-protection specialists. In water control, EPA offers environmentally oriented personnel diverse and stimulating careers in the areas of water supply, waste treatment, pollution control, water planning and standards, and construction management.

"The best opportunities for employment in the water program are in the EPA regional offices, and in the EPA research laboratories serviced by the EPA personnel offices in Cincinnati, Ohio, and Las Vegas, Nevada. Job opportunities in this program are best for sanitary, chemical, and environmental engineers; chemists, and life scientists."

For further information about jobs in the water-control program of the EPA, write:

National Employment Center
Code PM-212
EPA-HQ
401 M Street SW
Washington, DC 20460

More information about careers in water conservation is available from:

American Water Resources Association
206 East University Avenue
Urbana, IL 61801

Chief Hydrologist
Mail Stop 409
Geological Survey National Center
Reston, VA 22092

National Watershed Congress
Room 1105
1025 Vermont Avenue
Washington, DC 20005

Personnel Office
Tennessee Valley Authority
Norris, TN 37828

Water Resources Council
Suite 800
2120 L Street NW
Washington, DC 20037

8
FISH AND WILDLIFE MANAGEMENT

"My biggest problems are not with animals, but with people," says Paul Rogers, one of nine game wardens working for the Delaware Division of Fish and Wildlife. "When I started this job a few years ago, I'd get only a few animal complaints each week; now they're running in the hundreds—raccoons in the garbage can, skunks in the yard, groundhogs in the garden. People just don't know animal traits or habits. As soon as they see an animal acting in a way they think of as 'funny,' they assume it's got rabies. People who dream of having a job as game warden don't realize we have to trap squirrels in the attic. They think we're out there in the woods petting Bambi."

Game Warden

The radio in the car had just delivered another citizen's complaint—this one about a "rabid" skunk—and Paul had jotted down notes and added them to those already filling the clipboard attached to the dash of his car. He softly explained that he once handled every complaint by trapping the animals and releasing them elsewhere, but is unable to do that now because of the sheer volume of calls. "Now I limit my trapping to animals actually in the house, but I always call and give the citizens some suggestion on how to handle the problem . . . if a problem still exists."

His car was parked beside White Clay Creek in New Castle County, Delaware, not far from the Pennsylvania border. It was November, the deer season was open, and this car would serve as Paul's office at least until February, when the last of the various hunting seasons was at an end. We talked about his job as he drove, the car window down so he could listen for gunshots.

"Part of our problems are caused by what I call the 'extreme preservationists'—those folks who are so far out in left field you can't even talk to them about game management," he says. He talks for a moment about the need for regulation of hunting to insure survival of the species while preventing starvation caused by overpopulation in an area, then provides an example of this need.

"A year or two ago, I got a call from the folks at Brandywine State Park, asking me to take a look at a deer. It was lying on the bank of the river and when I approached, it didn't even try to stand up." He was obviously upset by recollection of the incident. "It was so weak its lungs were full of water from swimming that river, and our autopsy showed it had been trying to subsist on pine needles, which have absolutely no nutritional value."

He had spotted a station wagon parked off the edge of the road, and now he stopped long enough to jot down its description and license number. A few yards down the road, we stopped again, this time at the sight of a large man dressed in hunters' orange, a shotgun broken open and cradled in the crook of his arm.

The hunter quickly recognized the olive uniform, gold badge, and blue baseball cap showing a large Fish and Wildlife patch worn by Paul. The hunter explained that he had just given up an effort to follow the blood trail of a deer wounded by some other hunter. Paul says he will tell other hunters about it, then asks the man to unload his shotgun.

It is already unloaded, so Paul takes a short length of plastic tubing out of his pocket and slips it into the magazine to make sure the gun is plugged to hold only three shells. It is, so he checks the man's ammunition, verifying that it is a type permitted by Delaware law, and then asks for the man's hunting license. As we return to the car, I ask if he is bothered by the idea of repeatedly facing people who hold shotguns.

"Not at all," he says with a shrug. "If you're bothered by that, you don't belong in this job. My attitude is that if you treat people with respect, they'll treat you the same way. Besides, we prefer education to enforcement, and we make few arrests. But I did bust one guy who said he was going to tear my head off. I arrested him for fishing without a license, but when we got to court he apologized. I decided not to make an issue of the threat."

A short distance down the road, we come on two youngsters

walking up a road between two wooded stretches that Paul knows are off-limits to hunters. Both carry shotguns, so Paul stops the car to confront an example of what he has told me is a recurring problem: trespassing.

"Well, there just ain't any legal place to hunt," one of the boys complains. Paul shows sympathy, but is firm about the trespassing laws, and tells the pair where the nearest public hunting areas are. He takes their names, and warns them that if they are caught trespassing again they'll be cited into court.

These scenes, with some variations, are repeated several times this November day, but they represent only a part of the work done by Paul Rogers and others like him. At other times throughout the year he will be making court appearances, teaching safety courses, stocking trout streams, checking fishermen, and, of course, "trapping squirrels in the attic."

"Aside from the necessary degree in wildlife or fisheries management," says Paul, who earned his own degree at the University of Maryland, Eastern Shore, where he specialized in zoology, "I'd advise the beginner to concentrate on police science, basic psychology, and human relations. Too, I'd suggest courses in public speaking. About half of this job is enforcement, the other half educating the public. And even after getting the necessary training in school, or while getting it, I'd advise doing some volunteer work . . . with Ducks Unlimited, Audubon, or a similar group. That's not only a way of gathering some experience; it's also a way of finding out if you're suited to the work. Not everyone is, you know."

Game wardens, because they are the ones most visible to the public, could be called the "cutting edge" of fish and wildlife management—a career field that offers attractive employment to professionals and nonprofessionals alike. Most are employed by the individual states, at wages that vary widely but that are usually comparable to those earned by police officers in the region. Job requirements also vary, but increasingly needed is a degree in fisheries science or wildlife management, with hours in biological sciences, zoology, botany, and plant sciences, and related courses in the physical and earth sciences. A sound working knowledge of plant and animal ecology is the basic requirement, but as a day in the field with Paul Rogers clearly illustrates, skills in dealing with, and educating, the public are just as essential. It is, after all, our growing population that has created the need for management of our fish and wildlife resources.

Careers with the Fish and Wildlife Service

There was a time, according to scientific estimates, when America was home to 60 million buffalo, more than 1 million moose, 2 million wolves, 9 million elk, 350 million beaver, 35 million antelope, and billions of passenger pigeons. Some, like the passenger pigeons that once filled evening skies, are gone forever, and the rest are fewer in number and threatened in many ways. To some, the preservation of this part of our heritage is not important, but to the vast majority it is increasingly so.

We come to recognize that the very survival of mankind depends upon maintaining a healthy environment that allows our fish and wildlife to go on living, and we are faced with economic and aesthetic reasons for preserving these natural resources. Billions of dollars are spent each year by fishermen and hunters, and equal amounts are spent by the millions of Americans who simply enjoy observing these animals in their natural environment, in our parks, forests, wildlife refuges, and rangelands. They pay well for these rights.

But all other reasons aside, there exists a far more important basis for the preservation of wildlife: our moral obligation. Wildlife shares our trusteeship of this planet and has the right to exist. A large number of our activities interfere with this right of wildlife; thus it is morally demanded of us that we take other actions to maintain sufficient numbers of fish and wildlife for species survival.

We have not always recognized that obligation.

Until about 1933, when a forester named Aldo Leopold published the results of his wildlife studies in a book called *Game Management*, little in the way of scientific knowledge was applied to fish and game management. Those who worked with fish and wildlife were, until that time, simply game protectors, keeping fishermen and hunters away from restricted areas and within the limits set by law.

Leopold pointed out that the preservation of wildlife depends primarily on the preservation of habitat. He created the concept of providing refuge areas, improving the habitat, and stocking these areas with animals. He also pointed out that if the habitat is suitable, only a little stocking is needed; the animals will provide the rest. In addition, he noted the need for predators within the refuge, to strike a healthy balance between the habitat and the number of animals it supports—a balance we now recognize as essential to good wildlife management.

Because of Leopold's efforts Congress passed legislation for better management of these resources and created, at the same time, numerous career opportunities in the field we now know as wildlife management.

The first important law was the Migratory Bird Hunting Stamp Act of 1934. The Duck Stamp Act, as it is commonly known, created a fund for the purchase of wetlands—setting aside the natural habitat for which Leopold had pleaded. The Act also provided better enforcement by making it a federal offense to kill protected waterfowl and other migratory birds.

This law was followed, in 1937, by passage of the Federal Aid in Wildlife Restoration Act, then known as the Pittman-Robertson Act, which levied an excise tax on the sale of guns and ammunition. The funds raised under this bill are allocated to the individual states on a basis of 75 percent federal money to 25 percent provided by the recipient states. This money has allowed the states to enter into many management programs that might otherwise have been financially out of reach, and to hire thousands of wildlife specialists to carry out these programs; it has also been used to obtain and improve habitat, to develop and maintain related facilities, and to help establish cooperative wildlife research facilities at many colleges around the country. Research centers employ many wildlife-management specialists and provide facilities for graduate students doing research work in the field.

Because fishing as a sport has long been more popular than hunting in America, protective laws dealing with fisheries go back much further than those dealing with game animals. As a result, funds raised through the sale of fishing licenses have long been available for use in fisheries work—but these funds have not always been put to the best possible use.

Fisheries research still lags behind the science of game management, though much has been done in recent years. The first major step in this direction was the belated recognition of the fact that good habitat is critical to fisheries management. But not until 1950 were significant federal funds made available for fisheries research.

These funds were authorized under the Dingell-Johnson Act, which provides matching funds to the states for use in fish conservation. These funds have saved sport fishing in many areas, have enabled the states to add thousands of fishery specialists to their payrolls, and have done much to create an environment in which our aquatic life can survive. The program has also paid for research that has brought about more realistic fishing laws and created new concepts in fisheries management.

This remains a developing science. Researchers are only now beginning to understand what constitutes good fisheries management. For that reason, most future jobs in this field will go to scientists able to supply answers to the as-yet-unknown. Fishery specialists will be essentially researchers, with a deep knowledge of many very complicated but relevant subjects. Training in limnology (life in lakes, ponds, and streams), ichthyology (the study of fish themselves), fish culture, fishery management, fishery biology, and fish nutrition will continue to be required of every researcher and manager; but increasing emphasis will be placed on related knowledge, such as water-pollution control, fish diseases, and control of fish parasites. Courses in oceanography will certainly be required of those wanting to work in marine fisheries.

Wildlife management and fisheries management are two distinct sciences, with literally dozens of specialties found within each. But they can be grouped together for many reasons. The work done by a specialist in one field often has a rippling effect on current work in the other—the wildlife specialist must be aware of and understand what is going on in fisheries management: On the state level, where funds are limited, fish and game management is sometimes combined. The advice given by Don Perkuchin, manager of the Prime Hook National Wildlife Refuge on the Delaware Flyway, deserves attention.

"If you are eager to enter the field of wildlife management and are just starting your schooling or are already in college," he says, "my advice is to get as broad an education as you possibly can.

Branch out. Become a specialist in your first interest, sure; but don't become too narrow a specialist, no matter what your first love. Study everything even remotely connected to wildlife and its management. Think of it like hunting: Broaden your aim and you'll have a better chance of hitting your target."

Nonprofessional Jobs

The Fish and Wildlife Service of the United States Department of the Interior is the agency with the prime responsibility of conserving and managing the nation's fish and wildlife resources. It is also charged with doing this in a manner that will allow the public to understand, appreciate, and use this part of the national heritage.

The Fish and Wildlife Service employs a large number of fishery and wildlife biologists; many nonprofessional workers assist them. For those still in school and preparing for a career in fish and wildlife biology, the Service offers a number of student trainee programs, conducted on a short-term basis through its regional office. Information about those currently in operation may be obtained from the Fish and Wildlife Service, Department of the Interior, Washington, DC 20250.

For nonprofessionals wanting to work with the Service, the best opportunities lie in the Maintenance Division. At most of the fish hatcheries and refuges operated by the Service, jobs exist for those with skills in maintenance, carpentry, plumbing, etc. The term "maintenance," as used here, is a little misleading, however, for those employed in this capacity often assist refuge managers in maintaining the natural habitat of the refuge, or in other projects. When I visited Prime Hook National Wildlife Refuge, for example, workers from maintenance were helping to trap and band waterfowl. Pay for these jobs is usually based on local wages.

Fishery aides and wildlife aides are also employed, though in smaller numbers, at the refuges and hatcheries. They are hired specifically to assist the professional biologists conduct the field programs, and most have at least a year of technical training that is related to the work. As of 1978, these aides earned salaries ranging from $7,422 to $10,507 for beginners to $13,657 for those with technical training and several years' experience.

Seasonal jobs are also sometimes available with the Service.

These are filled from a list of names provided by the U. S. Civil Service Commission of successful candidates in its seasonal employment examinations. Literature about the exams is updated annually and may be obtained from the nearest office of the Civil Service. Summer workers, as of 1978, earned $3.15 to $4.51 per hour, but even more important than their wages, these workers were gaining experience that would count heavily as they pursued their outdoor careers.

Biologists

Sue Kadalka is one young person using seasonal employment to better her chances for a rewarding career in fish and wildlife management. I met Sue at Chincoteague Island National Wildlife Refuge, off the coast of Virginia, near the end of her second summer as an aide with the Fish and Wildlife Service. This was actually on Assateague Island, which adjoins Chincoteague, and where the famous wild ponies also roam. One of the ponies, a beautiful roan-colored stallion, had been badly injured on the neck during a fight with another male. Sue and two other aides had managed to get a rope halter around its neck and were attempting to lead it into a van so it could be taken to a vet for treatment. It took the best part of an hour to accomplish this, with the pony bucking, kicking, and snapping nearly every minute of that time. Sue was happily exhausted by the time we were able to talk.

Sue is a student at Rutgers University, where she is majoring in wildlife management. As the van and its captive drove off she laughingly pointed out, "What you've just seen is something they can't teach in a classroom."

During her two summers at Chincoteague Sue has helped manage the famous wild ponies that reside there. She also assists in management and improvement programs involving the Sika deer, a species of antelope imported from Japan; the Delmarva squirrel, which was once nearly extinct but now flourishes throughout the region; and in many waterfowl programs, always working alongside experienced professionals. She finds this outdoor work enjoyable and believes it is as important as any work on the face of the earth. After graduation, she hopes to continue with Fish and Wildlife as a full-time employee.

"This is where it's at for biologists today and in the foreseeable future, if only because Fish and Wildlife has the funding so many agencies lack," she told me. "Name almost any type of project related to the field and you'll find the Service deeply involved. No matter what interests you, or what might, chances are that you can do it with Fish and Wildlife."

Those two summers at Chincoteague have helped Sue improve her grades at college, adjust her courses to strengthen weak areas she might not have detected, and have increased her chances of stepping out of college and into the job for which she has trained. She is almost certain to be accepted by the Fish and Wildlife Service as a full-time biologist, probably in a position at one of its wildlife refuges.

The Fish and Wildlife Service maintains 384 national wildlife refuges and 20 wetland management districts encompassing 34 million acres and providing properly managed habitat for mammals, migratory and nonmigratory birds, and endangered species, as well as observation and recreation facilities used by millions of Americans. Each refuge is under the direction of a manager and may, depending on its size and activities, also employ one or several assistant managers, all of them graduate biologists. Temporary programs at a refuge may also require additional biologists who are not a part of refuge management.

As of 1978, a biologist just out of school could expect a starting salary of $10,507, with quick advancement to $12,257; but for biologists with advanced degrees and long experience, earnings in that same year approached $50,000. Average earnings were just below $30,000.

The nature of the work done at each refuge depends greatly on the location of that refuge, its wildlife population, and the purposes that caused it to be set aside as public lands. Of the 384 refuge areas, however, 276 are managed specifically for ducks, geese, or swans, with 100 million waterfowl depending on these areas for survival—so the odds are good that the beginner will be working on a refuge for nesting birds.

The largest nesting population of bald eagles in the northeastern United States is found in Maine. But because of repeated nesting failures, this population has gradually declined from more than 60 pairs in the early 1960s to about 40 pairs by 1976. Studies have revealed that nesting failure is caused largely by chemical contamination of eagles' food—which gave rise to an experiment to see whether the Maine population could be artificially maintained until the environment can again support a self-sustaining population.

Biologists of the Service, in cooperation with several other agencies, began transplanting eggs from successfully producing pairs of eagles in other areas to nests in Maine. Within two years the eagle population in Maine had been increased 12 percent by this method.

Major emphasis has been placed on prompt diagnosis of disease outbreaks and quick corrective action to prevent large losses of migratory birds. When several dead snow geese were found at Squaw Creek National Wildlife Refuge in Missouri, workers acted quickly to disperse the remaining flock of more than 12,000 birds. Examination revealed that the deaths had been caused by avian cholera—and a major outbreak had been prevented by this quick action.

In August of 1976, refuge personnel at Waubay National Wildlife Refuge in Wisconsin detected the early phase of botulism poisoning among pelicans. By promptly rushing specimens to Service laboratories, they were able to isolate the toxic agent causing the botulism, develop a program to bring it under control, and thus save large numbers of pelicans.

The National Elk Refuge in Wyoming, as the name implies, is one of the areas set aside primarily as habitat for mammals. One of its principal objectives is to provide wintering habitat for elk, and a major problem has always been the high cost of supplemental feeding—formerly as much as 1,600 tons annually.

Various techniques are now being employed to achieve better distribution of this elk herd and the subsequent better utilization of native forage. The most successful technique has been the controlled burning of worthless sagebrush—which covers nearly one fourth of this 24,000-acre refuge—and the establishment of grasses suitable for use by the elk. These converted areas now produce as much as 1,000 pounds of hay per acre.

Fishery biologists with the Service were also busy during 1976. During that year, approximately 216 million fish weighing more than

4 million pounds were produced at 70 hatcheries operated by the Service. They were provided to other agencies for stocking in our 58,000 square miles of water deemed suitable for sport fishing.

The Service also maintains development centers, fishery training schools, research laboratories, and field stations. Biologists at these work together to improve fish productivity, increase efficiency of hatchery production, determine effects of pollution on fishery resources, and develop more effective methods of controlling undesirable species of fish. They also provide technical assistance to other agencies and individuals across the country.

Enforcement Officers

Although enforcement has traditionally been left to game wardens of the individual states, 728 refuge employees are vested with law-enforcement authority, and the Fish and Wildlife Service also employs 185 full-time special agents who concentrate on enforcing the laws designed to protect our wildlife.

These special agents, who are highly trained police officers, handle major cases involving lengthy investigation, such as the 1976 case in which a fur company was fined $5,000 and placed on probation for the possession and sale of alligator skins, or the one involving a parrot smuggler who was sentenced to 5 years in jail. No matter what their other qualifications, new special agents receive additional training in this field at the Federal Law Enforcement Training Center at Glynco, Georgia.

While other Fish and Wildlife personnel are unlikely to become involved in long investigations or undercover work, they did collectively make more than 6,000 arrests in 1976, so the Training Center in Georgia has developed a special curriculum for them. This shows how important police training can be to your career in fish and wildlife management.

Linda K. Gintoli is one of the Fish and Wildlife employees with the powers of arrest, but her background also provides a good example of the variety of skills needed for advancement in this highly competitive field.

Linda is a 1970 graduate of the University of New Hampshire, where she earned a B.S. degree in wildlife management. Even with that degree, her first job with the Service was as a biological technician. She later spent a few months working as a naturalist, and in 1971 was selected for a trainee position, which led to three assignments as assistant refuge manager. Her next promotion made her the first woman to become a refuge manager for the Fish and Wildlife Service.

In this position, she supervises the Great Meadows, Monomoy, and Oxbow wildlife refuges in Massachusetts. Great Meadows lies scattered along several miles of the Sudbury and Concord rivers; Monomoy is a barrier island, with dunes, salt marshes, and flats; and Oxbow consists of freshwater marsh, swamp, and fields, so each area has its unique forms of life and equally unique problems.

Programs she currently heads include farming food for the Canada goose population, water-level management for ducks, various banding efforts, and enforcement of waterfowl hunting laws along the rivers. The refuges are also used as study areas by students in nearby schools, as well as for nature study and photography by hobbyists, so she also works with these groups.

In addition to all this, Ms. Gintoli recruits, trains, and supervises the refuge staff, including permanent and temporary personnel; maintains fiscal accounts, statistical and operational records; prepares reports of refuge operations; is responsible for the planning and carrying out of refuge maintenance; is responsible for the prevention of fire and trespass, and must constantly keep the wildlife and its habitat under investigation. It is a big and demanding job, requiring a large number of skills, but Linda Gintoli prepared herself well and has proven she can handle it.

Youth Conservation Corps

In addition to its wildlife refuges, fish hatcheries, and experimental labs and stations, the Fish and Wildlife Service is heavily involved in the Youth Conservation Corps program, operating 103 camps at refuges and fish hatcheries throughout the nation. These camps provide youngsters between the ages of 16 and 23 with an opportunity to be gainfully employed in outdoor activities directly relating to the use, management, and protection of natural resources while accomplishing needed conservation projects. A quick glance at some of the work done by these young people provides some idea of the many jobs for adults this program has created.

In 1976 alone, these young conservation workers completed 73 timber management projects appraised at $92,000; 262 recreation-development projects valued at $315,862; 8 visitor-information-center projects valued at $6,453; 163 visitor-services projects valued at $206,118; 92 range-management projects valued at $211,029; 34 wildlife-habitat improvements worth $43,530; 293 wildlife projects worth $315,628; 206 engineering/construction projects valued at $351,862; 26 water-quality projects valued at $7,351; and 152 soil- and water-conservation projects with a value of $221,461. Total worth of these projects exceeded $2,500,000.

Aside from the savings to the public, these projects required the assistance and supervision of adult workers with any of hundreds of skills, thus creating thousands of well-paid outdoor jobs. More projects of this type will soon be undertaken by the National Park Service, Bureaus of Reclamation and Land Management, the Bureau of Indian Affairs, and the Office of Territories, so the job outlook in this program should be bright in the years just ahead.

The needed electricians, carpenters, plumbers, and other nonprofessional workers in this program are usually hired on the local level, at wages comparable to those prevailing in the area. For a complete list of camps and projects, as well as information on specific job openings, write the Division of Personnel Management and Organization, Fish and Wildlife Service, Department of the Interior, Room 3452, Washington, DC 20240.

Professionals and nonprofessionals alike in this program work under the supervision of a camp director, almost always a fish or wildlife biologist. In addition to their scientific training, however, these camp directors usually have credentials that make them exceptionally qualified to work with youngsters. M. Noel Fitzgerald is one director who certainly possesses those credentials.

Ms. Fitzgerald heads the newly established Youth Conservation Corps camp in Olympia, Washington. This is a nonresidential camp, consisting of an area headquarters and 23 field stations throughout Washington. It provides work for a staff of about 20, as well as more than 100 Corps members at the satellite camps.

While earning her B.A. degree from Sonoma State College, Ms.

Fitzgerald worked as a park aide for the California Department of Parks and Recreation, with an assignment at Pismo Beach State Park. She held that position until she had also earned her M.A. degree in social science from Porterville College.

In 1968, she began working with the Tulare County Department of Education in the environmental education field with elementary, high-school, and college students at their resident outdoor education camp, and later ran a similar program for the mentally retarded.

She left this job to become assistant manager of California Conservation Corps camps at San Luis Obispo and Camarillo, assisting in the establishment of both. From there she moved to her present job with Fish and Wildlife's youth program.

As camp director at Olympia, Ms. Fitzgerald is responsible for the planning, programming, scheduling, and supervision of the staff and Corps members. She assigns work, evaluates performance, advises, counsels, and instructs subordinates on work and administrative matters, and plans and recommends work projects for the future.

She also arranges for administrative services pertaining to procurement, storage, and distribution of supplies; maintains financial management controls and records; supervises on-the-job training and work projects; and disciplines enrollees who represent many varied backgrounds, attitudes, and levels of maturity. Not all of it is outdoor work, but she gladly trades total freedom for the chance to help youngsters develop a better understanding of conservation work through actual experience. And she has some advice for others who would like the chance to do the same.

"The competition for professional positions in the Conservation Corps is keen, very keen," she notes. "You will need a degree in environmental studies, preferably. You will also need experience working with people, and the ability to communicate. Teaching and administrative credentials are required in most programs, and social studies are a big plus."

More Careers with the U.S. Government

Not all fish and wildlife specialists with the federal government are employed by Fish and Wildlife; not by any means. In virtually all agencies that are involved in the management of public lands or waterways, positions for professional and nonprofessional fish and wild-life workers exist, though in more limited numbers.

Denise Meridith, for example, is a wildlife specialist with the Bureau of Land Management, working out of its Eastern States Office at Silver Spring, Maryland.

Her original goal in life was to be a veterinarian. "But halfway through my four years of college," she says, "I decided I would not be content to set up a veterinary practice in a big city, where my main clientele would be canaries and poodles. So I switched my major to wildlife biology and began studies in entomology, whitetail deer, up-land game, and waterfowl."

Denise began work for the Bureau of Land Management in 1973, as a natural resource specialist at Las Vegas, Nevada. While there, she wrote the wildlife sections of a published study called *Unit Resources Analysis and Management Framework Plans* and was a member of a team compiling environmental-analysis reports and impact statements. She also wrote brochures for the public, conducted seminars, and gave slide shows about wildlife.

In her present position, she reviews environmental-impact studies from other agencies to determine whether there should be any input from her own agency, and she travels to lend her expertise where it is needed. She also provides guidance to other offices in preparing their own impact statements, and she conducts training sessions for new wildlife specialists. Information about jobs with her employer can be obtained by writing the Division of Personnel, Bureau of Land Management, Department of the Interior, Room 3619, Washington, DC 20240.

Biologist Virginia Carter often works closely with the Fish and Wildlife Service, but her employer is the Geological Survey, an agency that hires a small number of natural-resource specialists. Her specialty is remote sensing, which is the study of objects through photography, using the miscroscope, telescope, X ray, and other highly specialized equipment. Her training has opened the way to many exciting experiences.

That training includes a B.S. degree in biology from Swarthmore College and an M.S. degree in the same field from American University. It has been applied to research involving the application of remote sensing technology to the analysis of wetland ecology and hydrology. Her work includes the determination of characteristics of wetland vegetation and the interpretation of aerial photography and satellite data for wetland classification and mapping, wetland hydrology, and studies of vegetation.

In projects involving her own agency, Fish and Wildlife, NASA, the Tennessee Valley Authority and others, she has studied the Great Dismal Swamp and Dismal Swamp Canal in North Carolina and Virginia; done experimental wetland mapping in Sapelo Island, Georgia; and, by using high-altitude, color infrared photography and personal exploration, assisted in mapping and classifying the wetlands of Tennessee. She is currently working on the development of a wetland classification system to be used for the National Wetlands Inventory, and she also lectures on a regular basis at several universities. More information about jobs with her employer can be obtained from: Personnel Division, U. S. Geological Survey, 12201 Sunrise Valley Drive, Reston, VA 22092.

The National Park Service also employs fish and wildlife managers, most with additional training or experience in the areas of recreation and park management. In some instances, the duties of the biologist are combined with those of another job in the system, such as that of ranger.

Jerry Baldacchino is one biologist who left the Fish and Wildlife Service to work for the National Park Service. The trail he took in getting there is an interesting example of the twists and turns an outdoor career can take.

Jerry earned his B.S. degree in wildlife biology from the College of Charleston, South Carolina, and his M.S. in wildlife management from Virginia Polytechnic Institute. But even while earning these degrees, he worked as counselor at several summer youth camps, including the South Carolina Conservation Camp, which gave him his first full-time job after graduation.

He left this job to fill an opening with Fish and Wildlife in its public-use program, working first as a recreation aide and later as a refuge manager in charge of public use on three national wildlife refuges—Chincoteague, Virginia; Okefenokee, Georgia; and Blackwater, Maryland. In this capacity, he planned interpretive trails and pamphlets, conducted information programs for the public, and worked with teachers and students using refuge facilities for educational purposes. During this period, he also participated in the Department of the Interior's Management Training Program and a naturalist trainee program sponsored by the National Audubon Society.

With this training and experience, Jerry was extremely well qualified to transfer to the National Park Service when a better job became available there—a job that takes him from his Washington office to the shores and marshes of Assateague to the mountains and woodlands of inland parks.

He is today responsible for conducting field investigations and making evaluations of the potential impact of proposed projects on the fish and wildlife resources in various parks. After each investigation, he submits recommendations designed to reduce or to eliminate any adverse impacts such projects may have on fish and wildlife and associated habitat. Specific information about similar opportunities with this agency may be obtained from the Division of Personnel, National Park Service, Department of the Interior, Room 2328, Washington, DC 20240.

The Forest Service of the Department of Agriculture provides employment for several hundred fish and wildlife biologists, many of whom share the duties of the foresters. It employs other biologists who have branched out and assumed regular administrative jobs such as that of forest supervisor. Positions for biological technicians and aides are also available.

Management efforts in the national forests and on the national rangelands consist primarily of protection and improvement of habitat for game and nongame species. A major part of this work is directed toward maintaining a balance between the needs of wildlife and other legitimate uses of resources, such as the grazing of cattle and the harvesting of timber.

Work done at the Chippewa National Forest in Minnesota, which is a commercially important producer of timber and pulpwood, shows that our natural resources can be harvested without destroying the wildlife dependent upon them.

Staff biologists at Chippewa have won wide recognition for preserving more than 100 pairs of endangered bald eagles that nest in the forest. Awards have also been presented to them for their work in planning and establishing nearly 60,000 acres of wetlands for migratory waterfowl, and for a highly successful fish program that is still under way. The renown of Chippewa's wildlife program is such that graduate students come from all parts of the country to do research related to their individual specialties and for the chance to learn from these experts of the Forest Service. Nine regional offices have employment jurisdiction over positions in their geographic regions. The address of the nearest regional office can be obtained from any Federal Job Information Center (which can also provide information about openings), or by writing: the Office of Personnel, Forest Service, Federal Center, Building 85, Denver, CO 80225.

The Tennessee Valley Authority, with more than 36 million acres of land and 650,000 surface acres of water under its control, is another relatively large employer in this field. As of 1978, its management efforts were being greatly expanded, so prospects here may be bright for several years to come. More information about working with this agency may be obtained by writing the Personnel Office, Division of Forestry, Fisheries, and Wildlife Development, Tennessee Valley Authority, Norris, TN 37828.

Those with a specialty in marine biology or related fields should not overlook the opportunities found with the National Marine Fisheries Service of the United States Department of Commerce. It serves as the major adviser to our commercial fishing industry. A major part of its effort is in programs designed to determine the consequences of man's activities on our natural marine resources, and to accomplish this it has established a large number of regional centers for fisheries work and research. A complete list of these centers, as well as detailed information about jobs, may be obtained by writing the Office of Personnel, National Marine Fisheries Service, 3300 Whitehaven Parkway, Washington, DC 20240.

Further information may be had from the following sources:

American Fisheries Society
Fourth Floor Suite
1319 18th Street NW
Washington, DC 20036

American Institute of Biological Sciences
3900 Wisconsin Avenue NW
Washington, DC 20016

North American Wildlife Foundation
709 Wire Building
Washington, DC 20005

Sport Fishing Institute
Suite 801
608 13th Street NW
Washington, DC 20005

Wildlife Management Institute
709 Wire Building
Washington, DC 20005

The Wildlife Society
Suite S-176
3900 Wisconsin Avenue NW
Washington, DC 20016

9
FISHING AND FISHERIES

Fishing is the oldest industry in America. Long before the first settlers at Jamestown were able to harvest their first crops, they were catching seafood and trading it to the Indians. In 1623, the Plymouth colonists, using a single boat, were able to catch enough striped bass to support the colony throughout the summer, and a colonist named William Wood was at work developing new and better ways to catch them.

Oysters sometimes measured 2 feet in length in those days, and lobsters measuring 6 feet in length were reported. The James River of Virginia sometimes became so crowded with fish that Captain Smith and his party were able to dip them from the water with skillets.

The colonists were quick to recognize the value of this natural bounty and the fact that it must, inevitably, be limited. This recognition was demonstrated by an act passed by the General Court of Massachusetts Bay Colony in 1639, which ordered that neither striped bass nor cod should be used as fertilizer for farm crops—probably the first conservation law in America. A subsequent act of the Plymouth Colony in 1670 provided that all income from the Cape Cod fisheries for bass, mackerel, or herring would be used to establish free schools in the area. As a result of this legislation, the first schools of the New World were built with funds provided by the fishing industry.

But despite some early attempts at conservation, our fishery resources have been badly abused over the years, and we are now beginning to pay the price. The history of the lobster industry provides just one sad example.

Well into this century, lobsters as small as four inches in length were being captured and marketed, with as many as two dozen being cooked to obtain a can of meat selling for only a few cents. While it was known that lobsters are slow-growing creatures that can reproduce only after many years, and that stringent conservation measures were needed if the fishery were to survive, many lobstermen resisted all attempts to change the laws until quite recently—and the changes now coming may be too late.

The lobster fishery is troubled as few others. The inshore waters have almost been stripped of lobster of marketable size, to the extent that most lobstermen are reduced to part-time fishing, and an Associated Press article recently predicted that we are approaching the day when lobster meat will retail for as much as $70 a pound.

One could easily provide a long list of abuses by the industry, but watermen of today also face many problems not of their own making, especially the problem of pollution.

The great James River fishery described by John Smith in his diaries is closed now, at least temporarily, as the result of the infamous Kepone dumping; its closing placed an estimated 3 percent of all Virginia workers on the unemployment lines, and scientists say it may be a century or more before the fishing grounds are cleaned.

In similar manner, clam and oyster beds along both coasts have been closed to fishing because of pollution, and crab populations have been reduced by the unwise use of pesticides. Inland fisheries have not escaped such contamination, as witness the case of the mercury in Lake Erie.

Thoughtlessly constructed dams have caused other problems, preventing important species such as shad, alewives, and striped bass from reaching their spawning grounds and thus reducing their population, and giant trawlers from the Soviet Union, Japan, and other countries—some of these ships actually floating canneries—have ignored our fishing laws and further depleted our fish populations.

But attempts are being made to stop such abuses, progress is being made, and fishing remains a viable career for anyone who wants to meet the challenge of open water.

Tougher laws against pollution are beginning to have an effect. Many fishing grounds, some of which had been closed for years, have been reopened to fishing. And fisheries scientists have found other ways of combating the problem, at least as a temporary measure that is of interest to fishermen.

For example, in New Jersey, which has some of the worst pollution problems in the country, clammers now remove clams from polluted waters and transplant them to bays that are clean. After a few months, when the clean waters have rendered the clams safely edible, the clammers are permitted to harvest and sell them. During one 10-day harvest in 1978, 76 clammers raked out 1,216,500 clams under this transplant program. Oysters are also being transplanted.

Where dams have denied fish access to the spawning grounds, "fish ladders," often costing many hundreds of thousands of dollars, are being constructed, thus saving many species from extinction. No longer will foreign trawlers be able to strip our fishing grounds bare; our fishing boundaries have been extended to 200 miles, and a week before I sat down to write this chapter, representatives of Japan were in Lewes, Delaware, negotiating to buy seafood taken by our watermen.

The fishing industry is a strange collection of the old and the new. Along the Pacific Coast of Washington, Indians still fish from dugout canoes exactly like those used by their forefathers; but divers also go down and use powerful hoses to blast giant geoduck clams from the bottom. In California, underwater television guides divers to the highly prized abalone, yet small fishing boats sometimes use methods and equipment that have not changed over the centuries.

Fishing is not a single industry—it is a large number of industries, each with its own product, equipment, techniques, and market. Most crabs and lobsters, for example, are taken by methods more like trapping than fishing—yet some of both are brought up from the bottom with dredges. Modern oystermen are very much like farmers, planting the young bivalves and harvesting them when they are grown. Clams are sometimes dug, sometimes raked, and sometimes dredged. The swordfish is usually hunted and harpooned, but in some areas it is taken on hook and line. Many finned fish are netted. A few examples will show how varied the equipment and the methods can be.

The shrimp fishery is one of our largest, with boats operating out of ports from Alaska to California, Maine to Florida, and across the Gulf of Mexico. Its boats go out equipped with otter trawls.

The otter trawl was invented by biologists in 1912. It is a long, funnel-shaped net, so constructed that its mouth remains open as it is drawn through the water. It frequently measures hundreds of feet in length and width. When the shrimp gather in their offshore spawning grounds and have been located by the boat, the otter trawl is simply let out and drawn over the bottom, then brought in by winches. Most flounder and other bottom fish are also taken by these trawls, which, along with the boat, can represent a huge investment.

If you are familiar with the delicious pompano of the Southeast, you may be surprised to learn—as I was—that most pompano, which is a favorite of gourmets and commands the highest prices, is caught by surf fishermen who do not even use boats. The commercial catch is supplied by sport anglers who supplement their incomes selling this delicacy directly to seafood houses and fine restaurants.

The sea trout, which ranks fourth in importance among the commercial species of the Gulf States, is taken by yet another method that shows the diversity of techniques and equipment used in fishing. This is known as "splash pole" fishing.

The boat may be a small one, with only the owner aboard, or it may carry a large crew of fishermen. Moving in among the schooling fish with baited lines attached to long bamboo poles, the fishermen draw the trout to the bait by slapping the poles against the surface of the water. A single fisherman using this technique can sometimes catch several hundred pounds of trout in a day.

The red snapper is another popular species taken by methods that have changed but little over the years. The industry began in 1870 at Pensacola, Florida, when a fish house was built by an enterprising New Englander, one S. C. Cobb. Smacks equipped with live wells were sent out into the Gulf, most of them carrying crews of nine men with handlines.

The lines were baited with dead mullet or other fish bait, then lowered to a point just over the bottom, usually around a reef or sunken wreck. When schooling fish were present, it was simply a matter of pulling them aboard, and the action could be furious. One man might catch 4,000 pounds of fish in an hour by this method, depending on depth of water and other factors. The method of fishing remains the same—and the catch sometimes is spectacular—but today many of the boats used are schooners capable of ranging over hundreds or even thousands of miles, though many independent fishermen still work the Gulf from their smaller boats.

In talking about equipment and techniques, it must be remembered that many fishing boats will use a variety of both during the course of a year. It is true that some fleets—such as those that fish for shrimp—will follow a migrating species, but many other boats must be content to fish for whatever is in the area at the time.

Fishing boats on the mighty Chesapeake, for example, may go after bluefish, striped bass, mackerel, and flounder during the warmer months, but during the winter, when these migratory species have moved on, the whiting makes up almost all of the catch. To keep a boat busy throughout the year and earn maximum profits, these watermen must know when, where, and how to go after each fish, and they must be equipped to do so.

Learning to operate a fishing boat and its equipment is a matter of experience. The fisherman usually needs a variety of skills that are acquired on the job, not through study. Many universities do offer courses in marine science, navigation, and other studies helpful to fishermen, but one really only learns to use fishing equipment by getting out on the water and using it.

Perhaps more than any other industry, fishing tends to be followed by generation after generation of the same families. In the fishing villages that dot our coasts and the edges of our major inland waters, youngsters may be out on the fishing boats before they are in their teens. Many use fishing to pay for a college education, and many others become independent fishermen at an age when others are still in school. To those born and raised in such an environment, acquiring these skills is no problem. They are acquired in the natural course of living.

For those not born to the industry, however, other routes must be taken. Seamanship, navigation, communications, boating safety, and emergency procedures are as basic to most fishing as soil conservation is to farming. The Navy, Coast Guard, and Merchant Marine teach these skills to many who eventually become fishermen. Others learn these skills while using a boat for recreation, and others pick them up by actually finding a job in the industry.

Employment in the Fishing Industry

While the total number of jobs in the fishing industry has been steadily declining in recent years, for a number of reasons, the competition for those that remain is so light that anyone with a real interest should be able to find one. The vast majority of these jobs occur along the coasts, especially in the great fishing centers of Maine, Cape Cod, the Chesapeake, Savannah and Charleston, Pensacola and the Gulf, California and Puget Sound. Fisheries are found on most major inland waters, such as the Great Lakes, the Ohio, Mississippi, St. Lawrence, and Tennessee rivers, but as a general rule these use smaller boats and thus need fewer employees.

Competition for these jobs is light for a variety of reasons. Pay for the entry-level jobs is extremely low, usually the minimum allowed by law. Fringe benefits are almost nonexistent. The work is always hard, sometimes frightfully so. Working conditions aboard a boat may be intolerable to some. Fishing crews must work in every extreme of weather, in most regions, and the work ranks high on any list of dangerous occupations. Some jobs require that you spend days, even weeks, away from home, and a fishing boat may change its home port several times during the course of a year, following the movements of the species it seeks.

Chances for promotion are also slim, because the number of better-paying jobs on most boats is very limited. But even though the odds against promotion are high, they are not insurmountable. Don Leonard, an old friend, is living proof that these odds can be overcome.

Don grew up in Dayton, Ohio. During service in the Navy he learned some seamanship, fell in love with the open water, and decided that was where he wanted to spend his life. But after receiving his discharge, circumstances forced him to return to Ohio and take a job as a structural ironworker, a job he despised.

Don never quite lost his yearning for the sea. Several years ago, while laid off as an ironworker, he drove to a port near Savannah, Georgia, and signed on as a hand on a shrimp trawler. It paid about one third of what he had earned as an ironworker, but at least he was doing work he loved.

Structural ironwork almost always come to a stop during the winter in Ohio, so this annual move became a regular part of Don's life. Each winter he learned more about shrimping, and in his spare time he studied navigation, naval engineering, and other related subjects. After a few years he was able to meet the Coast Guard requirements for a captain's license, and today he no longer returns to Ohio and the job he abhorred; he captains a shrimp trawler owned by a large corporation. He draws a guaranteed salary against a percentage of the catch, and that salary, he tells me in a recent letter, is far better than the one he earned as an ironworker.

Investment Required for Fishing

Simply because of the large financial investment required, few beginners will be able to buy and operate one of the large boats required for offshore fishing. Most of these today are owned by corporations, though some experienced fishermen do pool their resources and enter this fishery. Our inshore and freshwater fisheries, however, offer almost unlimited opportunities for getting started with a relatively small financial investment.

The inshore saltwater fishery is usually defined as that which is found in the intertidal zone—in bays, coves, estuaries, tidal streams, and rivers. These relatively shallow waters produce a huge percentage of our seafood—almost all of our crabs and lobsters, clams, oysters, mussels, and many of our finned fishes. But here I am extending it to refer to all of this and any commercial fishing that can be done within a few miles of shore, where the fishing can be done from a relatively small boat not costing a fortune.

For this type of fishing the investment need not be huge. How much, exactly, will depend on your financial resources, the type of fishing you decide to do, and the kind of boat you decide to buy, as well as its condition. Clammers, crabbers, and oystermen can be seen using almost anything that will float, and sport-fishing boats are suitable for many types of inshore fishing. Even the larger, more elaborate boats used for inshore fishing cost no more than you might pay for a house, and certainly less than you would pay for a farm.

Buying used equipment can reduce the size of your investment. In recent months, I have seen a crab boat, complete with power winch, offered for $800, a lobster boat for $2,000. Add to these prices about $1,200 for crab traps or lobster pots, plus the cost of a license (which can vary widely), and you will have a very good idea of the investment required for these types of fishing. In looking for a used boat, however, remember that its condition must be such that it will pass a safety inspection.

If you intend to fish on any major body of water (and that is where most commercial fishing occurs), you, too, may be required to meet standards set by the Coast Guard or by the state. The requirements vary according to the size and type of vessel, its crew (if any), etc., but you can find out about these by placing a call to the nearest Coast Guard station. If you lack certain skills that may be required (such as navigation), the Coast Guard can often direct you to places where these are taught.

Laws governing the inshore and freshwater fisheries are set by the individual states, though the U.S. Fish and Wildlife Service sometimes has jurisdiction over sport, migratory, and protected species. With regard to most marine species, the Bureau of Marine Fisheries of the U.S. Department of Commerce also has laws with which the fisherman must comply. This overlapping jurisdiction means that the new fisherman must, first of all, find a way to comply with all these laws.

The starting place is with the state. Check with the state's bureau of fisheries. As a general rule, you will find that a license must be obtained if the catch is to be sold. Oyster and clam rights are usually leased by the states, and where pots or traps are used, as in crabbing, the license fee is based on the number of traps. A certain type of equipment (such as the gillnet) may be banned in one area but perfectly legal in another. Fishing may also be forbidden during certain seasons of the year. As another general rule, these state laws will be in accordance with federal statutes, but where there is a variance, the local authorities will tell you how to comply with other regulations.

Finding Fishing Opportunities

If you have not already decided on a certain type of fishing and are simply looking around for opportunities, the state's department of commerce, located in the state capital, is a good place to check. They can tell you about fishing industries that already exist in the area, provide information about markets, and sometimes refer you to other sources of helpful information.

If you live in an area where fishing is a major industry, you should also check with the state university. In these areas, the county extension agent often plays a dual role, providing agricultural information to farmers, and marine-science information to fishermen. Universities involved in the federally funded Sea Grant program are another terrific source of information and help. About a dozen universities are involved in this program at any given time, doing research intended to develop our fisheries and help those who earn their livings by working in them. A complete list of these universities can be obtained by writing the National Marine Fisheries Service, whose address is given at the end of this chapter.

Most industries have dozen of trade journals, publications that are devoted to informing those who work in the industry, but commercial fishing has only one. This is *The National Fisherman*, available by subscription from the publisher (at $7.50 per year), located at 21 Elm Street, Camden, ME 04843. It is essential reading for anyone seriously interested in commercial fishing.

In this trade journal you will find ads offering new and used fishing boats and equipment for sale, as well as ads offering jobs in the industry. Other ads are placed by buyers of fish and seafood, thus offering you an outlet for your catch.

Articles describe new fishing equipment and techniques, and they also keep fishermen informed about changes in fishing laws and the over-all industry. Most important of all, at least to the beginner, these articles tell how fishermen in all parts of the country are earning money at their chosen profession: what they are catching, how they are catching it, where they are selling it, and what prices they are being paid.

No matter where you live, these sources will guide you to ways to earn money by fishing, many of them surprising to the novice. Perch, pickerel, walleye, and other species that most think of as gamefish are fished commercially in many parts of the country. Shallow lakes in the Plains States annually produce many millions of dollars' worth of buffalo, sheepshead, and other fish. Freshwater crayfish, long used as bait but ignored as food, are the basis of a booming fishery that extends from St. Louis to New Orleans. White sturgeon are being taken from the Snake River of Idaho, as well as from other rivers across the

Midwest. Mussels are being taken by the ton from the Tennessee and other rivers of the south. Even carp and suckers are being profitably fished and marketed, and the shark fishery is booming along most coasts.

Marketing the Catch

In looking for opportunities to earn money by fishing, you must, above all else, be looking for a market to sell the catch. It may be stating the obvious, but because of the need for freshness and the high possibility of spoilage, the market for fish or seafood must be found before the first fishing is done.

If you live in a major fishing area, this represents no problem at all. Fish and seafood houses in these areas readily take the entire catch of the local fishermen, usually at prices that are negotiated in advance. If you are doing a type of fishing that involves a large boat and a catch measured by the ton, these processing houses may be the only buyers able to offer a steady market for your entire catch.

If you are in an area where no major fishing industry exists, and therefore have no bulk buyers for the catch, you will have to create your own markets. This is easier than it sounds, however, because of the huge demand for fresh fish and seafood; and because of the great difference between retail prices and the prices paid by large packing houses, direct marketing may be preferable. This difference in prices is so great that most commercial fishermen—even those whose daily catches are huge—sell at least part of their catch directly to fish and seafood markets, restaurants, or even to the consumer from their own seafood shops.

By talking to the owners of retail outlets and asking what they are buying from fishermen and at what prices, you should have little difficulty in finding buyers. Middlemen are involved in most sales to these outlets, so by cutting out those middlemen, you can probably offer the catch at a lower price to the buyer while earning greater profits for yourself.

In talking to these potential buyers, it is also important to see what they are *not* already selling. A seafood shop may not be offering a certain species simply because the owner does not know that species is available. If you know of a species that you can take in commercial quantity, then you can probably create a market by offering to fill that gap in the seafood case or on the menu.

In marketing seafood, the price is frequently determined more by what that seafood is called than by what it really is. While the laws covering the actual fishing are fairly strict, those governing how it is sold are very, very lax.

About half the "swordfish" sold in this country, for example, is actually mako shark. Freshwater mussels are generally offered to the public as "clams." The fish from skates and rays reaches the consumer as "scallops." The gourmet item known as "sea squab" is a cut of meat from the common blowfish. Almost all of the "sole" sold in America is, in reality, flounder. The list goes on and on, and any fisherman who sells his catch through direct marketing must remain aware of these realities and use them to his best advantage.

After studying the fishing laws, the fishing opportunities, and the markets around you, you may or may not face the problem of financing your fishing venture. If you have decided to try a type of fishing that can be done with a boat and equipment that you already own—or a type requiring only a nominal investment—then no problem exists.

But if you have in mind a fishing enterprise requiring a large boat, expensive equipment, and an investment of many thousands of dollars that must be borrowed, obtaining financing can pose some problems. Because so many factors make it impossible to accurately forecast how much a fisherman will earn in any year, bankers tend to look on commercial-fishing loans as risky ones. The amount you will be able to obtain will depend very much upon your personal credit rating, the collateral for the loan, and the approach you use in asking the bank to make that loan.

How to Find Credit

Like the new farmer, your chances of obtaining a loan for getting started will be better if you enter the business on a part-time basis and are able to show another source of income. Be prepared to discuss not only the amount of money you will need, but also the type of fishing you will be doing, the costs of doing it, and the profits you can reasonably expect to produce. Be ready to use statistics to show why and how you believe you can produce those profits, have a realistic budget prepared, and the odds in your favor will become far better.

Those odds seem likely to improve before this book goes into print. A bill has been introduced before Congress that will, if passed, extend to fishermen long-term, low-cost government loans similar to those available to farmers. If it passes, as now appears likely, the loan program will be administered by the Bureau of Marine Fisheries and will make it far easier for you to join the more than 100,000 people licensed for commercial fishing. Joining them, for most, is like entering an entirely different world, a world where the demands are great and the existence rugged—but one that few fishermen would be willing to trade for any other.

Crabbing

"There ain't never been a better time for a youngster to get started in fishing," Fred Wilhelm told me just after dawn one day in 1978, "nor there ain't never been a worse time. Look anywhere along this old bay and you'll see good boats selling for maybe half what they're worth. Old folks die off, or just have to quit, and the young ones in the family just don't seem to want to take over and carry on, not like they used to. Maybe they're just afraid of hard work, maybe they just itch to move off to the city; I don't know. I do know the towns along here just keep shrinking, except when the tourists are in, and it wouldn't be hard at all for somebody to pick up a boat and get started."

We were leaving a dock near Crisfield, Maryland, a tiny town but also one of our great seafood centers, the major outlet for Chincoteague and Tangier Sound oysters, Chesapeake Bay fish, and especially the blue crabs we were going after that morning. In exchange for the chance to talk with him, I had offered to spend the day working as a "culler" aboard Fred's crab boat, the *Jimmy*.

"Retail prices are high—higher'n I've ever seen them," Fred continued as we headed out toward the first line of crab pots we would be checking. "Problem is, we ain't gettin' much out of what the customer is paying. Catching plenty of blue crabs ain't hard—anybody could learn it in a few days—but getting paid the proper price is a different matter. When we're catching plenty of blues, the packing houses pay a low price because they say we're catching too many. When the crabs ain't there, the retail price goes up—but that sure don't mean we're seeing any of it."

Fred Wilhelm, one of about 2,000 licensed crabbers in Maryland, has been fishing these waters for nearly 30 years, learning the business, like many others, from his father. His crab boat is stripped of all frills—a boat clearly intended for business. It has no head, no seats, and the decks are nearly filled with empty barrels for the catch and boxes of bait—scraps of fish—for rebaiting his crab pots.

His bait costs $7 per box. Wilhelm uses 2 boxes per day, and fuel this morning has cost him another $20. As we headed out to his crab pots, he talked with some bitterness about rising costs and low returns.

"Costs me about $40 a day to operate," he grumbled. "And since the bad winter of '77, there ain't hardly been any crabs at all. But I've gotta go right on meetin' those costs, no matter what. People see crabs retailing at $18 a dozen, they figure we're gettin' rich! They don't know that's what we're gettin' for a hundred-pound barrel of 'em."

Like other crabbers in this area, Wilhelm sets his pots around the first of April, then works them until cold weather sets in and the crabs have burrowed into the mud, usually in November or December. He sells his catch to a processing house because he has no family to help with direct marketing and feels he could not handle that work alone.

"Can't get that price off of local folks," he told me, referring to the high retail price of crabs. "But during the summer, the tourists'll pay just about all you ask. And a smart youngster could run a few pots, then truck the catch over to Baltimore or Washington, and . . ." He let the thought trail away, for we were now approaching the first of his marker buoys.

I had already struggled into rubber boots and a rubber apron, for crabbing is wet, sloppy work. I waited near the stern as Wilhelm pulled the boat closer to the buoy, his eyes roaming the nearby water.

"I always keep an eye out for pots that might have been hauled away by boats or barges," he told me, his expression making it clear how he feels about boaters who carelessly run their boats through his pot lines, tangling them or cutting them loose.

Crab pots are dropped about 50 yards apart, in fairly straight lines, to the bottom of the bay. They are linked by nylon lines to floating buoys, with each buoy bearing the special mark of its owner. Wilhelm's buoys are yellow plastic jugs, painted black across the bottom, and each bears a number assigned by the state when he pays the $25 for his yearly license.

As we approached the first of those buoys now, Wilhelm swung the stern around and I used a long wooden pole fitted with a hook to snag the nylon line and pull it aboard. Then I slipped the line into the winch (or "pot puller"), set the pulley whirling, and brought the crab pot aboard. It held 15 or 20 crabs, a pair of fish of some unidentifiable species, and the billowing blobs of a jellyfish.

The crab pot used in these waters is a wire-mesh trap about 2 feet in length, width, and height. Four funnels lead into the bait, attracting the crabs, which are unable to escape from that compartment. I unpinned the bait compartment on this one, dumped the old bait in the water, replaced it with new, and then unhooked the rubber strap holding the trap closed. The crabs went into an old washtub that we would be using for culling.

The job of a culler is to quickly go over the crabs from each pot, tossing back any females bearing eggs, any crabs smaller than the legal size of 5 inches between the broadest points of the upper shell, and other species that may have wandered into the pots.

The second part of the job involves sorting out the "shedder" crabs—those that will soon lose their hard outer covering and become much more valuable as soft-shelled crabs. These go into a barrel reserved for them, the hard-shells into another. The boat was heading for another buoy as I worked frantically to accomplish all this.

"Best way I know to learn crabbing—doing exactly what you're doing," Fred called back as I was hooking the second pot. "Pays maybe $25 or $35 a day along here, seven days a week. Do it a summer or two, then get your own boat. Trouble is, most crabbers can't find anybody wants to work, so most go it alone."

This pot came up with about as many crabs as the previous one, and Wilhelm looked disappointed. "In a good year, pots average about half a bushel each time they're raised. My guess, it'll be about three years before we get over the freeze that killed them off."

The pace of the work remained frantic for the next couple of hours. Then we came to a gap in the line of buoys—a missing crab pot—and Wilhelm decided to take a break, angered and obviously wanting to discuss it.

"That pot cost me $11.52. Out a couple of hours and I'm already out that much more. Thievery is about the worst problem we've got these days." He paced, letting the boat drift a little. "Some just take out the crabs and leave the pot; they're the better ones. Others follow your line. It's a real problem for everybody on the water, not just crabbers. Oyster piracy is a big thing along here. And vandalism. Fishermen find their nets cut, or find them filled with rocks. You just watch—that won't be the only pot I lose today," he predicted—and it turned out to be the first of three that would be found missing.

The first line of pots—about 75 of them—had been raised by about 9:30 A.M., producing more than 2 barrels of crabs, but still Wilhelm was less than satisfied. We moved to the second line of pots and returned to work, raising a trap about once every 3 or 4 minutes.

"It's picking up a bit," he conceded, glancing at a pot that was loaded with some of the largest crabs I had seen in this area. "But it still ain't what it used to be. One good year, I brought in three dozen barrels in a single day. Today, I only came out with ten barrels and we'll be lucky to fill nine."

Hours and hours later, though, when finally we eased the boat back alongside the dock, all 10 of the 100-pound barrels were full, and a smaller barrel was loaded with shedders. To the novice, a glance at this catch would cause visions of great wealth. That is not exactly the case.

During a year when retailers have received an average price of $7.78 a pound for crabmeat and as much as $18 a dozen for live blue crabs, the price paid to fishermen has dipped as low as $.16 a pound for live blue crabs and has never exceeded $.50 a pound when the catch is sold at a processing house.

There are two major reasons why this is so. The first is that about 10 pounds of crabs in-the-shell are required to produce a single pound of meat. The second is that a great amount of hand labor is required to pick out the meat.

A machine has recently been patented that, according to its owners, will not only pick out the crabmeat without all this labor, but will also obtain more meat from each crab. They believe it will make it possible for the processers to pass along some of their savings in the form of higher prices to the fishermen, but Fred Wilhelm doesn't see it happening that way.

"Only the fisherman is going to look out for the fisherman," he told me emphatically. "That's the way it works. I'd tell any beginner to find some way around all these middlemen. Do that, and one barrel of crabs would be worth more than I'm getting for ten or twelve."

Like many other businessmen, Mr. Wilhelm is reluctant to go into detail about his income. But on the day I went crabbing with him his catch sold for just over $245, leaving a net profit of about $150 for the day, even after deducting the cost of the missing crab pots. His earnings could be much greater if he were able to sell directly to the consumer, as many crabbers are now doing.

Clamming

Across the Delmarva Peninsula, along Delaware's Rehoboth Bay, I talked with several clammers and fishermen who are already doing exactly as Fred Wilhelm suggests. One in particular, Norman Jewett, has built a very lucrative seafood business around the clams he rakes from the beds leased from the state.

The clam taken along these shores is the quahog, which, when smaller and more tender, is also known as the cherrystone or littleneck clam.It lives in great colonies in the bays of the East Coast, lying buried an inch or two down in bottoms where enough mud mixes with the sand to give the sand a blue-black color. Although some states permit dredging for this species, Delaware does not, and clammers along these shores still take the species by drifting over the beds in small boats and bringing the clams up with bull rakes—long-handled rakes with baskets behind the tines that catch the clams as they are raked from the mud.

"I sort of got forced into the retail business," Norman Jewett told me on the day I visited his small shop, a converted garage beside his house. "Couple of years back, the retail price of clams started climbing and just kept on going. Cherrystones hit a peak of about fifteen dollars a hundred—but the brokers and packing houses wanted to go right on paying what they always had: about six dollars a bushel."

Rather than continue to accept that price, Jewett says, he decided he would leave his clambeds largely unharvested, taking out only the few he thought he could sell by placing a small sign in front of his house. As it turned out, he was able to sell more than a few.

"There are several hundred clams in a bushel, depending on their size," he points out. "And they keep pretty well, just as long as they're kept cool. I found out that by offering them to customers just a little cheaper than they could get them elsewhere, I could sell just about all I could find—at a price that's about triple what they pay at a packing house."

Jewett still works the clambeds while his wife and son handle the retail end of the business, delivering to restaurants and grocery stores as well as selling to those who visit their own shop. They sell not only the 2,000 or so clams Jewett rakes out daily, but about that many more he buys from other clammers. To attract more business, the shop also offers flounder, oysters, bluefish, and other popular local seafood that the family buys from other fishermen. In all instances, Jewett insists, they are able to pay the fishermen top prices while increasng their own earnings.

"One good thing about clamming," Jewett points out, "is that you can always leave the clams in the mud until you're able to get a fair price. I'm taking out less clams but making more money than before, which also means the clams have a better chance to multiply and I've got more out in the beds."

During the winter, when the tourists are gone and the demand for clams shrinks, Jewett goes clamming only two or three days a week, devoting the rest of his working hours to running the eel pots that he sets in local rivers and streams. The eel catch he *does* sell to a broker, who transports the live eels in a tank truck designed for that purpose. This is because the market for eels in this country is a fairly new one, only now beginning to develop, and Jewett is unable to sell large quantities locally. But he is working to build markets, and foresees the day when his eel catch will be sold alongside his clams.

"They used to figure a clammer had to bring in at least a thousand clams a day to scratch out a living," Jewett says. "That can be done, but doing it can be tough. But with prices and demand the way they are, a clammer can make out pretty well with a lot less clams than that. It's all in how you sell them."

I asked for suggestions about getting started.

"I'd say to start doing it as sport," he suggested. "Look, getting started as a clammer doesn't cost all that much—a thousand or two thousand dollars for everything. But nobody wants to lose that kind of money, which is what they're going to do unless they know where the clams are and how to get them. It costs almost nothing to wade around and dig them for your own use, and that gives you a chance to check out the beds and get an idea of how well they're going to produce. After you know that—then you're ready to start thinking about a license. Only then."

Unlike many other commercial clammers, Jewett feels that sport clamming causes him no problems and should be encouraged. "They have the same rights to the water that we have," he says, "and the truth is, sportsmen just don't take that many clams out of the mud. I don't believe a clam population is likely to be destroyed by raking. If anything ever does destroy the clambeds, it'll be the dredges; they destroy everything on the bottom that gets in front of them. I usually try not to worry about my problems, but that problem—well, it's one that does worry me!"

Oceanography

Perhaps you want a career on the open water, but prefer to work at finding solutions to the many problems facing fishermen and other watermen today, rather than actually fishing. If so, you may be interested in the exciting field of oceanography—which may prove to be the science of the future.

Oceanographers employ the techniques and principles of modern science, mathematics, and engineering to study the oceans—their physical properties, movements, plant and animal life. Their research helps develop new ways of forecasting weather, helps control and develop our fisheries, aids in mining the ocean floor, and may even help to improve our national defense.

Although some oceanographers do work in laboratories on land, for most of them the sea is the laboratory. These scientists explore and study the oceans with a variety of surface ships, aircraft, and a number of types of underwater craft. Specialized instruments are used to measure and record the findings, and special cameras are used to photograph marine life and the ocean floor.

The Scripps Institution of Oceanography at La Jolla, California, has long been a leader in this field. It operates a fleet of oceangoing vessels and small craft that has served as a model fleet for many other schools of oceanography. Its vessels have made many major expeditions, mostly in the Pacific and Indian oceans, and two of its ships have circumnavigated the globe.

Scripps also has a unique vessel, *FLIP (Floating Instrument Platform)*, which is the envy of most other schools of oceanography. This vessel is towed to the experimental station, then inverted by flooding its ballast tanks, so that 300 feet of her 355-foot vertical tower is underwater. In this position *FLIP* is said to be remarkably insensitive to motions caused by wind and wave, and provides a stable underwater lab from which delicate measurements may be made.

If this type of research is exciting to you (and with only a few rare exceptions, all oceanographers are involved in research), you must face the fact that the minimum requirement for a job in the field is a bachelor's degree in oceanography, biology, earth or physical science, mathematics, chemistry, or engineering. About 35 universities presently offer undergraduate degrees in oceanography or marine science, but training in a basic science may also open the way to graduate training in oceanography.

Most oceanographers specialize in one branch of the science. Biological oceanographers study plant and animal life in the ocean. Physical oceanographers, who are essentially physicists and geologists, study the physical properties of the sea. Chemical oceanographers study the chemical composition of ocean water and sediment, as well as the chemical reactions that occur in the sea. Oceanographic engineers design and build instruments used in oceanographic research. About half of all oceanographers are marine biologists, but explorations for offshore oil and other needs could alter that percentage in the very near future.

College courses needed to prepare for graduate study in oceanography include mathematics, physics, chemistry, geophysics, geology, meteorology, and biology. This is when specialization begins.

"In general," advises Howard Seymour of the Marine Science Center of the University of Delaware, "students should plan to specialize in the particular science that is closest to their area of oceanographic interest. For example, students interested in chemical oceanography should obtain the bachelor's degree in chemistry, then go on to graduate studies in oceanography."

About 65 colleges presently offer advanced degrees in oceanography and marine science. Like the University of Delaware with its research vessel, the *RV Delaware*, most of these schools provide seagoing laboratores for use by their students. Graduate students spend much of their time aboard these vessels, doing oceanographic research and becoming familiar with the sea and the techniques used in obtaining information about it. Many offer summer courses in diving, seamanship, and navigation.

Some oceanographers are employed in almost every state; the vast majority of them find work in one of the states bordering the sea. Even that job market can be narrowed down. Forty percent of the 2,700 oceanographers in this country can be found working in three states—California, Maryland, and Virginia.

About half of all these oceanographers work in colleges and universities, either as teachers or as researchers, with most of the researchers in federally funded programs such as Sea Grant. A few oceanographers work for private industry or for fishery laboratories of various state and local governments, but about 25 percent of the total are employed by the federal government. The Navy, the Coast Guard, and the Bureau of Land Management employ some oceanographers, but far more are hired by the Bureau of Marine Fisheries and the National Oceanic and Atmospheric Administration.

To become an oceanographer requires many years of study and hard work, but it is work that is well rewarded. This is one of the best paying of all career fields, with wages that are about double the average earned by nonsupervisory workers in all other fields.

In 1978, starting salaries for oceanographers ranged from $11,523 a year to $20,442 a year with most government agencies, depending on the degree held and the grades. In that same year, the average annual wage paid to oceanographers was $23,800. But according to a publication of the Department of Health, Education, and Welfare, many oceanographers were able to double their earnings through the sale of writing, photography, and lecture fees—which again demonstrates that you should make a special effort to sharpen your skills of communication.

The subject of lecture fees brings us to one of the more interesting fringe benefits I discovered while doing research for this book—free luxury travel for oceanographers. Virtually every ocean liner that leaves port these days will have an oceanographer aboard, providing regularly scheduled lectures that inform the paying guests about the mysteries of the sea.

Pay is nominal, but the oceanographer trades the lectures for free travel that includes the right to take along a spouse or companion. The positions are obtained through contacts with large travel agencies.

In 1978, in an instance of this, a ship of the Cunard Lines had an oceanographer and his wife on board during its 55-day cruise to South American ports—a cruise for which passengers paid prices ranging from $6,000 to nearly $14,000! It is hard to imagine a better vacation for one who loves the sea—but it is only one of the many fringe benefits offered by this exciting career in the great outdoors.

For more information contact:

American Fisheries Society
Fourth Floor Suite
1319 18th Street NW
Washington, DC 20036

International Oceanographic Foundation
3979 Rickenbacker Causeway
Virginia Key, Miami, FL 33149

National Marine Fisheries Service
Department of Commerce
Washington, DC 20235

National Oceanic and Atmospheric Administration
Rockville, MD 20852

10
PHOTOGRAPHY AND JOURNALISM

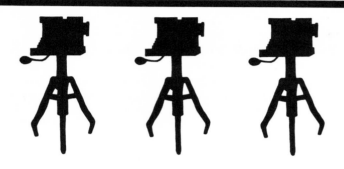

More than thirty years ago, Bradford Angier, tired of the city, gave up a promising public-relations firm in Boston and moved to the wilds of British Columbia. He bought land on the banks of the Peace River, built his own log cabin, and settled in to live the kind of life he loved.

This move required a certain amount of cash income, so Mr. Angier spent almost as much time at his typewriter as he did in the woods, sending out a virtual torrent of manuscripts that began to appear with regularity in leading outdoor magazines and then as books.

The first of those books, *At Home in the Woods,* served as a guide to those who might want to follow in his footsteps; and the next, *How to Build Your Home in the Woods,* made it just a little easier for them to do so. Later books, such as *Wilderness Cookery* and *How to Go Live in the Woods on $10 a Week,* resulted from the experience and knowledge Mr. Angier gained as the result of his wilderness adventures. The list of books has continued to grow over the years, making Bradford Angier one of the better-known outdoor writers, and all of those books have certain elements in common: They dealt with subjects the author was acquainted with, through personal experience or through research, and they provided a service to the reader.

Opportunities to earn a good living as an outdoor writer and/or photographer have never been better, but you must remember that the booming nonfiction market of today is keyed toward service to the reader and that such service can only be provided by those who really understand their subject.

This does not mean that you must be a forester to write about forestry, or a farmer to write about farming. And it does not mean that you are limited to writing about the single subject you know best—though that is always the best place to start.

But it does mean that you must be willing to work hard to know all you can about your subject before attempting to write about it. This means doing lengthy research at libraries, universities, and other sources of information, and it means going to experts on the subject and asking for their help. Above all, you must have a real interest in your subject and in providing a service to your readers.

Information specialists are in great demand at almost every agency mentioned in this book, with annual salaries in excess of $30,000. Most of these jobs go to applicants with degrees in journalism, but some are filled by those who couple good skills of communication with other training or experience; an information specialist with the Forestry Service, for example, is likely to be a forester or forestry technician who just happens to have acquired training in journalism somewhere along the way, or who added those skills knowing they would help further his or her career.

These people do the vastly important work of informing and educating the public about the important work being done in forestry, soil and water conservation, fish and wildlife management, and other areas. Their jobs are crucial to the conservation effort, because only an informed and educated public will continue to support it. But for those seeking outdoor careers, it is important to remember that most of these information specialists write about the work of others and spend only a very small amount of their own time outdoors. An information specialist is paid to write, not to participate—writing only about the work of others is a deskbound job.

With some exceptions, the same situation exists in the newspaper industry. Many of the larger dailies have staff writers who specialize in outdoor subjects, and some of our very best outdoor writing is being done in that field, but these writers have other assignments that tie them to their desks, and only a small amount of their time is spent outdoors. All of these jobs are worthwhile and provide an excellent chance for the new writer to begin a career, but your first love must be writing.

Most careers in outdoor writing come about as a natural result of the outdoor interests of the writer. The late Rachel Carson was an ecologist first, a writer second. Alfred Charles Kinsey, long before he became famous for his surveys of sexual attitudes, was a botanist and naturalist whose interests caused him to write *Edible Wild Plants of Eastern North America*, a classic in the field of popular botany. Euell

Gibbons gained fame as a writer, but only after becoming accomplished as a botanist, biologist, and naturalist. Bradford Angier was skilled as a writer before he made his move to the wilderness, but his subsequent career was possible only because he was skilled as a woodsman, naturalist, and general outdoorsman.

Opportunities for Free-lance Writers and Photographers

Aside from the jobs already mentioned, the opportunities in outdoor writing and photography are available, for the most part, only to those willing to work as free-lancers. These opportunities are great and growing, but the business, like any other, takes some time to learn and will produce only a small income at first. Most writing careers begin as part-time endeavors, producing an income to supplement the earnings from other sources.

There is a strong trend in the publishing industry toward specialization. It is a rare magazine that attempts to cater to all the reading interests of the American public. Instead, we have a growing number of specialized magazines that single out one interest. For instance, among the specialty magazines devoted to boating, one finds *Bay and Delta Yachtsman,* which publishes articles aimed at small-boat owners and yachtsmen, but only those who enjoy their recreation in the waters off northern California; *Boatmaster* aims at an audience of fishermen, but seeks to attract them by publishing articles on boat buying, boat maintenance, boat insurance, or any other subject that will help the fisherman get greater value out of a boat.

This trend toward specialization has, in turn, created a real demand for writers who are specialists. This is not to say that a farmer, forester, fish biologist, or commercial fisherman can immediately begin to earn a good living by writing about his or her specialty, but that specialty does make it much easier to begin earning good money in the spare time—and once you've used that specialized knowledge to establish yourself with a few editors, you've taken a giant step toward establishing yourself as a professional in the field.

You will notice that I have constantly linked writing and photography. That is not because you must be a photographer in order to sell your writing, nor is it because you must be a writer in order to sell your photography; it is quite possible to sell either one without the other. I have linked the two skills because written material is far easier to sell when it is accompanied by good visual material, and vice versa.

Another trend in magazine publishing is toward the use of more pictures and fewer words. The well-written outdoor article, even when unaccompanied by illustrations, will usually find a home at some publication, but often at a lower price. Some magazines will refuse to consider any piece not properly illustrated—and the beginning writer simply cannot afford to reduce the number of markets for the work. And the photographer who cannot provide the text for a photo story has also picked a tough row to hoe.

The one thing I can't give you is a promise that a career in this field will allow you to spend all of your time in the outdoors. During the last year, I have fished for shad at the famous Enfield Dam in Connecticut; fished for mako shark in the depths of the Baltimore Canyon, off New Jersey; hunted morel mushrooms in Michigan; spent time crabbing and clamming in Delaware; and toured the Pennsylvania Dutch country—all as part of my magazine work. When doing magazine articles, I would estimate that about half my time is spent in the outdoors.

When working on a book such as this one, even that amount of time is reduced. Books require an enormous amount of research, which is often sheer drudgery. But even so, while working on this book, I have managed to visit national parks and wildlife refuges, forests, and farms, and I have spent time on the water with a commercial crabber and another who goes after clams. I have also managed to spend time (too much of it, my editors will probably say) surf fishing, tonging for oysters, and just generally pursuing my own interests at places I've had to visit in order to do this book. Writers like to tell others that theirs is a lonely life, but I find it anything but that. It can be exciting, challenging, sometimes frustrating, but a day-to-day adventure unlike few other jobs on the face of the earth.

Art Spikol, editor of *Philadelphia* magazine and columnist for *Writer's Digest,* says he believes that only rarely can a writer earn more than $8,000 per year through the sale of magazine articles. My own experience tells me that his estimate is far too low. I have earned nearly that much in my spare time, and for several years a single magazine paid me about half that much—for work that was produced in two or three days each month.

Top magazines will pay into the thousands of dollars for articles that will help them build their circulation. Outdoor writers whose names become household words—for example, Jacques Cousteau, Cleveland Amory, or the late Rachel Carson and Euell Gibbons—can write their own ticket. Many writers whose names would not be recognized by the average reader are earning incomes of $50,000 or more—and in today's market the advance for a single book can be several times that amount. But books are for later. The magazine market is the logical place for the beginner to start, and before you tackle that, there are many things you need to know.

The Market for Outdoor Reporting

The first is that the bulk of the market lies in nonfiction. This is true in both magazine and book publishing. For example, according to *Publishers Weekly*, of the 30,004 new books published in 1975, only 2,407 were fiction. This trend continues today.

This does not mean that any training or experience in writing fiction would be useless. Many of the techniques of fiction, such as the setting of scene, the creation of suspense, and the proper use of dialogue, can be applied to nonfiction in ways that will transform an ordinary article into a small masterpiece. By all means, study the techniques of fiction—but unless you are another Hemingway, don't count on earning a living from it.

Remember, too, that the bulk of the magazine nonfiction market is in reportage. You can sell articles based on your own personal experiences, but those experiences must be *presented as reportage*. *Writer's Market*, in defining this matter of reportage, says, ". . . Generally magazines clamor for reporting: how to start your car when all else fails; how to keep your cool when . . ." It is, as I mentioned before, a matter of service to the reader. For the outdoor writer, I would alter that definition to read: "How to catch more or bigger fish; how to grow a better crop; how to protect an endangered species; how to find more enjoyment in your favorite outdoor activity." Let the reader learn from you.

No matter what your expertise, you should work to supplement it with the reporter's skills of digging and interviewing—skills that are largely self-taught. The writer who acquires these skills, according to *Writer's Market*, "should find himself in demand, and find his story possibilities almost limitless."

These skills will not only make it possible for you to give depth to articles about your own outdoor specialties, but will also make it possible to sell articles about what other outdoor people are doing. Sportswriter Red Smith once said, "A good reporter can cover anything," and by becoming one you multiply the number of markets willing to pay for your work.

What are those markets? And how many would be receptive to articles and photography dealing with outdoor subjects? The answers to those questions were partially provided in a survey done by *Writer's Market*.

According to that survey, the general-interest magazines buy about 6,800 manuscripts from free-lancers; the sports magazines, 3,800. This is a very conservative estimate, according to the publishers, for nearly half of the magazines queried failed to report how many manuscripts they intend to buy. And those magazines listed as sports publications account for only a small part of those publishing outdoor-oriented material.

Writer's Market lists 4,095 publishers who will pay for written material and/or photography. These are divided into categories according to the main interests of the publishers. Sport and outdoor magazines, devoted to everything from archery to tennis, skiing, and mountaineering, represent the obvious targets for the outdoor writer. But these represent only the tip of the iceberg.

It is my honest belief that almost any magazine is a possible buyer of the outdoor article. At a casual glance this may not appear to be so, for often these outdoor articles are disguised as something else. The travel article—which is acceptable to a very large percentage of magazines—is a good example of the outdoor article in disguise.

Some travel articles devote themselves to the means of reaching a destination; most are published with the goal of helping the reader get maximum enjoyment after he has arrived. Outdoor recreation, in all its various forms, is probably the major reason for travel in America today, and the writer who can help these travelers enjoy better fishing, hunting, hiking, skiing, surfing, backpacking, or whatever, can almost always find a market among the hundreds and hundreds of magazines which publish travel articles.

Few writers would think of *Gourmet* as a market for the outdoor article. As you probably know, most of its readers are affluent urbanites, with a strong interest in fine food and cooking. But a careful study of the magazine shows that most of its articles are devoted to travel, with each article serving to introduce specialized or regional recipes that can be duplicated by the reader. It was by knowing and recognizing this simple fact that I was able to sell them an outdoor article disguised as a travel piece.

I had just arrived on the Delmarva Peninsula at the time and had been keeping myself busy clamming, crabbing, fishing, tonging for oysters, and just generally exploring. This area attracts many tourists, and all of these seafoods are ones relished by gourmets. I checked with *Gourmet* to see if they might be interested. They were.

I wrote about my experiences in a way designed to help any travelers who might want to duplicate them, thus providing a service to the readers. Tested recipes, which could be used even by those not wanting to make the trip, provided another service—and the publishers responded with a check for several hundred dollars.

Another writer sold this magazine an article on how to forage blue mussels, disguising it in almost exactly the manner I have described; and my account of my mushroom-hunting adventures in Michigan was sold as a travel article to another publisher.

This is only one of many ways in which the outdoor article is presented as something else. The *Wall Street Journal* might be the last place one would expect to see such a piece, yet one writer recently did just that by touring Vermont while the maples were being tapped, talking with farmers, watching the process, and then adding enough facts and figures to make his piece an acceptable business article. Another writer recently placed an article on rattlesnake hunting with the Sunday magazine section of the *Philadelphia Inquirer* by doing it as a profile of the beer-drinking, gun-toting types who engage in this so-called sport, and by making his article a social-interest one when he pointed out that the snakes die a cruel death when released.

A book could be filled with such examples. I have seen carefully disguised outdoor articles in *Playboy, Esquire, Redbook, New Times, Better Homes and Gardens,* and scores of other magazines where one would not expect them to appear. No market is off-limits to the outdoor writer; the real key to success in writing lies in studying the market. I am firmly convinced that the lack of marketing skills is the greatest cause of failure among would-be writers.

Writers are constantly advised to read the magazines for which they hope to write, and most of them just as constantly ignore this advice—to their own regret. Take that advice a great deal further—analyze the magazine and its markets.

Start by obtaining a copy of *Writer's Market,* which is available at most libraries and bookstores, or from the publisher at 9933 Alliance Road, Cincinnati, OH 45242. The book is a must for anyone wishing to sell writing or photography, and most pros buy the new issue each year and keep it near the typewriter.

In it you will find most of the major magazine and book publishers in the country. The individual listings provide not only the addresses of the publishers and the names of the editors, but also information about the types of articles they use and their length, the kind of photography they require, and how much they pay. Some listings include tips from the editors on how best to get started with that magazine.

Backpacker Magazine, which pays as much as $500 for articles on subjects that include: "How to make and repair equipment; profiles of conservationists who have made a mark on the world; interviews with photographers and leaders in conservation or land management; personal experience; and mountain profiles," offers this bit of advice to those hoping to sell articles there: ". . . Generalized articles just don't work here. Our readers are terribly sophisticated backpackers, and can spot writing by someone who does not intimately know his subject within ten seconds. Articles on trips must have an angle. We don't want to see diaries: where you went, what you took, when you ate, etc."

Aside from its listings of publishers, *Writer's Market* will guide you to sources of information that every writer needs at one time or another; to syndicates and other buyers of material; to writers' clubs, colonies, organizations, and more.

Read the book from front to back. Learning to use this guide is an essential part of selling your material. About half of the publishers it lists are ones whose magazines are not sold on newsstands, so the only way to locate each and every possible market for your work is by going through the entire book. After you have done this—and it is admittedly no small job—go through the book again.

On this second trip, make a list of the magazines that might conceivably be interested in the type of articles you hope to write and sell. And don't just limit them to those listed under the category most closely related to your own special interests. Make the list as long as possible, and plan on adding to it later.

For example, if you are a farmer, don't just list those magazines you find under farm publications. Your knowledge of farming can probably be used to sell articles to magazines published by companies who manufacture tractors, fertilizer, or other farm supplies, and perhaps you can use it to tell the readers of women's magazines how to grow a better rose garden, or to tell hunters and fishermen how to obtain permission to hunt and fish on private farmland. Remember, you are making a list of *possible* markets—don't hesitate to add any magazine that appears to offer even a remote possibility of buying your material.

If the magazine is a popular one and for sale on most newsstands, buy it. Almost all the magazines listed in *Writer's Market* will send free sample copies to writers, but I have a hunch that editors are less than excited by the writer who hopes to sell to them, yet is unwilling to spend a buck or two to buy the magazine.

Even with publications that are locally available, write to the editors and request a copy of their guidelines for writers, if such guidelines are mentioned in *Writer's Market*. Most magazines do offer these, and the guidelines present more detailed information than that found in *Writer's Market*.

With many magazines, these guidelines can be critical to your hopes of selling. Those offered by *Outdoor Life*, for example, let writers know that article ideas must be submitted at least a full year in advance of the article itself. All magazines have a lead time such as this, though it varies in length, and you must always keep that lead time in mind if you are to have any hope of selling.

In most cases, these guidelines offer information that is more detailed and more current than that found in *Writer's Market*. Some, such as those sent out by *The Mother Earth News*, are like minicourses in creative writing, offering a wealth of tips on how to research and write your article. But the time to ask for them is *before* you approach the editor with your article idea. If you ask for them in the same letter in which you suggest an article, it is the same as saying that you are totally unfamiliar with the magazine, and it will almost certainly kill your chances of making a sale.

Most magazines, if unavailable locally, will send free sample copies to writers. Where this is the case among those on your list, write the editors a *short* letter asking for the sample copies and the guidelines. Type it neatly (as you must with all your correspondence), tell them you are a professional writer, make your request, and add only return postage. Tell them nothing else; now is not the time.

As those magazines and guidelines come in, compare them carefully with the listings in *Writer's Market*. Let the listings and the guidelines supplement one another and you will begin to get a better picture of what the editors really want. As time passes and some editors have not responded to your request for guidelines or sample copies, I advise you to put a checkmark beside their name on your list of markets and look at them with a more critical eye. This does not mean you should remove them from the list of markets, for often there are good reasons for the failure to respond. But I have found this lack of responsiveness to be a pretty fair indicator of how actively the publisher seeks free-lance material.

Now you must analyze each magazine—not just read it. The idea is to develop the best possible picture of those who read the publication, so you can provide articles that will serve their interests.

The advertisements are one key to doing this. Are the products offered most likely to be bought by the affluent, or by those who are just getting by? In the latter instance, the readers are likely to be interested in your money-saving articles. Where health foods are advertised, you can bet there are organic gardeners among the readers. If sonar fish-finders are advertised, this magazine is probably reaching very sophisticated fishermen who take their sport seriously, not just the casual angler.

Aside from trying to identify the readers, there is another very good reason for studying these ads: They are the main source of income for the publisher, and that magazine is not going to print articles that will drive them away. If the magazine has several pages of advertising from tobacco companies, for example, it is not likely to buy your article called "How the Smokers Are Poisoning Your Air!" Take that one to another publisher.

Go over the masthead, which will be printed on one of the first pages. Check this against the Table of Contents. If most of the articles are written by staff members, the market for free-lance material may be limited. But if the writers are listed as contributing editors, have heart—these are free-lancers who have worked their way into the position of selling regularly to this magazine, and they usually indicate a very active market.

As you begin to analyze the magazine's articles, as a matter of fact, you should pay particular attention to the material done by these contributing editors, for they have found the key to selling to this market.

When magazines have an editorial page, or publish a statement from the editors, its content often helps provide part of the picture you are trying to develop, for this is where the editor talks to the reader.

You must certainly study the photos, to see how many and what type are used, for these can sometimes solve the problem of identifying the readers. When magazine photos (especially if those photos are taken by a staff member) show people, those people are almost certain to be from the same group who reads the magazine; and their activities, as shown in the photos, will be in line with the readers' interests.

Now dissect the articles, one at a time. Aside from trying to identify the readers to whom they are addressed, pay careful attention to the magazine's approach. What are they for and what are they against? What is the purpose of each article? How long are the articles? Do they take the form of essays? Are they features? Does the magazine prefer an investigative approach? Do the articles open with quotes, anecdotes, or a presentation of facts? Are the articles objective, or do they take a strong stand on one side of an issue? Above all, what service do they provide to the reader? When you can answer all these questions, and only then, you can begin to think about approaching an editor with your article idea.

To keep up with these trends and changes, you should subscribe to one of the writers' magazines. Not only do these contain useful articles about writing of all kinds, but they also provide updated market information, often including requests from editors for articles on certain themes. There are several, including *Writer's Digest*, which is available at libraries and bookstores, or by subscription from the publisher at 9933 Alliance Road, Cincinnati, OH 45242.

You should also study *Publishers Weekly*, which is available at all libraries or from the publisher at 1180 Avenue of the Americas, New York, NY 10036. Though largely devoted to the book market, this publication does a magnificent job of predicting trends in the entire industry. Ken McCormick, now a senior editorial consultant at Doubleday, has said of its market forecasts: "They are marvelous. If you read them regularly, you begin to see what the flow of ideas are, what's coming."

Reading book reviews, either in major newspapers, magazines, or *Publishers Weekly*, can also help you spot trends and take advantage of them. When a book, or several books on one subject begin to sell like hotcakes, you can safely bet that magazines will start showing heavy interest in articles on the same and similar topics. The point of the study is this: You can tailor an article to the market, but you can never tailor the market to fit the article.

How to Sell Your Idea: the Query Letter

You will notice that I have mentioned approaching editors with your article *ideas,* not with actual articles. That is because in today's market, the idea usually must be sold before there is any real hope of selling the article. There are exceptions, of course, just as there are exceptions to all rules, but the chances of selling your material will almost always be greater if you take the professional approach and use a query letter to convince the editor of the value of your idea.

Most editors prefer to see a query letter rather than a finished manuscript, and many refuse to read material that has not been preceded by such a letter. This is a sore point with some writers, yet the query is not for the convenience of the editor alone; it can be a real time-saver for the writer, as well as the most valuable sales tool.

The query letter is a one-page summary of the article you hope to sell, telling the editor its subject, title, approach, what photography is available, and providing any other pertinent information the editor should have. The query letter can be a powerful sales device that creates a desire to read the full article, a sense of urgency to read it *now*, and a conviction that the editor is dealing with the writer best qualified to handle the idea.

When you have developed a powerful idea for an article, carefully compose a query letter. Like the manuscript that is to follow, this letter must be neatly typed, carefully proofread, and professional in all respects. It must get quickly to the heart of the matter, not waste the editor's time with trivia. It should show evidence that you have researched your subject, and it must also convince the editor that you are familiar with the magazine and its objectives. Above all, it must convince him that his readers will be interested in the full article.

It will be easier to achieve that goal if you spend some time studying a good book on how to write sales letters. Such books are available in most libraries, and they can be of enormous help in making your query letters the powerful sales devices they should be.

On the other hand, there are certain errors in the query letter that can cost you sales. The most common among beginners is the letter that begins (or concludes), "I have never sold any writing, but . . ." Never advertise your lack of experience. Let your professionalism speak for itself. And if you intend to write about a subject that is new to you but that you intend to base on heavy research, emphasize the latter and omit any mention of the former.

On the other hand, if you have sold previous material, or if you have strong experience with your subject matter, don't hesitate to emphasize it. The query letter is no place to be humble.

Near the end of the letter there are two things you should do: Ask the editor for any suggestions he or she might care to offer on how the article should be handled, and *ask for an assignment*.

By asking for suggestions, I do not mean that you should ask for help in researching or writing the article; you will get neither, and you will probably kill your chances of a sale. Just invite the editor, in a general way, to offer suggestions that might strengthen the article. As often as not, if the editor is really interested, your invitation will be accepted—and you will have taken a giant stride toward a sale.

I once queried the editors at Ford Times with an article idea. My daughter and I were going to spend a week on a coastal island, living entirely off foraged foods and seafood from the surrounding waters. I proposed a personal-experience piece, with emphasis on how it was done, but I invited suggestions.

Even though I was unknown to the editors there, they responded by asking me to submit the article on speculation, and suggesting that I emphasize the family relationship and certain other factors. I did, and that article will have been published long before you read these words.

There is, I think, a bit of psychology at work here. When an editor makes suggestions for change, even the most minor ones, that article becomes, in part, the editor's article. I believe it increases the desire to see it published.

It is also important that you ask for the assignment. Students in the Dale Carnegie sales courses are taught that the biggest single cause of lost sales is the salesman's failure to ask the customer to buy. Asking for an assignment is your way of asking the customer to buy.

Asking for an assignment will not always get you one, but you will almost never get one without asking. More than likely, you will be asked to submit your article on speculation, but just asking for the assignment is another way of showing your professionalism, and it is the only way you are going to get expenses and all the other niceties that go to assigned writers.

When asking to see your article on speculation the editor has taken a psychological first step toward buying it. That editor has asked that you do a job of work, and the last thing he or she wants to do is feel guilty about your going unpaid for your work. That does not mean you are going to sell unsatisfactory material, but it does mean you have gained a weak commitment to buy. It now becomes your job to write an article so superb that the editor will feel good about making that commitment—and be eager to see more of your work.

Aside from its potential as a sales tool, there are other good reasons for using the query letter. A long list of them could be made, but they can be summed up as two: Query letters save time; and before you can steadily sell articles, you must first sell ideas.

"But how do you get your ideas?" is the question most often asked of any writer. When friends asked it of me early in my writing career, I used to reply by pointing to the funny little dent near the top of my typewriter—the spot where I pounded my head as I searched for ideas. That was before I realized that the key lay hidden in the question itself.

How?

Kipling once said that the writer has six honest serving men— who, what, when, where, why, and how. They all continue to serve the writer well, but in today's service-oriented market, I feel that *how* has become the most faithful servant of all. Just by asking yourself questions that begin with the word *how*, you should be able to produce in an hour enough article ideas to keep you busy for months. But while asking yourself these questions, you must also be asking yourself another: "How can I be of service to the readers of this magazine?"

Those who read *The Mother Earth News*, for example, are folks who want to escape the city for a rural environment. They are interested in organic gardening, solar energy, protecting the environment, a simpler way of life, and much more. In seeking ideas for them, just ask yourself questions related to their interests: How can I find and finance a place in the country? How can I grow a better garden organically? How can I help stop the pollution of the environment? How can a country home be built for less? When you can provide the answer to your question, it will no longer be a question—it will be material for an article.

Newspapers are other good sources of ideas, for what is printed there often forecasts what will follow in the magazines. But two frequently overlooked sources of ideas are found in the magazines themselves.

The first is the letters-to-the-editors column. Not only will these help you identify the readers of the magazine, but often you will find readers asking questions and thus almost begging you to do an article that answers those questions.

The magazines "fillers"—those tips, recipes, news items, and anecdotes that most magazines use to balance their pages—are other good sources of ideas, for often they are like little miniarticles that can be developed and expanded.

These fillers also deserve your attention as a market—not because the pay for them is high, but because they are often the easiest sales to make, and it is extremely important that the new writer see his or her name on a check as soon as possible. If a lack of marketing skills is the prime reason for failure in this field, it is not far in front of frustration.

The first check I received was for such material—fifty dollars that arrived just when I had decided to admit that I would never make it as a writer. That check renewed my confidence, sent me back to my typewriter, and was followed by a sudden burst of sales. I have been at it ever since, and when other work is slow, I put a few of my tips or recipes on paper and send them off.

Once you have the basic idea for your article in mind, it will usually need further development. Mort Handler, who was for many years editorial director at Publishers' Development Corporation, once gave me some advice that I have never forgotten.

"Find a theme and narrow it down," he told me. "But never make it too narrow for your intended audience." Assume that you have studied *Outdoor Life* and have decided to try to sell them an article that will be of service to fishermen. Assume, also, that your first "idea" question has been, "How can I catch more and bigger fish?" That question sounds okay, because it would be of interest to the nationwide readership of this magazine, but the theme is too broad. Entire books have been devoted to answering that question.

So you narrow it down by asking, "How can I catch more and bigger bass?" which is better but still too broad, for this fish requires different techniques in different places and at different seasons of the year. Now try coupling *how* with one or two of Mr. Kipling's "honest serving men."

Try asking yourself when and where, as well as how, in this example. Do you know a certain body of water that constantly yields big bass during a certain season of the year, and how those bass are *taken*? Better yet, do you know certain fishing techniques that will produce steady catches of bass from certain types of water during one season of the year? Assume that you do, or that you know where to find information that would make this possible. Your article idea then becomes something like, "How can I catch more and bigger bass from small creeks in the spring of the year?" and would result in a title such as "Big Bass from Little Creeks—Springtime's Hottest Fishing!"

An article such as that would have a good chance at a nationally circulated magazine, because it has broad appeal without attempting to cover too much. However, if you were developing the idea for a magazine with only a regional readership, the theme would need to be narrowed down just a little bit more, perhaps to: "Big Springtime Bass from Pennsylvania's Creeks—and How to Catch Them!"

Research for Success

The next step is in research—the most important and the most neglected part of the writer's job. The thing to remember about research is that you can never do too much. This means reading all you possibly can on your subject, talking with as many experts as possible, and digging out facts and figures. Become a walking encyclopedia on the subject.

"Write for the reader who is exactly as intelligent as you are," John Shuttleworth, editor and publisher of *The Mother Earth News*, advises writers. To this I would add: Work at research until you are far better informed than most readers of your own intelligence could possibly hope to be.

Aside from the fact that you must do this research if you really hope to help the reader, there is another very good reason why it is of special importance to the beginner—it is a matter of confidence in your writing.

There is something intangibly wrong about writing that is done with a lack of confidence. It gives editors a vague feeling that all is not right with the manuscript, though they cannot tell exactly why they feel that way. Confident writing is the writing that sells, and research will provide that confidence. Always approach an article with the assumption that you have a lot to learn about your subject, then learn through research, and you will be amazed at how comfortable you will feel as you begin the actual writing.

Manuscript Preparation

A free booklet, *The Mechanics of Writing*, which fully describes preferred methods of submitting manuscripts and photography, provides copyright information, and contains other helpful information, can be obtained by sending a self-addressed, stamped envelope to: Mechanics Editor, *Writer's Market*, 9933 Alliance Road, Cincinnati, OH 45242.

Actually, it is not all that complicated. The manuscript must be neatly typed, double-spaced, on a good grade of standard-sized bond paper. Use only a standard typeface—either pica or elite—and a black ribbon.

Your name and address goes in the upper left-hand corner of the first page, the page number in the upper right-hand corner. The title is centered about halfway down that first page, the word "by" is centered under that, and your name is centered on the next line.

Leave wide margins at the top, bottom, and both sides, for the editor's notes, and go on with the article, doing your best to make it look professional in every respect. Too much emphasis cannot be placed on neatness and care in spelling, for this is your product and it must compete with other products being offered for sale.

Not only should you keep a carbon copy of every manuscript you send off to the marketplace, you should also retain your notes and research material, as well as the negatives of the photography. Long after this article has been accepted and you have been paid, you are likely to find yourself working on a related topic, and that material could prove invaluable—especially if you move to writing books.

More then 80,000 writers buy a copy of *Writer's Market* each year, most with some thought of doing a book. Books are the big income producers for writers, so the competition is fierce. But the odds against you are not impossible to overcome, especially if you have built up some credentials and keep yourself informed about the market and its needs.

Write to a few publishers and request their catalogs, so you can see what they have done in the past and might be interested in doing in the future. The next step is to pay a visit to the library to check your idea against similar books listed in *Subject Guide to Books in Print*.

Selling a Book

If you still feel that your idea is fresh and new, or that your approach to it would make your book exceptional, the next step is to write a query letter that will sell the idea. As in the magazine market, books are usually written after the idea has been sold, and many publishing houses simply do not have the staff that would be needed to read all the manuscripts that come in without a previous query.

If your query letter does a good job of selling, you will probably be asked to submit an outline and two or three sample chapters of the book, plus sample illustrations. If these live up the promises made in the letter, you will be offered a book contract, with terms that are fairly standard among publishers, and an advance against royalties.

No one can predict exactly how much you will earn in royalties from a given book—but, "Providing they sell well at all," says Ross Olney, who has sold more than 80 books and should know, "you draw royalties over a long period of time, like money in the bank."

That "money in the bank" can give you the freedom offered by few other careers. Provided he or she can pay the rent, a writer can live anyplace that has mail service, following a work schedule of one's own choosing. And the writer earns a living by actively participating in pursuits that he or she would likely be following even without pay. All in all, it is a pretty wonderful way of life.

If we are to preserve any part of our natural heritage, we must have a public that is informed, aware, and concerned. Keeping the public so is the biggest job—and largest reward—of the outdoor writer. This is a fact that was recognized by Gifford Pinchot, father of modern forestry, who upon assuming his job as head of the U. S. Forest Service immediately hired a writer as his chief assistant. It is a fact that will not change: Outdoor writers will continue to be needed.

Perhaps you recall the furor created by the publication of Rachel Carson's *Silent Spring*, a book that stirred the American conscience and gave impetus to the conservation movement. If so, you may also look around you, as I do, and see that the furor has begun to die down, her warnings are being forgotten, and we desperately need another writer like Rachel Carson.

Maybe you will be the one to carry on her message. I hope so.

11
SELLING NATURE WITHOUT HARMING IT

Almost every outdoor field has its peak seasons. This fact means that those who pursue outdoor careers are, far more than most others, likely to need ways to keep productively busy year-round and supplement their earnings. For the beginner, who often must accept a seasonal job in the effort to later qualify for a year-round position, this part of outdoor work can pose a problem.

In most of these chapters, no matter which outdoor career you hope to follow, you will come across ways of adding to your income. As an outdoor worker, you are going to learn much that is of interest to others, so writing about your work is one way to supplement your earnings. Your choice of a career probably means that you are going to live in a rural area, where you can not only reduce your expenses by raising some of your own food, but also increase your cash income through beekeeping, worm farming, rabbit husbandry, or another of the low-investment ventures mentioned in the chapter on farming.

In pursuing a career in one field you will be gaining experience that will almost certainly qualify you for supplemental work in another. As a farmer, for example, you might find work during the winter doing snow surveys for the Soil Conservation Service, or you might earn money in fishing, as many farmers in coastal areas do. The ways in which these career skills can be combined are almost endless, limited only by your ambition.

In this chapter, though, I want to introduce you to some ways of earning money that are not so directly tied to any combination of careers—ways of earning money that are open to you simply because of your outdoor interests and because you are likely to be living in the type of place where they can be profitable.

Some of these methods I am going to describe are fairly new ones. Some are as old as America itself. Some require a lot of hard work. Others are as pleasurable as a walk on the beach. A few require some skills and knowledge, but usually these are going to be skills and knowledge that you will have acquired in preparing for almost any job mentioned in previous chapters. Some require only ambition. A few are simply pleasant outdoor hobbies that will pay for themselves, and others can be enormously profitable seasonal businesses. All can be pursued without destruction of the environment.

Supplying Insects for Serum Production

Let me tell you, first, about one of the more unusual earning opportunities—collecting and selling hornets, bumblebees, yellow-jackets, wasps, and other stinging insects. Medical centers and labs buy these to produce serum for those who are allergic to their stings, and it is quite possible to add several thousand dollars to your annual income by supplying them. According to one buyer, a California college student has been earning about $8,000 each summer for the past few years, working a couple of hours each night, several nights a week.

These insects, like all other creatures, are important links in the chain of life and should not be driven to extinction. But they do frequently build nests in areas where they can be annoying and dangerous to humans, and collecting them to produce life-saving serum is a logical way to utilize a natural resource.

To collect them, you'll need gloves, a beekeeper's veil, and two layers of clothing, firmly tied at neck, wrists, and ankles. You'll also need a bag made of fine mesh, into which you can drop the nest and from which the insects cannot escape. The smoker used with honeybees is of little use with these insects, for the smoke is as likely to infuriate as to soothe.

Collecting is usually done at night, when all the insects are in the nest and they are less likely to sting. The entire nest is cut from its moorings, dropped in the mesh bag, the bag securely tied off, and the whole kaboodle transported, as quickly as possible, to a freezer. Leave it at below-freezing temperatures until the insects have had time to die a peaceful death; then—and only then—remove the bag and shake them from the nests.

Finding nests is no problem. Simply let people know that you are willing to remove these nests from their property—for a reasonable price. Run a small ad in the local newspaper. Place mimeographed notices in country clubs, laundromats, small stores, and other places where they will be seen. Not many people are willing to provide this service, so you'll have no trouble getting $10 or $15 an hour for your time.

You'll have even less trouble selling the insects. A. W. Benton, professor of entomology at Penn State University and head of Vespa Laboratories located there, pays $250 a pound for hornets, $375 a pound for yellowjackets and bumblebees, and $400 a pound for wasps. There will usually be at least 1,000 insects to the pound, depending on the species and the time of year; and the number of insects to the nest can be as few as a dozen or as many as several hundred, so gathering a pound requires some initiative. But it does pay, and pay very well.

"It's not easy getting people to do it," says Benton, who actively recruits suppliers. He assures new recruits that if they work five or six nights each week they can depend on earnings of several thousand dollars per year, but he also warns, "You can get the hell stung out of you if you're not very, very careful."

If you are still interested, write Mr. Benton, request more information about getting started, and ask for a list of current prices. He can be reached at Vespa Laboratories, Penn State University, State College, PA 16801.

If selling hornets sounds farfetched to you, it may begin to sound ordinary when I tell you that long before I was aware of the market for them, I knew an Ohio farmer who sold abandoned hornets' *nests* at his roadside produce stand. These papery gray nests—many of them far larger than basketballs—were offered as unusual decorator items, presumably to those whose homes had a rustic decor, or to hobbyists who converted them into lamps, planters, and other crafted items. If you do decide to help supply the hornets needed for producing serum, it is possible that these nests—for which that Ohio farmer was getting as much as $40 each—could provide a supplement to your supplement. However, I am calling this to your attention for a far more important reason: to remind you that beauty is truly in the eye of the beholder—a fact that could add hundreds or even thousands of dollars to your annual income.

Collecting Driftwood

Consider driftwood. It is extremely popular for use in interior decorating. Hobbyists and craftsmen buy it for use in making unusual home decorations. It is sold in gift shops, shell shops along the seashore, even in furniture stores. At Ocean City, Maryland, during the summer of 1978, shops along the boardwalk were asking as much as $100 for some of the more beautiful pieces.

But what, actually, is driftwood? It is nothing more than a piece of wood—of any species—that has been made beautiful by the processes of nature. Perhaps bleached white as bone by the sun, perhaps not; eroded by wind and sand; gracefully curved, beautifully burnished, naturally sculpted—it is simply a piece of wood that appeals to those who look upon it. Most people incorrectly assume that the wood has spent time in the water, especially the sea. Most would be surprised—as I was—to learn that the major source of "driftwood" is the high mountain country of Arizona, and that most of that driftwood sold on the boardwalk at Ocean City is supplied by an enterprising family that lives many miles inland. The truth of the matter is that if a piece of wood has been aged, weathered, and formed until it has visual appeal, it has become driftwood. If it is attractive to you, it may be attractive to others—and it can put dollars in your pocket.

This is not to suggest that you should go out daily and scour the countryside in search of driftwood. But it is to suggest that you should be aware of its monetary value and keep your eyes open for it while you are engaged in other outdoor activities. Just take a second look at a hillside, roadside, or woodland floor and you will be surprised at the striking forms that seem to materialize before your eyes. Collecting the most beautiful of those forms then becomes a pastime that can be as profitable as it is pleasant.

If you are already involved in selling some product directly to consumers, you will have little difficulty in selling driftwood. Just check the local prices, mark a selection of driftwood accordingly, and place it where it can be seen by customers. It will usually sell itself.

You might consider offering it at crafts shows, flea markets, county fairs, or at a booth at a farmers' market. Booths at such places usually are available at a very low rent, the traffic is heavy, and they are good outlets for many of the natural products mentioned in this chapter.

Some people sell driftwood to gift and craft shops, furniture stores, and other retail outlets. Smaller stores, especially, are always on the lookout for highly profitable additions to their line, and by offering them the driftwood at a good discount and on consignment, you should be able to interest several local dealers in your wares. This means you will receive a far lower price for each piece of wood, but it also means you may be able to sell it more steadily.

Decorator Items from the Woods and Shore

Mistletoe and holly, with the shiny evergreen leaves and bright red berries that are familiar to all as Christmas decorations, may also catch your eye as you walk the woodlands. The demand for these is such that in New Jersey, farms of several hundred acres are devoted to raising them for the market; yet, especially in the East, American holly is among the most common shrubs of the forests, often crowding out other trees and shrubs. Cuttings can be taken from either without destroying the plant.

The demand for holly wreaths soars around Christmas, of course, and if you are interested in crafts, you will have little trouble selling all the wreaths you have available at that time. Books on handicrafts at your local library are filled with plans for making them, as are pre-Christmas issues of many magazines. But if crafts do not hold an interest for you, remember that shops that sell materials to craftsmen will probably be glad to handle all the holly and mistletoe you care to supply. Americans seem to have had enough of the artificial, and they are eager for items that help them recapture the true meaning of Christmas.

In thinking of the market for Christmas decorations, keep in mind that many other items can be sold. For instance, many hundreds of thousands of dollars' worth of pine cones are shipped out of Tennessee and Georgia each year, along with pine cuttings for making boughs. Left in their natural state, or perhaps touched up with a bit of spray paint and glitter, the pine cones find their way into all sorts of Christmas decorations. Conifer trees, as a group, are the most common trees in America, and in most regions you can easily pick up bushels of the cones. Since no shipping costs are involved, you can probably offer these to craft shops cheaper than they can buy them elsewhere, adding a few more dollars to your seasonal profits. Other decorator items from the wild, such as acorns, dried milkweed pods, and even sheaths of wild wheat or oats, also produce some income for those who are able to recognize their beauty and make it available to others.

The collection and sale of seashells is an industry that produces millions of dollars of annual income in most coastal states. Some shells are sought by collectors because they are rare, not just beautiful. For these, collectors have been known to pay hundreds, even thousands, of dollars. For that reason alone, if you spend a lot of time along the shore, you would be well advised to spend some time studying any one of the dozens of good books that will help you to identify the various shells, the only way to avoid letting an extremely valuable one slip throught your fingers.

But these rare shells account for only a small part of the retail trade in seashells. Many of the seashells sold in America once housed marine creatures that are among the most common animals in the ocean. The scallop shell, which serves as the roadside logo of a major oil company, is probably the most popular seashell in America. People buy the larger ones for use as ashtrays, baking dishes, or serving dishes, the smaller ones for making crafted items. They are commonly found along most seashores, and where they are fished commercially, huge piles of empty shells can be picked up. The shell can sometimes be sold for a higher price than the meat it once contained.

This is not an unusual example. Abalone shells of the West Coast are so eagerly sought by collectors and hobbyists that most western states now forbid their transportation across state lines. I have a huge conch shell that was bought for me as a present by a friend who visited Key West, Florida, where they are common enough to be fished commercially. She paid forty dollars for it—yet the flesh from it could not have earned a fisherman more than a dollar or so.

The quahog clam provides another example. It is one of the most common clams along eastern shores. Drab and unattractive on the outside, the shell is beautifully creamy and marked with purple splotches on the inside. The shell once served as the most valuable wampum of many American Indians. Whole shells are seldom offered for sale today; instead they are broken and the bits and pieces are used to make beautiful jewelry, belts, and other items of handicraft.

Your chances of collecting a quantity of shells is always better following a storm. When winds have driven the waves high on the beaches, the sands are sometimes left littered with hundreds of thousands of shells, ranging from the plain and common to the exquisitely beautiful and rare. In good collecting areas, at such times, it is entirely possible to pick up truckloads of shells.

Shell shops thrive in most coastal areas. They will buy shells in quantity from you, but probably at only a fraction of what they will bring at retail. In marketing seashells, a better rule seems to be: Take them where they ain't.

I learned that many hotels along the East Coast of Florida, where seashell collecting is not exceptionally good, buy large quantities of seashells from sellers along the Gulf Coast, where it is among the best in the world. To keep their visitors happy, the hotels on the East Coast scatter these on their beaches, thus allowing the tourists to go home with "natural" souvenirs of their visit.

The seashell that is regarded as common and worthless in one area may bring several dollars in another, so if you have friends or relatives in other parts of the country—especially inland—who will help with the marketing, you may be able to earn exceptionally good profits by shipping even the most ordinary shells of your area to them.

Following this principle, my own daughter has built a thriving little business in jewelry made from the shells of quahog clams. She obtains all the shells she needs from a nearby clam cannery, where tons are dumped each week. She breaks the shells into bits, drills a hole in each selected piece, and places it on an inexpensive chain to make a pendant or charm bracelet. Several local stores handle these on consignment, but they account for just a small part of her sales.

Most of her production she ships to a young cousin in Ohio, who markets them for her. These shells are anything but common in that area, and the jewelry not only brings a higher price in that market, but also sells at a much faster pace. The two youngsters are not getting rich at this, but they do earn a small but steady income, and a similar business might be developed into something large by enterprising adults. Certainly the margin of profit is high enough to warrant investigation.

Collecting and Selling Rocks, Minerals, and Gemstones

The same rule of beauty makes many common rocks and minerals valuable. Rock shops are found in most parts of the country, often selling bits of stone and mineral that have no commercial value as gems, or no industrial value, but that are simply beautiful to behold. Some of the stones are cut and polished, and some are made into jewelry, but many are sold in the natural state.

Amateur rockhounds really need no formal training in geology, though knowledge of the subject would certainly help. Most libraries have field guides to the common rocks, gems, and minerals, which will help you acquire a general idea of those likely to be found in your area, but there are other ways to acquire more specific help.

The best source of this help is the nearest museum of natural history. Almost all of these museums have displays of stones and minerals that are common to their own region, including a great deal of information about the natural occurrence of each. Actually seeing the stone in its natural state will be more helpful to you than anything else, but most museums also have a geologist who can answer any questions you might have.

Rock shops offer more help. A visit to one not only offers you the chance to see various rocks in both their natural and polished states, but also to see which ones the shops are selling, at what prices, and in what ways. Many of these shops also offer helpful magazines and booklets for those who pursue this hobby, as well as equipment for pursuing it. But most important of all is the advice you can get from the owners of such shops—usually hobbyists who have built a business around their outdoor interests.

A small pick is the only piece of equipment absolutely essential to getting started. Later, if you really become interested in this possibly profitable hobby, you will want to add a stone polisher and a cutting device of some sort. Both of these can be obtained for well under $100, but they are not really needed until you have begun to collect on a regular basis.

Abandoned quarries and gravel pits are especially good places to begin the hunt, for in such areas various layers of the earth have been exposed, thus making it possible for you to reach various rocks and minerals that might otherwise be buried. But the best place for hunting is the place you happen to be at any given moment—some of the best discoveries are made by accident, by amateur prospectors who wisely keep their digging equipment close at hand.

No matter where you begin to dig, be sure to immediately label each and every sample you take home, marking it with the exact location from which it was taken. This could be of extreme importance. After building up a collection of hundreds of stones and minerals, which can be done rather quickly, it often becomes difficult to remember exactly where each was found. Identifying each sample can take some time—though the museum and rock shops may help you do it more quickly—and you are going to be very disappointed if you discover that you have a highly valuable sample but cannot remember where it was found.

In prospecting around, just keep an eye out for that which is naturally beautiful, or which might be made beautiful with a little cutting or polishing. That fossilized fern? Might it not make an interesting paperweight? That nugget of "fool's gold"? Would it not be of interest to someone? That piece of rose quartz? Might it not be truly beautiful when cut and polished?

You would also be well advised to keep a sharp eye out for the geological formations known as geodes—which can usually be sold with no cutting or polishing and can be worth only a few dollars each, or several hundred dollars apiece. They may be as small as a pebble, or they may measure several feet across. They are found in all parts of the country, usually in sand or clay.

Geodes are nodules that, when broken open, are found to be hollow and the cavity lined with one or more minerals, frequently in the form of beautiful crystals that are faceted and formed in ways that make them as beautiful as any gem ever cut and polished by man. The crystals come in all sizes, shapes, and colors, with varying degrees of value.

Before a geode can be formed, there must have been, in the first place, a cavity in the surrounding rock. Over the centuries, as water leached through the rock, it became saturated with one or more minerals, and then, dripping into the cavity, deposited the minerals, usually as crystals lining the hollow. You can then recognize it as a geode by the fact that it is far too light in weight to be a solid rock, and then it may be carefully broken open. Where one geode is found there will frequently be many, many others, so the discovery of one can lead you to a bed that could be worth many hundreds of dollars at a rock shop.

Rocks and minerals of beauty can easily be wholesaled to gift and hobby shops, or even to jewelry stores, but once you have a large selection, you might want to set aside a small space to retail them yourself. You need not sell a lot of them, because the margin of profit is so large. According to an article in *The Mother Earth News*, one young couple followed almost exactly this route and turned their hobby into a business that nets $1,000 per week.

As an amateur prospector you are by no means limited to looking for the common rocks and minerals. Many extremely valuable gems and minerals do occur in this country, and you may just be lucky enough to come across one or more while out in the field.

Topaz, which is usually some shade of yellow but may also be brown or blue, is not at all unknown in this country. It occurs in cavities or seams, in or near granite, and has been found in such diverse places as Connecticut, North Carolina, Utah, Colorado, Missouri, and California.

Perhaps you are familiar with tourmaline, the lustrous red, green, brown, black, or colorless crystal that has been prized as a gem for centuries in India and that occurs in association with either copper or granite. In 1820, two young boys found a bed of it near Paris, Maine, that yielded more than $50,000 worth of quality stones. It is dug from fields in New Hampshire, Massachusetts, New York, Colorado, and California.

Emeralds and rubies, which are among the most valuable of all gems and which have a hardness approaching that of the diamond, have been found in North Carolina and Montana. They are found in association with corundum, which is found from Massachusetts to California, so other fields of these precious gems may lie undiscovered.

We tend to think of gold as being limited to the states of the Far West, yet it was once commercially mined in Georgia, as well. Silver? When the first white settlers reached Ohio, the Indian tribes living there had tons of jewelry, trinkets, and other ornaments fashioned from it. The source of this silver has never been determined, even though Simon Kenton, among others, tried again and again to buy that information from the Indians.

If you decide to start looking for any of these more precious gems and minerals, you would be well advised to do a little additional research at the library. Ask to see the state history books for the state in which you intend to prospect. Where valuable discoveries have been made, or where mining of a certain mineral has been of importance, these will almost always be recorded in the state history. By knowing what has been found in the past, you will have a better idea of what may be found in the future—and you will be able to give better direction to your prospecting.

The soaring price of gold and silver does mean that part-time prospecting for them is once again profitable. For many years, as you know, the price of refined gold was set at about $32 an ounce. In 1979, as I write this, the price is at more than $400 an ounce—and climbing. The price of silver has not risen quite so dramatically, but it, too, has climbed steadily over recent years. These prices mean that many old mining claims, abandoned because they were not profitable at the old prices, might now be reopened successfully, and that even primitive mining techniques, such as panning for gold, might pay very, very well.

Gold is among the most precious of all metals. It usually holds the metallic state, even in nature, and is recognized by its color, considerable weight, hardness, malleability, and the fact that it never tarnishes. It most often occurs in quartz veins in fine to thick threads, scales, or grains, and occasionally in larger masses that we know as nuggets. From these quartz veins it is often washed down the streambeds, to be found later in the sands or gravels, or even in the beaches of the sea. When mixed in this manner it is known as "placer gold," and its recovery is placer mining—using water to remove the lighter sand and gravel while retaining the much heavier gold. Panning is placer mining in its most basic form.

Most of the great gold discoveries began with this simple form of mining. When gold began to show in the pan, the prospector then attempted to trace the gold back to its source, the vein from which it was weathered. When a deposit was found, the size of the particles there might be as fine as dust, or, like the largest ever found in California, they could be nuggets weighing as much as 161 pounds. You may never find a nugget approaching that size, but you may, like many others who pursue the hobby, be able to create a small but steady income by panning out dust and tiny nuggets. Your chances of doing so are best if you live between California and Alaska, or in Colorado, Nevada, Arizona, Utah, or South Dakota; but slimmer chances do exist in Georgia and both of the Carolinas—all of which have produced gold in the past.

Silver, when found in its native state, is usually in wiry, flaky, or mossy masses, but sometimes nuggets of considerable size do occur. The largest known nugget weighed in at 800 pounds, and another topped 500 pounds. When such nuggets do occur and are exposed to the air, they quickly tarnish and take on a black color, which must be scraped away to reveal the silver below—one way of testing suspected ore.

Silver, especially in the nugget form, is usually found in association with other metals like iron, copper, lead, and zinc. In nuggets, it has most often been found near the copper-mining regions of Lake Superior, and those in Idaho, Nevada, and California.

Using a Metal Detector

If this amateur treasure hunting really interests you, you might also want to add a metal detector to your outdoor equipment. Such a device is, of course, useless in searching for rocks, minerals, and gemstones, and of little more value in seeking gold or silver, which are better found by other means. But a metal detector can lead you to other treasures, large and small, and using one is a fascinating hobby that usually pays its own expenses and always provides the thrill of discovery.

Metal detectors come in many designs and degrees of sophistication, with some available to fit every budget. Kits for building them may cost as little as $30, while the more sophisticated assemblies may set you back many hundreds of dollars. The detector sends out an electronic signal—when it encounters the density of metal, it bounces back and registers on the detector, either as a flashing light or as a movement of a needle. Most hobby shops sell them, and they are also offered through ads in many magazines.

Wherever large crowds gather in the outdoors, they are likely to be followed by someone sweeping the area with one of these metal-seeking devices—an almost sure way of finding items of value. On a visit to Delaware's Cape Henlopen State Park, where the beach attracts many thousands of visitors each summer day, I found Sue Begley, a young park aide, doing just that.

Hoping to interview one or more employees about their outdoor careers, I had timed my arrival to coincide with the evening closing of the park, when they would be more readily available. I soon found myself walking the beach beside Sue, talking about her hobby, and watching in eager anticipation each time the light on the handle of the detector flashed and she knelt to dig out a dime, a quarter, or, as frequently as not, a metal tab from a beer can.

"My father let me borrow the detector for the summer," she told me. "And if he was trying to get me hooked on the hobby, he's surely succeeded. You wouldn't belive the things people lose at the beach—necklaces, bracelets, watches, rings. Twice I've found purses that were purposely buried and then forgotten; and on those we were able to contact the owners, who claimed them. But I found one coin purse with a fifty-dollar bill tucked inside, and no identification. It was never claimed. It's amazing!"

At the Park office, Sue, who says she is more interested in the hunting than the money but who estimates her daily find at about $5 in coins, showed me a shoebox containing rings, watches, costume jewelry, and trinkets she was holding on the chance their owners might return. If no one claimed them before the end of the season, they were hers to keep.

Throughout the year, but especially as winter approaches and northeast winds send angry waves high up on these shores, beaches in this area yield treasure of another kind—gold and silver Dutch coins that almost certainly come from the sunken wreck of the *DeBraak*, a ship of the seventeenth century that went down with a cargo that was known to include hundreds of millions of dollars' worth of these metals.

The *DeBraak* has never been found, nor the bulk of its treasure, though many ambitious searches have been undertaken over the years, and it is known to lie somewhere on the bottom of Delaware Bay, its existence confirmed by a steady trickle of coins it releases to settle on the beaches and taunt those who search for the source.

These coins are not easily visible to the eye. They come up encrusted with marine and mineral deposits, and are quickly covered by a crust of sand. Most of those recovered are found by modern beachcombers equipped with metal detectors. According to an article in a local newspaper, one such beachcomber has, over the years, collected several hundred of them, with an undisclosed value upon which one can only speculate.

This is not the only such treasure. Certain beaches in New Jersey also produce old coins from sunken ships. So many coins have been found along the shore below Ocean City, Maryland, that the sands there are know locally as "Money Beach," a name that is shared with another shoreline in Virginia. Old coins of value are often found on Padre Island in the Gulf of Mexico, as well as on dozens of beaches in Florida.

All our coastlines are dotted with sunken ships, some holding treasure, some without. Even those holding no gold and silver frequently give up artifacts of value, pieces of weaponry, old belt buckles, and fishing and sailing gear of another era. The antique value of some of these renders them even more valuable than gold or silver, and they are very likely to come into the hands of a beachcomber who uses modern equipment in hunting them.

Such treasures exist just as abundantly inland as they do along the edge of the sea. No one can accurately estimate how much treasure lies hidden across the width and breadth of America, but its dollar value certainly runs into the billions.

The American Indians hid gold and silver from the first white settlers. Settlers hid treasure from both Indians and thieves. The thieves who managed to steal enough to deserve concealment then hid their booty from the lawmen who followed. Plantation owners of the South, as the Civil War drew to a close, buried many of their valuables to hide them from the invading armies of the North. In hundreds of instances, these treasures have never been recovered.

Many of the treasures likely to be found with a metal detector are not gold and silver at all, nor were they always hidden; many were lost or thrown away. Americans have always been quick to discard that which is of no use at the moment, yet we are also a nation of collectors. No matter what the object, it is probably collected by someone, and the metal detector can sometimes turn up a staggering number of such collectibles and antiques.

Old bottles, bits of barbed wire, glassware items, old coins, weapons, ancient farm utensils—all of these are eagerly collected by many people. The detector will give no reading on old bottles and other glass, of course, but often such items will be found alongside the metal that causes the indicator to flicker. For example, long before we had a modern trash-collection system, farmers buried their trash on their own land. When such an old dump is located with the detector, your digging is likely to turn up all sorts of items from yesteryear, some of which may prove valuable. Keep in mind that yesterday's junk is often today's antique. Never discard any old item that is found until its identity has been established and its worth verified by comparing it to the many books for collectors that will be found at your library.

If we are a nation of collectors, we are also a nation of movers. Across all of rural America can be found abandoned farmhouses by the thousands, traces of small settlements whose inhabitants have moved on, foundations where houses once stood, even entire ghost towns with their buildings intact. These provide especially fertile hunting grounds.

The houses need not be ancient. The coins that were dropped just a few years ago, or the items that were squirreled away by a child, can be very valuable to the modern collector. Where people have been, in most instances, they leave items behind—items that may mean dollars in your pocket.

Some research will also get you started in the right direction. Visit your local library and carefully read books on the history of your state, or, better still, your own county. Old newspaper files, if they are available to you, can also provide much information that will be helpful. And don't ignore local folklore and legends, for those often are rooted in truth.

Such research may reveal that a skirmish between the Indians and the settlers took place near you, or a minor battle of the American Revolution, the Civil War, or the War of 1812. Many of these small encounters have been largely forgotten, but relics from them can be just as valuable as any found at Concord or Gettysburg.

But not all valuable relics come from war. Such research can lead in many directions. Perhaps it will disclose the site of an old settlement, a building that was destroyed by fire, or a spot where crowds of people once gathered—and possibly left behind items that are of great value today. It was exactly this type of research that guided one Ohio woman to a find worth several thousand dollars.

Darke County, Ohio, is the birthplace of the famous Annie Oakley. "Little Miss Sure-shot," who often returned there to stage her famous Wild West Show. During the course of some research at the library in Greenville, Ohio, Wilma Dees, an amateur prospector, was able to locate the site where those shows had been held and was smart enough to put that information to use.

The land was now owned by the county, bordering a township dump. After obtaining permission to explore it and to keep what she found in her digging, Ms. Dees went to work. Almost immediately she began finding articles of value: old coins, including some of gold that were minted in the last century; an old plowshare; a watch fob. Then she began turning up items that were obviously connected to the Wild West Show.

Most of these—a couple of spurs, bits and pieces of bridles and other harness, a belt buckle—were of only nominal value. Then she dug from the earth a .36-caliber Colt revolver, which was later authenticated as having belonged to Buffalo Bill Cody. She sold this for $2,500 to Don Foreman, a collector of guns, who later donated it to the Annie Oakley Collection of the Garst Museum in Greenville, where it is now on display.

So many variables—including a certain amount of luck—are involved that no one can tell you how much you can expect to earn by such prospecting. However, if you are not afraid of some truly hard work, the cutting and sale of firewood is one way you can almost certainly boost your annual income by several thousand dollars.

Cutting and Selling Firewood

There are more wood-burning fireplaces in America today than at any time since the American Revolution. Wood-burning stoves are again being used for heat as people seek an alternative to fossil fuels. Wood-burning cookstoves are making a comeback. Even in areas where fuel is not needed for heat and other practical purposes, the sale of firewood is possible, for many folks simply enjoy the beauty of a blazing log fire.

The demand for firewood is such that the price is soaring, making its supply extremely profitable. Where only a few years ago a cord of the very best firewood could be bought for as little as $20, even the least desirable woods are now selling for twice that amount, and the price for quality firewood is approaching $80 a cord in some parts of the country. Better still—for those who supply it if not for those who pay for it—even at those prices many woodcutters are unable to meet the demands of their customers. A small ad placed in the newspaper, or a few notices tacked on bulletin boards, offering split and seasoned firewood at competitive prices, will probably attract enough business to keep you busy in every spare moment you have.

If you own wooded land, then you already have the trees to cut. But even if you own no land at all, this money-making opportunity remains open to you. Many farmers who own wooded land may be more than glad to have your help in clearing it, or they may allow you to cut the wood on a profit-sharing basis. Trees that are highly desirable for use as firewood frequently have little or no value as lumber, so even private forest owners in this industry may allow you to cut dead, dying, diseased, or undesirable trees from their forests on a similar basis.

Public lands are an even better bet. Most forestry agencies will issue permits for cutting firewood, frequently charging a fee for the right to do so, but sometimes charging no fee at all. Trees may need to be cut as part of a timber-stand improvement project, or in the fire-control effort, or to better wildlife habitat, or for numerous other reasons. By cutting the trees the forester has marked for removal you may be doing important conservation work as you are earning excellent pay.

By keeping informed about what is happening around you, you may also come across other opportunities to harvest firewood. For instance, the Army Corps of Engineers, when it acquired and condemned the land that would be flooded as a result of its Caesar Creek Dam project near Xenia, Ohio, opened 20,000 acres of mostly wooded land to woodcutters. Permits costing $20 were issued, and for several years, while the dam was being built, woodcutters were able to haul away thousands and thousands of cords of wood that would otherwise have been lost beneath the rising waters. Any major building project may present a similar opportunity.

Aside from the legal right to cut the wood, you will also need certain equipment. A power saw, which will cost in the neighborhood of $100, is clearly essential. You will also need a portable log-splitter. Several types are available at farm stores, most of them capable of splitting half a cord to a cord of wood per hour and costing about $400. You will also need a truck or other means of transporting the wood. The total investment will be decided by your choice of new or used equipment, as well as by your available resources, but in most instances you should be able to recover this investment rather quickly.

As a general rule, the hardwoods, which provide comparatively steady fires and lasting coals, command the highest prices when sold as firewood. The resinous softwoods, especially the pines, bring the lowest prices, yet pine is nevertheless the principal wood fuel in many communities.

Hickory, oak, beech, birch, hard maple, ash, elm, locust, and cherry are the sources of the very best firewood. A cord of wood from any will yield about as much heat as a ton of coal. Shortleaf pine, western hemlock, red gum, Douglas fir, sycamore, and soft maple are excellent also. To match the heat given off by a ton of coal, one must burn 1½ cords of wood from these trees. Least desirable for burning are cedar, redwood, poplar, catalpa, cypress, basswood, spruce, and white pine. Two cords are needed to obtain the heat obtained by a ton of coal.

There is no real secret to felling a tree, by the way. But before you attack one with ax or saw, you should always look and check it for "widowmakers"—hanging branches, sometimes from neighboring trees, that have been broken loose by lightning, disease, or wind. If you carelessly attack a tree holding one of these, the vibrations are all too likely to bring it crashing down to demonstrate how such branches got their common name. Such trees are best left alone until nature has removed the suspended branches.

To drop a tree in the general direction you wish, start by cutting a small safety notch on the side away from the direction of fall; this will minimize any possibility of the butt kicking back or the trunk splitting. Below this, on the side facing the direction of fall, a wide notch is cut. When this wider notch is about three fifths of the way through the tree, return to the first cut and saw until the tree topples. It is as simple as that.

Next comes the job of cutting the trunk and the larger limbs into suitable lengths and splitting those that need it. The most common length is about 18 inches, with a diameter of 6 inches or so the best. But don't throw away any pieces not conforming to those measurements, because nobody is going to object if the cord holds a few logs that are shorter or longer, thicker or thinner, as long as they are reasonably close in size.

Larger pieces from the trunk will probably require splitting. How this is done depends on the type of log-splitter you have bought. The most popular type is simplicity itself—a metal cone, with a sharp point, that attaches to the drive wheel of almost any vehicle. The vehicle is jacked up until that drive wheel is off the ground, the wheel set to spinning, and the end of a log is held against the sharp point of the spinning cone. This will split even the largest log in a matter of seconds.

The logs can be stacked for seasoning. This is simply the process of allowing them to dry. With most wood it will require at least 3 months; with some varieties, 6; and with a few kinds, a year may be required. The wood is properly seasoned when you can no longer see a darker core at the center of a log. If you need the money urgently, you can raise it by offering unseasoned firewood at a slightly lower price, but that stacked firewood is a bit like having money in the bank—its value will be steadily rising, and the longer it ages, the better the product will be.

One woodcutter, in an article about the cutting and sale of firewood, estimates his earnings for this work at about $20 per hour. But if the demand for firewood continues to rise as it has in recent years, even higher earnings may be possible.

Wildcrafting

Not only the forests and woodlands of America, but also the fencerows, fields, roadsides, and all other outdoor places offer the chance to earn money by "wildcrafting"—an activity nearly as old as the country itself but one that has largely been forgotten by modern-day Americans.

Strictly speaking, wildcrafting is the collection of wild plants for use as drugs, home remedies, or experimental purposes. Because of the increasing popularity of specialty foods in recent years, however, the term has come to include the gathering of wild fruits, berries, nuts, and other edibles. It is a craft that requires excellent knowledge of the plants of a given region, but that knowledge is fairly easy to acquire, and it can easily add hundreds or even thousands of dollars to your annual income.

If you follow any of the outdoor careers mentioned in this book, you are soon going to be able to identify many of the plants that are common in your region. Those common plants may often be worth money to you, as a wildcrafter, but if you are really going to make this pay, you should be continually adding to the list of plants you are able to positively identify at a glance.

Start by writing to one or all of the buyers I am going to list below. Tell them you are interested in wildcrafting, and ask for their price list and shipping instructions. The printed lists they send back will include basic instructions for curing the plants you find, as well as other valuable information. Most of these dealers will also look at a sample of a plant to verify your identification, but their lists include many plants so common that you will need no help along those lines. In addition to the more elusive species, you will find that they buy such common plant materials as roots from dandelion, may apple, poke, blackberry, sassafras, and wild ginger; bark from willow, cherry, and certain elm trees; and leaves from many common plants you are likely to know.

The dealers are:
Frank Lemaster & Co.
Route 1
Londonderry, OH 45647

S. B. Penick & Co.
100 Church Street
New York, NY 10007

St. Louis Commission Co.
4157 N. Kingshighway
St. Louis, MO 63115

F. C. Taylor Fur Co.
227 E. Market Street
Louisville, KY 40202

Wilcox Drug Co., Inc.
P.O. Box 391
Boone, NC 28607

In checking these lists you will find the buyers offering as little as a few cents a pound for some of the most common botanicals to many dollars per pound for those that are more difficult to obtain. You will also find that one dealer may be the best market for certain plants and the worst for others, so you should compare the prices carefully before you begin to gather, dry, and ship the product.

Collecting Ginseng

Ginseng is, of course, the most famous of the plants gathered by the wildcrafters, and of course it always fetches the highest price.

When I began work on this book wild ginseng root was bringing about $85 per pound . . . and that price has now jumped, only a few months later, to $140 per pound. But the price paid for a pound of wildcrafted plant material can often be misleading to the novice. A more common plant may bring only $1 per pound, or even less, but you may be able to find hundreds of pounds of it far easier than even a few ounces of ginseng.

Several years back, in Ohio, I watched a pair of youngsters prove this. Several acres of hillside were being excavated for a construction project. Dandelions grew thickly over almost every inch of that hillside. Their roots were, at that time, worth about $.75 a pound, dried, but digging them out of the hard soil where they commonly reach down to a depth of 2 feet can be, as most know, tremendously hard work. This boy and girl were avoiding that work by following the bulldozers and picking up the dandelion roots left in its path. They had about a dozen burlap bags full of the forking roots that, they estimated, would bring about $200 when dried.

The root of the plant commonly known as poke or pokeweed is another that brings a low price per pound, yet is so common that gathering it can be worthwhile. The dried root typically brings less than $1 per pound, but the plant commonly occurs in thick groves, and a root can be as large as a human's leg. When a field is being cleared for cultivation or other purposes, it may be possible to collect this in amounts that will bring hundreds of dollars.

By harvesting some of the plants you already know, then, you should be able to earn some money right from the start. But if you are to achieve the highest earnings possible from this craft, you will probably have to expand your knowledge of botany and plant identification. Several books can help you with this.

For a permanent reference you will want a copy of *American Plants of Medicinal Importance*, which is available through the extension office of the United States Department of Agriculture, or from the Superintendent of Documents, Goverment Printing Office, Washington, DC 20401.

You would also do well to borrow from the library a copy of *Recognizing Wild Flowering Plants* by William C. Grimm, which is a book for wildcrafters. If not locally available this can be obtained for $7.95

from Stackpole Books, Cameron and Kelker streets, Harrisburg, PA 17105

The Herbalist, originally written in 1918 but recently revised, is the classic in this field and can be of further help. It is available at larger libraries, or for $4.50 from Sterling Publishing Co., Inc., 419 Park Avenue South, New York NY 10016.

On a more technical level but available at any library deserving the name is Gray's *Manual of Botany,* published by Harvard University Press. This standard reference work uses a complex set of keys to identify virtually every species of plant life found in North America, though it gives little information about their uses. At $34.50 a copy it is probably a little too expensive for most private libraries, but you should learn to use its keys as a positive means of identifying those plants that you are unable to classify by other methods.

These books, with their descriptions and illustrations, will put you well on your way to profitable wildcrafting, but you should do more to speed your learning—get out and look at the plants of your region, see and handle them, ask questions about them, and get to know them as they are. This can make you far better acquainted with the plants than any illustrations could possibly do.

Ask your neighbors, especially any farmers, about the local plants. Many are really knowledgeable on the subject. They are not likely to know the plants by the botanical names, but the books I have listed identify the plants by their common names as well as by their Latin ones.

Just taking a nature walk at an Audubon Center, wildlife refuge, or park can help increase your knowledge. The naturalists who lead these are experts, and as they point out the various flora, you will see species after species that can be marketed.

Take notes about the plants during these early explorations, paying special attention to the type of soil and terrain in which each species thrives. When it is possible, take home samples of plants and compare them to the text and illustrations in your books on botany. Even where the species has no commercial value, the process of identifying them will add to your knowledge, making it easier and easier for you to identify each unknown species you encounter.

Learning about the plants that grow around you may turn out to be one of the most exciting things you will ever do. And how much you earn will certainly be determined by how well you learn. But the number of plants with commercial value is such that, no matter what part of the country you call home, you should soon be able to find, identify, and sell plants from at least a dozen species. Among them, perhaps, will be that most famous of the botanicals, *Punax quinquefolius*, better known as ginseng.

As you may have heard, several government agencies, including the U.S. Forest Service and the Fish and Wildlife Service, are attempting to determine exactly how much wild ginseng exists in the United States. If the plant is found to be extremely rare and endangered, as some conservationists believe it to be, then laws will be passed to protect it, and ginseng will no longer be listed among those plants gathered by wildcrafters. This is not to say that ginseng is known to be endangered, but, rather, that no one knows exactly how much of it we have.

A little over a decade ago, the late Euell Gibbons stated his belief that America had more wild ginseng at present than at the time the continent was discovered by Columbus. He believed this largely because ginseng has been cultivated for years in all parts of the country and like many other plants, will escape cultivation and continue to grow in the wild.

I do not know if Euell Gibbons was correct in this assumption, but I believe that ginseng is far from extinct, and I am convinced that wildcrafting, when properly done, has never posed, and does not pose now, a real threat to the species. The threat comes from destruction of the plant's habitat, and from those few who call themselves wildcrafters but who are really vandals in the woods, digging for dollars and giving no thought to conservation.

To know the difference between a wildcrafter and a vandal, you must understand a little about ginseng, and information that applies to some other plants as well.

It is the root of the plant that is valuable. The root sends up a distinctively shaped herb that seldom exceeds 18 inches in height. This rises as a single stem, which branches once in the first years of its life, but which branches three, four, or even five times as the annual plant grows older. The plant is considered fully mature in its fifth year, when usually it will have three branches. The branches bear dark green leaves that are almost exactly like raspberry leaves in shape but that grow in clusters of five . . . three large and two smaller. Directly in the center of each fork of the plant is the flowering stem, which produces a yellow blossom sometime between May and August. The blossom later drops off and is replaced by bright red berries, each about the size of a cranberry, which remain on the plant until late September or early October.

The root of the ginseng is thick when mature, with many arms or branches. In very rare instances these branches may cause the root to resemble a human form; and because much of our ginseng goes to the Orient, where a great deal of superstition about longevity and powers of aphrodisia surround the plant, such a rarity can be extremely valuable, a single man-shaped root once selling for $3,000.

Ginseng almost always grows in colonies. Its natural range is from Quebec to Manitoba and south to Georgia, Tennessee, and Oklahoma; but because it has been so extensively cultivated, it may turn up in any location where the soil is rich and the shade is deep. A single colony may yield 10 or more pounds of dried root . . . and yield it without destruction of the ginseng patch.

Now let me demonstrate the difference between wildcrafting and vandalism. The *Philadelphia Inquirer* recently carried an article about what it called the former but I call the latter. The article was based on an interview with a Pennsylvania woman who lightly talked of collecting "hundreds of ginseng roots to make a pound," and it was illustrated with photos of roots so tiny they had to come from plants in their first or second year of growth.

Now compare that bit of destruction to the method described by Sherman Huff, who has wildcrafted in the mountains of southeastern Kentucky for many years:

"In this part of the country ginseng grows in hilly or semi-hilly terrain, never in the bottoms. I usually find it around hardwoods, and most of the patches are hidden in underbrush and protected by nettles or other herbs. The patches I know of are almost all on western or northern slopes.

"I dig ginseng only in the fall, partly because it's easier to find at that time and partly because the roots are heavier and will fetch a better price, but mainly because the plants have had time to produce seeds and I won't kill off a patch by digging in it.

"Along about the last of September, after a good stiff frost has dropped some of the lesser plants and made the others easier to spot, I'll outfit myself with a clean burlap sack and a small shovel and take to the hills.

"I'll poke around in the rough country where I know the ginseng grows, walking slowly, parting each patch of dense vegetation, keeping a sharp lookout for the red berries that mean 'seng.

"When I find a patch, I count the plants that have at least three forks, trying to calculate how many ounces I can expect to harvest. Between thirty and fifty average roots make a pound, and if the patch looks like it has only a few roots in that size range, I won't dig any of them; I'll leave them for a later year.

"The first thing I do—once I've decided to dig—is to pick all the berries and set them aside where they won't get lost while I'm digging. Then I carefully dig down to the top of the root of each individual plant. If a root looks too small, I cover it back up and leave it alone. Those that are big enough I dig out carefully, brush free of dirt, and place in the sack. But even when all the roots in a patch are big, I leave at least one third of them right where they are, 'cause that way the patch will have a new start, even if the seeds I'm going to plant don't 'take.'

"That's how I finish the job. I take the seeds I've set aside and carefully plant them three or four inches deep in the earth, covering them well and patting the soil down so the rain won't wash them away. Then, to finish up, I blanket the bed with all the leaves I find close at hand. There's ginseng scattered all through these hills that I've planted back like that.

"Roots are mainly what you'll sell in the business. With most of them you can give them a chance to reseed just by waiting 'til late in the year to dig, and by always leaving behind some of the plants in a patch. With others, like ginseng, you can pick the seeds and plant them. It's the only way of being sure you'll have plants to keep you in business in the years ahead."

Mr. Huff says he has found as much as $500 worth of ginseng in a single day (at a time when prices were at less than half their present level), but adds that this was an exceptional day. He wildcrafts only a month or two each year—as much for pleasure as for money—and says he usually earns enough to pay about half of the annual rent on his small farm in Kentucky. And he does it without destroying the species that provides his income.

Wildcrafting is a time-honored pursuit. Its practitioners provide about 100,000 pounds of wild ginseng alone each year, most of which is exported to the Orient. The demand for this herb will probably soar as a result of our new relationship with China, and this seems to be a logical use of a natural resource—but only if steps are also taken to preserve that resource.

No matter what the results of the ginseng census being taken, I believe that we should take steps to assure the survival not only of ginseng but also of all other plants that are collected for sale. Laws should be passed imposing stiff penalties for the possession of immature plant materials. Size limits should be imposed. Wildcrafting should be allowed only on a seasonal basis. In other words, we should extend to these plants the same conservation measures we use to preserve our fish, our wildlife, and our other natural resources, allowing them to be utilized but not destroyed. Until such measures are taken, however, those who practice the old art of wildcrafting should lead the way in showing that it can be done without wiping these valuable plants off the face of the earth.

Collecting and Selling Wild Edibles

In gathering wild edibles for sale, no such problems confront the wildcrafter. Although many root vegetables and leaf vegetables are listed among the hundreds and hundreds of wild edibles used in this country, those most likely to be sold at a profit are fruits, nuts, berries, and mushrooms, all of which can be picked without damage to the parent plant.

In picking and selling that which is to be used as food there is absolutely no margin for error, for you are dealing with human health and, possibly, lives. The rule to follow is: *Never pick for human consumption any wild thing that has not been identified beyond a shadow of a doubt and that does not have a long history of use as food!*

Learning about the wild edibles is far easier than learning about the plants that are collected as botanicals. Any library will have several field guides on the subject, including, probably, those by Euell Gibbons and Bradford Angier. Hundreds of thousands of people have reduced their food costs by using these guides as their introduction to the foraging of wild food. They will not only help you to identify the wild edibles but will also acquaint you with their uses, which can be helpful knowledge as you begin to market them.

Most of the more popular wild foods have been used as food for centuries, and in all parts of the country there are those who go out and collect their favorites. Just keep an eye open to see what your neighbors are gathering for their own use and you can acquire a lot of knowledge about the edibles that thrive locally.

Oddly enough, even a visit to the supermarket can be very helpful to the beginner. The raspberries, blueberries, huckleberries, currants, gooseberries, cranberries, blackberries, and many of the nuts and other edibles you will see displayed there are very similar to their wild relatives, and, in many instances, they are identical. If you have any doubts at all about the appearance of a wild species that you know is also cultivated, the very best way to resolve those doubts is to take a look at the cultivated fruit, nut, or berry.

Relatives of the cultivated plants are enormously abundant from one coast to another. In many parts of the country one can easily collect bushel after bushel of blueberries, blackberries, cherries, plums, and other delectables that are little different from those cultivated by farmers. Where these are plentiful they can be very profitable, for they are already widely known as food, and a ready market for them exists.

Other wild edibles are often worth seeking because, even though they are excellent as food and eagerly sought by consumers, they cannot be cultivated, at least not on a profitable basis. If you have ever visited Cape Cod and tasted the beach plum jelly sold to visitors there, you have experienced one example of this, for the small shrub that bears the beach plum is a plant that has absolutely defied all attempts at cultivation.

Morel mushrooms provide another example. About a dozen species occur in all but the most arid parts of the country, popping up in the spring when few dangerous mushrooms are present. Known also as "sponge" or "spring" mushrooms, these are probably the most widely collected of all mushrooms, known to hundreds of thousands of collectors. Long used by gourmet chefs at finer restaurants, who eagerly pay as much as $10 per pound for them, they have thus far defeated all attempts at cultivation, and those that appear on any menu are gathered from the wild.

"Each and every spring I hear from a few folks who think they've solved the problem of growing the morels," I was told, in the spring of 1978, by Dr. Alexander Smith, professor of mycology at the University of Michigan and author of *The Mushroom Hunter's Field Guide.* "Then these people just vanish and I never hear from them again." During that same conversation he also told me, in all seriousness, that only weeks before, in Idaho, he had seen mushroom hunters gathering morels "by the truckload."

Other wild mushrooms have long been sold in farmers' markets. Few bring the high prices commanded by the morels, but because they are frequently more abundant, gathering them may be just as profitable. Giant puffballs, for example, may bring less than $1 per pound, but single specimens often weigh 15 pounds or more, making it possible to gather hundreds of pounds in a few hours. The common meadow mushroom, which is the parent species of the common mushroom of cultivation, also grows so abundantly that I have seen more than 10,000 picked from a 4-acre field in a single afternoon.

Elderberries, famous for use in wine, pies, and jelly, thrive in most parts of the country, the shrubs producing millions of blue-black berries in umbrels that may be a foot or more across. As well known as elderberry products are, they are seldom, if ever, cultivated. While the law will not permit you to sell elderberry wine, you *can* sell the berries to home winemakers, as well as to those who want them for other purposes. You can make and sell some of the other delicious elderberry products.

Hickory nuts and black walnuts are always in great demand, especially as the holiday season approaches. The trees that produce these are among the most widespread in America, but they are seldom planted for nut production, largely because the trees must be very, very old before they begin to bear. But a single tree often produces many bushels of nuts which—at the extremely low price of $.50 per pound, in the shell—would bring a price of more than $20 per bushel.

Other less common nuts, such as pecans, butternuts, beechnuts, and hazelnuts, will sell at even higher prices.

Stressing the word "wild" will often help sell these edibles. Visit a few gourmet shops, health-food shops, and specialty-food stores, and you will almost certainly see displays of small tins and jars of jams and jellies supposedly made from wild fruits and berries. These frequently sell at prices more than double those asked for their more common counterparts, even though the wildness of their ingredients might rightly be questioned.

What you collect for sale will be determined, largely, by where you live. Each region of the country has its own distinct group of wild edibles, though some species appear in most parts of the country. By making yourself utterly familiar with all the edibles that grow abundantly in your own region, you should be able to create a list of marketable edibles that can be harvested, one after another, in all but the very coldest months of the year. You might gather morels during the spring, blackberries, raspberries, elderberries, and more during the hottest months of summer, blueberries as the weather cools, and nut crops around the first frost. And always, you should keep an eye out for new crops to harvest.

Seek out the edibles that grow very abundantly in your region, because they are the ones that will provide quantities large enough for you to market. Common as these plants might seem to you as you are walking the woods, remember that city folk and others who might like them as food may not have the time, the skills, or the inclination to go out and gather them. That is why you can get paid for gathering them.

Southwestern Ohio, for example, is an excellent area in which to gather morels, so good that anyone should be able to walk the woods in April or May and find all a family could use. Yet, according to an article in *the Dayton Daily News*, one man from that area earns as much as $500 per week, during the season, by finding them and offering them for sale through small grocery stores. Many other common edibles could be just as profitable.

With the wild edibles that have good keeping qualities, such as the nut crops, a small ad in the paper is an excellent way to market them, for this will allow you to obtain the full retail price. With those that must be sold faster, or where you have gathered them in extremely large quantities, you may find it better to offer them at a wholesale price to produce stands and small groceries. You might also consider converting part of the harvest into jams, jellies, and preserves.

In making jams, jellies, or other food products for sale you must be in compliance with the local health laws, which usually is a matter of cleanliness. The Food and Drug Administration will, ordinarily, not become involved unless the product is sold in interstate commerce, or unless the local laws are so lax that health hazards are obvious. But you should check the local laws before you begin.

With either the fresh foods or with cooked food products, such as jellies and jams, it may be profitable to rent a stall at a county fair, flea market, farmers' market, or even a craft show, especially if you have a variety of goods to offer. Letting people know that these wild edibles are available is frequently the biggest problem in selling them, and such areas of high traffic allow you to display your wares very effectively and at a low cost.

Many millions of dollars' worth of wild food goes to waste each year, primarily because the public does not know it is available and no one places it before them. Harvesting this natural bounty can be a fascinating hobby that will provide many hours of pleasure as well as a small but steady income throughout most of the year.

Obtaining Permission for Access to Public and Private Lands

In addition to the outdoor skills needed to earn money by the methods I have described in this chapter, there is one other thing you are going to need very often—permission from landowners, either public or private.

You would not venture onto a farmer's land and begin cutting trees or picking garden vegetables without his permission, yet all too many people ignore one simple fact—the landowner possesses all the rights to all the natural resources on the property, not just to the crops he or she has planted. Trespassing may very well be the most frequently committed misdemeanor in America—yet it is often a needless offense, committed out of thoughtlessness rather than intent.

Most landowners are surprisingly good about granting permission for pursuits that will do no damage, as millions of fishermen and hunters can attest. But the time to get that permission is before you go onto private property; otherwise, you may find yourself facing an angry landowner, as well as a fine for trespassing. Where goods of obvious value are to be removed from the property, obtaining this permission will almost certainly mean sharing your profits, but many landowners may allow other uses without asking a cent in return.

In certain places and in some of these pursuits, such as strolling a public beach to look for seashells or other collectibles, permission is automatic, for these are among the activities for which some areas are made public. But in using the public lands for any but the purposes for which they were most obviously intended, you should always check ahead with the representative of the agency charged with the management of that land—the ranger in a park, for example.

The laws about how these public areas may be used vary wildly, and each law may be interpreted differently by the individuals charged with administering it. In most instances, however, one answer to one question will decide whether or not you will be given permission to pursue your activity on the public lands: Will it do harm to the natural environment?

If followed wisely and with caution by persons of concern, the moneymaking methods I have described in this chapter pose no threats to our natural resources. They are ways to sell the wild without destroying it and are better off in the hands of the conservationists than in those of the mindless profiteers.

Nature has many treasures to offer. But the laws of nature also demand that these treasures be given the chance to restore and replenish themselves, that they be utilized only in ways that will allow them to offer the same bounty to future generations. Nature and its bounty is offered to you; respect of its ways is demanded of you.

Take the offering only if you can meet the demands.

INDEX